Industrial Conflict in Modern Britain

James E. Cronin

CROOM HELM LONDON
ROWMAN AND LITTLEFIELD TOTOWA N.J.

©1979 James E. Cronin
Croom Helm Ltd, 2-10 St John's Road, London SW11

British Library Cataloguing in Publication Data

Cronin, James E
    Industrial conflict in modern Britain. — (Croom
    Helm social history series).
    1. Industrial relations — Great Britain
    I. Title
    331'.0941   HD8391
    ISBN 0-7099-0120-8
    ISBN 0-7099-0214-X Pbk

First published in the United States 1979 by
Rowman and Littlefield
81 Adams Drive
Totowa, New Jersey

ISBN 0-8476-6188-1

Printed and bound in Great Britain

CONTENTS

TABLES

FIGURES

PREFACE

Historians seldom have the privilege of treating topics of obvious current interest. A book that takes the story of British strikes up to the mid-1970s, however, is surely an exception, and its author must confront the problems attendant upon relevance. Perhaps the greatest problem facing academics who write about industrial relations in the twentieth century is that their analyses seldom lend themselves to handy prescriptions and tend, inevitably, to disappoint those who want understanding to be immediately translated into policy. This is especially the case with historians, whose preference to the long view often seems infuriatingly aloof and whose penchant for explanations unique to each situation appears utterly useless. Though I have sought to steer a middle course between the pessimism of the focus upon the long term and the confusion and bias of the contemporary chronicle, the result may nevertheless fail to satisfy the reader who wants clear and simple solutions in the here and now.

Disappointment is liable to be still more acute because of the specific nature of my argument. For what I shall assert and attempt to show is that strikes, though they have a long history, are at any given moment a response by ordinary working men and women to quite discrete and concrete problems. Waves of industrial unrest keep recurring for two reasons: strikes are normally the most effective way for workers to communicate their discontents and desires; and new discontents and desires are constantly created by the 'dynamism of industrial society. Workers strike because striking works and because they have grievances. As it is probable that many workers will continue to feel aggrieved, and because no better means of pressing their demands has yet appeared, I see no reason to expect, or even to wish for, a waning of industrial strife.

So there will be nothing prescriptive about this study, except perhaps by implication. Still, I hope it will prove of some use in furthering our collective understanding of the evolution of labour in British society, and in clarifying some of the issues and difficulties that beset both labour historians and students of industrial relations. One of the major difficulties will be obvious to even the most casual reader: the labour historian, especially if he seeks to bring his analysis very far into the present century, must somehow come to terms with a large body of theory and research conducted by sociologists, economists and random other social scientists working in the area of industrial relations and using concepts and methods quite different from those normally used by historians. This I have tried to do as tersely and painlessly as possible, but I would not for a moment be deluded into expecting universal approbation. Some historians will undoubtedly find too much use here of statistics and aggregate data and too little texture and local detail, while certain sociologists and economists will despair over my unwillingness to settle upon a single long-term model of strike determination. My defence is that, for good or ill, no one in either tradition has as yet made quite the argument developed here, and it is unlikely that anyone working solely within one or the other ever would have.

It is neither possible nor desirable to summarise the entire argument in this preface, but it might be useful to state in advance just what is different about it. Most accounts of labour's history see it as the progression through time of a body of men and women sharing a common social and economic location. Their shared lot sometimes improves and at other moments deteriorates; their conditions of life change and their ideas and culture adapt. Workers are a group to whom things happen, and the normal method of writing their history is to examine their shifting responses to the external environment.

This framework has two major disadvantages, and I depart from it on both counts. It minimises the creative element in labour's adaptation to external realities by ignoring or at least slighting the processes of ideological change and organisational innovation. Second, it falsely assumes a constancy, a stability, in the structure and membership of the working class when, in fact, its composition is continually being altered and restructured by geographical and social mobility, by technological change, and by the differential growth of various sectors of the economy. By emphasising the creativity of strikes and the social dynamics behind them I hope to have cast light upon a few aspects of industrial conflict that have until now been poorly illumined.

If I have succeeded at all with this project, some of the credit must go to those who helped me and it along. I owe a special debt of gratitude to Geoffrey Barraclough. His support was constant and his criticisms were immensely useful; and his own work has served as a model that attests to the possibility and necessity of contemporary history. Professor Eugene C. Black joined with Barraclough in directing the dissertation upon which this book is based, and provided all sorts of guidance and encouragement. Three good friends who happen also to be mathematicians kindly helped me to learn and utilise the statistical techniques employed in Chapters 4 to 6: Ronald Webber, Diana Spiegel, and Professor Stanley Spiegel. David Snyder, Douglas Hibbs, and David Sapsford also aided, by sending me then unpublished work or by discussions, in the technical aspects of the project. Institutional cooperation was given by the Computer Centre at Brandeis University and the Social Science Research Facility of the University of Wiscosin-Milwaukee, by the Baker Library at Harvard, and by the Institute of Historical Research in London. Financial assistance came via an Abraham Sachar Fellowship during 1975. For the graphics, I owe thanks to the UWM Cartographic Service and to Kevin G. Cronin.

Considerable aid and advice were given during the early stages of my research by Peter Stearns, Eric Hobsbawm, Dorothy Wedderburn, Harold Perkin, Dudley Baines and James Joll. Later on, I benefited from critical readings of portions of the argument by Joan Scott, L.P. Curtis, Emmet Larkin, Ronald Ross, R. Charles Wittenberg, Joseph White, Bob Holton and Melvin Dubofsky. The entire manuscript was read at one point or another by Charles Tilly, Edward Shorter, Richard Price, Robert Moeller, Jonathan Schneer, Reginald Horsman and James Green. Their criticisms were all helpful; Tilly's were invaluable. Mary J. Cronin provided early assistance in research and incisive editorial comments on successive drafts of this book.

Finally, it should be noted that the arguments of Chapter 2 were given previously in papers to the Social Science History Association and the Columbia University Seminar on the History of the Working Classes. Discussions in those two forums were stimulating and of considerable help in clarifying my ideas. An earlier version of the chapter also appeared in the *Journal of Social History*, XII, 2 (Winter, 1978), pp. 194-220.

I wish to thank all of these friends and colleagues and to absolve them of any responsibility for my errors. They are implicated only insofar as their warm support emboldened me to proceed.

1 INTRODUCTION: STRIKES AND SOCIETY IN MODERN BRITAIN

The balance of power in modern industry is sharply skewed in favour of management. Workers, in consequence, have scant leeway for self-activity. They do not determine what they produce, nor do they control the pace or pattern of its production. Creativity must therefore find outlets in other arenas, primarily in the enjoyment and interaction of family and friends, and through leisure. Occasionally, the workplace itself can and has become a focus of sociability as well, but for the most part self-expression at work is restricted to 'a crude and unpopular power of veto, depending ultimately upon systematic sulking (like working to rule) or striking'.[1] The industrial working class speaks its mind negatively, forced to communicate its fears, wants, grievances, hopes and aspirations through a weak and poorly developed language of industrial resistance. Deciphering its messages requires a systematic effort of translation, which is what this book is all about.

The first and most important step in decoding the language of industrial conflict is to reinterpret its negative terms positively. The negativism of working-class activity is an artifact of the distribution of social and economic power, reinforced by a 'public opinion' moulded largely in the interests of those who do not strike. V.L. Allen captures well the hostile institutional and ideological context within which striking workers operate:[2]

> Strikes take place within a hostile environment even though they are a common everyday phenomenon. They are conventionally described as industrially subversive, irresponsible, unfair, against the interests of the community, contrary to the workers' best interests, wasteful of resources, crudely aggressive, inconsistent with democracy and, in any event, unnecessary.

Even those who do strike, or engage in other forms of industrial conflict, view such action defensively, as a last resort forced upon them by circumstances alone. No one, it seems, likes to strike, but everyone does it. As one strike leader put it in 1937, 'The only man who desires a strike for fun is the man who wants to go to hell for a pastime.'[3] Indeed, to listen to some union officials, one would think that they would never sanction or participate in a strike willingly, let alone initiate one. If such disclaimers were true, of course, the analysis of conflict would be much simplified: predicting strikes would be an easy matter of totalling up employer provocations and employee grievances and constructing a straightforward index of discontent.

The reality is more complex, and requires subtler methods. Above all, it demands that we discount the rationalising rhetoric that surrounds strikes, and instead look upon the act of striking as a positive statement by working people. Strikes are not the defensive actions of desperate and downtrodden men and women. They are instead the means of communication and sources of political and economic leverage most readily available to industrial workers, and as such do yeoman service as flexible tools, reflecting the changing and often increasing desires and organisational capacities of the working class. Most strikes are essentially creative acts of an offensive kind, signs not of weakness but of collective resources, not of resignation but of an often hopeful and heightened sense of self-worth, raised within a context of institutionalised social inferiority. This positive nature of strike activity will be revealed throughout this study, and forms one of its basic assumptions.

A second assumption we shall be making is that strikes really do matter to those involved — indeed, it would be hard to overestimate the importance and significance of industrial conflict for working people. Since 1870 strikes have involved more workers in a more meaningful way than any other form of social or political action, particularly during the present century. Compare, for example, the number of workers who strike in a given year with even the most generous estimate of those who take part in the activities of the local Labour party or trade union branch. Most manual workers, and a growing percentage of non-manual workers, engage in strike action at least once over the course of their working lives, and many do so much more often. Only voting touches greater numbers of workers, yet who would argue that the commitment involved in casting a ballot is equal to that entailed in deciding to strike? The members of the South Wales Unofficial Reform Committee understood this well:[4]

An industrial vote will affect the lives and happiness of workmen far more than a political vote. The power to vote whether there shall or shall not be a strike, or upon an industrial policy to be pursued by his union, will affect far more important issues to the workman's life, than the political vote can ever touch. Hence it should be more sought after, and its privileges jealously guarded.

Even today, when workers' rights to organise are much more generally recognised, strikes still involve considerable risks and hardships. Between 1957 and 1970, 'the overwhelming majority of strikers' lost 'some 80 percent of their normal earnings', despite substantial increases in welfare measures.[5] Strikers often jeopardise their chances for promotion, or increase their chances of being declared redundant − as happened to militants at Ford in 1962 − or, in extreme cases, of spending time in jail − as did five dockers in 1972.[6] As Knowles explained in his path-breaking book of 1952:[7]

> The hardships suffered by workers in industrial struggles have, in the past, been too great to ignore; and even now, when the character of the strike seems to have materially altered, it is seldom a wholly frivolous act however trivial its immediate cause may appear.

To put it simply, the decision to strike is one of the most important decisions a worker ever takes. Because of this, and because of the structural constraints which modern society places upon other forms of plebeian self-expression, the record of strikes is clearly the critical source available for reconstructing the social history of the working class.

Practically speaking, there is no single record of strikes: many pieces of evidence lie buried in local newspapers, collections of pamphlets, police and other government reports as well as the official statistics, not to mention a rich oral tradition stretching back easily to before the First World War, and all of this can help to illuminate aspects of past industrial conflict. The type of evidence most useful in any particular study will depend upon the approach employed, of which there are basically two. Writing the history of industrial strife requires a serious methodological choice right at the outset: whether to treat strikes narrowly, in case studies of a particular strike or the strikes of a single year of industry; or whether to cast one's net more widely, in hopes that an aggregate treatment will yield insights and information of a more useful, because more broadly applicable, nature. The narrow tack has been taken most frequently in approaching British strikes, and has resulted in a series of admirably specific and subtle studies of individual strikes and of the strike propensity of various industries at particular times.[8] A distinctly different choice informs this study, and has dictated a perspective that is less restrictive, and that makes frequent and explicit use of statistical data. Strikes have been treated here, for the most part, either in the aggregate or at rather gross levels of dis-aggregation on the initial premise that the forces which most likely produced strikes would probably be those which affected more than one group of workers at a time. The usefulness of this assumption is practically confirmed by the particular temporal pattern of indu.trial conflict in Great Britain: strikes tend to fluctuate together in all industries, to cluster and bunch up in several, relatively short, periods of time. They come in waves; and it seems only logical that this type of variation must be studied statistically, by an aggregate approach which combines data from several industries over an extended period of time.[9]

The simultaneity and synchronisation of strike activity across industrial boundaries points to more substantive reasons for employing an aggregate approach. Before the industrial revolution, everyday life for the poor was embedded in a bewildering and complex network of local particularisms and exceptions. The dramatic social changes set in train by the industrial and urban revolutions, however, have tended to generalise and homogenise social conditions and trends, eradicating customary differences and displacing the sources of dynamism from local to national or even international levels. Studying the evolution of strike activity as a whole should enable us to follow the complicated transitions that have occurred in the structure and social location of the working class, its consciousness and collective organisation. It should also afford many glimpses of the general trajectory of industrial capitalist society since the late nineteenth century.

Returning to the linguistic metaphor, it should be obvious that the adoption of a broadly statistical method is only the first step in translating the language of industrial behaviour into terms more easily comprehended. Reading the message of working people out of the numerical codes and classifications elaborated by government statisticians requires further analytical devices. We shall have recourse to several in this book, but one will be primary: the technique of linking the timing and loci of strikes to the rhythms and incidence of other social and economic processes and events. This quintessentially historical method will colour both our critique of other models and theories and the logic of our own argument. What this means in practice will be shown later in the text, but for now it might be helpful briefly to locate this approach within the historiography of collective action and social protest.

Recent studies of riots, revolutions and crowd behaviour are instructive as to both the possible value of the study of industrial conflict and the methods and research strategy to be employed.[10] The best studies begin by deciding when and where action occurred and who participated, with timing, location and personnel, and use this information to reconstruct patterns of organisation and social structure and, finally, the mental world of the actors. The methodological implications are fairly obvious: even if it is true that purely economic and social explanations of conflict are not in and of themselves sufficient — because they ignore the point of view and state of mind of the actors in the situation — it may nevertheless be the case that studying the economic and social correlates of mass action can play a critical role in the process of rediscovering the parameters of a social and economic system and also in recreating the mentalities of strikers or rioters operating within it. Two examples should make this clear.

E.P. Thompson's stimulating essay on the eighteenth-century crowd, for instance, starts by acknowledging the 'self-evident truth' (as he puts it) that high prices produce food riots. He argues, however, that one must not stop at this level; one must not rest content with the construction of a social tension chart like Walt Rostow's, but rather should proceed to analyse the ways in which popular behaviour is provoked, justified, and 'modified by custom, culture and reason'. And what Thompson finds is that the pre-industrial poor operated within an elaborate and well-defined moral universe in which hoarding and price-gouging were proscribed, and where notions of a just price and fair wage prevailed over the market imperative of 'what the traffic will bear'. This 'moral economy' was therefore peculiarly sensitive to problems of price and consumption, and the spasmodic, price-related rioting it experienced was its uniquely apposite form of social conflict.[11]

The economic correlates of social movements can be, therefore, of critical analytical significance. In the supple hands of writers like Thompson, they may provide useful and suggestive evidence about the mentalities of social groups and their relations with one another, and help to define retrospectively the essential polarities of a society. Ernest Labrousse's work on the timing of the French revolutions of 1789, 1830 and 1848 offers another successful example of this sort of reasoning. The revolution of 1789 was born, he argues, of a fusion of three temporalities: the long-term expansion of the late eighteenth century, which intensified the imbalance between the prosperity and the political power of the bourgeoisie, a new-style industrial cycle which bottomed out in 1788-9, and an old-style harvest crisis which peaked in the spring of 1789. As Pierre Vilar recently pointed out, this is not simply a 'mechanistic' shuffling together of 'linear times as if they amounted to a causal explanation'. Rather, it is an attempt to decipher the precise stage of France's social evolution at the time of the Revolution from the specificity of its economic rhythms, and thereby to reconstruct the social psychology of 1789. In short, it is a method of using the relation between economics and protest to penetrate the structures and ideologies of a society\[12]

Just as the pattern of food riots reveals the inner dynamics of the eighteenth-century social order, and the timing of the revolutions in France provides a means to view social change in that country, so the unusual pattern of British strikes can reveal much about the rhythms of the modern economy and the behaviour of those who live and work in it. Unlike other forms of collective action, however, the meaning of the strike is more liable to change over time, and the analysis of strikes is less likely to reveal a stable 'moral economy' of the poor underpinning militancy than a series of different mind-sets, or constellations of beliefs and expectations, fuelling strike activity at different times. The reason is evident, and has to do with the essential dynamism of modern society. As Eric Hobsbawm has argued,[13]

the basic change brought about by the Industrial Revolution in the field of social thought has been to substitute a system of beliefs resting on unceasing *progress* toward aims which can be specified only as a *process*, for one resting on the assumption of permanent order, which can be described or illustrated in terms of some concrete social model, normally drawn from the past, real or imaginary.

Extrapolating from the incidence and patterns of industrial conflict to a 'moral economy' of the working class is thus extremely complicated; indeed, the instability of belief and behaviour in modern society guarantees that any useful model of protest since the industrial revolution must be inherently dynamic, and capable of explaining or at least absorbing the sharp breaks and odd twists and turns along whatever secular trend one may discern. We should therefore expect the persistent, rapid, and uneven character of social change since the industrial revolution to impart a noticeable discontinuity to patterns of belief and to modes of collective action.

Change, development, discontinuity — such are the terms increasingly used to depict economy and society in the modern world, and such will be the themes struck in this analytical history of British strikes. One could, in truth, summarise the entire thrust of this study by saying simply that strikes change: they fulfill different functions, mean different things as time progresses, and in the succeeding and different meanings of strikes can be deciphered the distinct stages of ideological and organisational growth through which the bulk of British workers have passed. But this would be too simple, for what is most interesting are these differences themselves — knowing that they exist is no substitute for understanding each on its own terms and in its own context.

The organisation of this book is uncomplicated. First, a chapter will be spent analysing various competing theories of strikes, trying at the same time to criticise the applicability of their formulations to the particular historical patterns exhibited by British strikes and to cull from them insights and guidelines for a new, more historically minded theory. From there, we will proceed to develop this new approach to strikes by an analysis of the significance of strike waves in the history of British industrial relations. Several subsequent chapters will test the theory using both quantitative and more traditional qualitative techniques. One final chapter will apply it to the rather thorny problem of inter-industry differences in strike activity, and the conclusion will summarise its implications for the historiography of the British labour movement. Technical discussion concerning the data and statistical techniques employed are relegated to an appendix, but should not for that reason remain unread.

Notes

1. *Management Today* (19 March 1974), p. 36, cited in J.D. Edelstein and M. Warner, *Comparative Union Democracy* (New York, 1976), p. 355.
2. V.L. Allen, *Militant Trade Unionism* (London, 1966), p. 27.
3. W. Payne, leader of busmen's rank-and-file movement in 1936-7, as quoted in K.G.J.C. Knowles, *Strikes: A Study in Industrial Conflict* (New York, 1952), p. 30.
4. Unofficial Reform Committee, South Wales Miners' Federation, *The Miner's Next Step* (Tonypandy, 1912), pp. 14-15.
5. J.W. Durcan and W.E.J. McCarthy, 'The State Subsidy Theory of Strikes: An Examination of Statistical Data for the Period 1956-1970', *British Journal of Industrial Relations*, XII (1974), p. 43.
6. H.A. Turner, Garfield Clack and Geoffrey Roberts, *Labour Relations in the Motor Industry* (London, 1967), pp. 281-2; M. Barratt Brown, 'A Trade Unionist's Diary', in Michael Barratt Brown and Ken Coates (eds.), *Trade Union Register: 3* (Nottingham, 1973), p. 275.
7. Knowles, *Strikes*, p. 6. Knowles' book is undoubtedly the best and most comprehensive work on British strikes, but it is mostly confined to the interwar period. Unfortunately it has been largely ignored by historians. Recently, Professor Harold Perkin proposed an extensive study of strikes in order to determine the relationship between economic development and class conflict. Unfortunately other work has forced him to postpone this project. Cf. H.J. Perkin, 'Inflation, Deflation, and Class Conflict in Britain since 1815', paper presented to

the Leningrad Congress of the International Association of Economic History, 1970.

8. Many such studies are cited in R. Hyman, *Strikes* (London, 1972); but see also J.E.T. Eldridge, *Industrial Disputes* (London, 1968).

9. E.J. Hobsbawm discusses the wave-like character of strikes in 'Economic Fluctuations and Some Social Movements since 1800', in *Labouring Men* (Garden City, NY, 1967), pp. 149-84. See also J. Cronin, 'The Peculiar Pattern of Strikes in Britain since 1888', *Journal of British Studies* (Spring, 1979).

10. Much of the recent literature of strikes, riots, and other forms of collective action in Europe is cited in Charles, Louise and Richard Tilly, *The Rebellious Century* (Cambridge, Mass., 1975).

11. E.P. Thompson, 'The Moral Economy of the English Crowd in the Eighteenth Century', *Past and Present*, no. 50 (Feb. 1971), pp. 76-136; 'Patrician Society, Plebeian Culture', *Journal of Social History*, VI (1974), pp. 382-405; and 'Eighteenth-Century English Society: Structure, Field of Force, Dialectic', unpublished. See also W.W. Rostow, 'Trade Cycles, Harvests, and Politics, 1790-1850', in *British Economy of the Nineteenth Century* (Oxford, 1949), pp. 108-25.

12. See the brief presentation of Labrousse's views in his '1848-1830-1789: How Revolutions are Born', in F. Crouzet, W.H. Chaloner, and W.M. Stern (eds.), *Essays in European Economic History, 1789-1914* (London, 1969), pp. 1-14; and the discussion in P. Vilar, 'Histoire Marxiste, histoire en construction. Essai de Dialogue avec Althusser', *Annales E.S.C.*, XXVIII, 1 (Jan.-Feb. 1973), pp. 165-98. Needless to say, this perspective may be as useful to non-Marxists as it is to Marxists such as Vilar. It would not be the first time that Marxian insights have fertilised the historical imagination.

13. E.J. Hobsbawm, 'From Social History to the History of Society', *Daedalus*, C (1971), pp. 38-9.

2 THEORIES OF INDUSTRIAL CONFLICT

Extended discussions of method and theory bore most historians, and they ordinarily eschew them, preferring instead to make do with the assumption that the narrative form dictated by the nature of their subjects will impose its own methodological imperatives and its own logic of explanation. It is clear, however, that a simple narration of the ups and downs of strike activity will not provide much enlightenment as to cause, and that the selection of proper tools is critical in this case for any serious causal analysis. So one must ask just how the study of strike data ought to be conducted. Technically, of course, the answer is obvious — one must supplement the traditional burrowing methods of historical research with the statistical techniques developed and applied so widely in other social sciences. But in terms of concepts and theories the answer is not so simple; and it would seem to be a mistake to borrow uncritically, along with the techniques, also the models and assumptions prevalent among industrial relations specialists whose disciplinary bases are in economics, political science or sociology. And yet when one surveys the literature on strikes, it becomes clear that concepts derived from the non-historical social sciences have long been dominant, and compete only with an impotent empiricism. More disappointing still, at least some historians of strikes have adopted such models virtually whole and even those who have been more critical or electric, as the case may be, have not ordinarily developed models of strikes which are explicitly and self-consciously historical in assumption and operation.[1]

The main purpose of this chapter is to submit various extant theories of strikes to both theoretical and empirical criticism, and to generate in the process the rudiments of an historical model. To accomplish this in a contextual vacuum would naturally be impossible, so the exercise will be conducted in a British context and the theories tested against the British experience. Whether the argument will have any broader relevance will be dependent therefore on its applicability to events and processes in the history of British industrial relations.

Before entering into critique, it might be useful to glance briefly at the main outlines of strike history in Britain. This is most easily done graphically, and Figures 2.1 and 2.2 have been constructed in order to provide a first approximation of the reality which any theory of strikes must explain. The graphs reveal that while strikes have varied in two dimensions — through time and across industries — for most of the period since 1888 the curves for different industries have run parallel and the most dramatic fluctuations have been those occurring over time. Strikes have tended to come in waves, clumping together in a few years, dying down in most others. Moreover, each strike wave also seems to represent a transition between distinctly different patterns of activity which persist for a number of years. Finally, it is worth noting that a comparison of this peculiar path of strike activity with the course of trade union growth (Figure 2.3) shows a substantial similarity; apparently strike waves are correlated with waves of unionisation.

These few facts have serious implications for a theory of strikes. The parallel movement of strikes in different industries, for example, suggests that what matters most in determining strikes are not those aspects of technology and organisation which differentiate one industry from another, but historical factors common to each other. Nevertheless, it remains that industries do differ, which indicates that the broad historical factors just referred to probably affect various industries to different degrees, or that workers in different industries possess unequal capacities for translating grievances into collective action. Consequently, any research strategy concerning strikes ought to begin with temporal variation and proceed to variations across industries.

The wave-like character of strike history provides more specific insights into the nature of the historical factors at work. There is, to be sure, a clear long-term trend in most industries and in the economy as a whole toward more strikes and ever-increasing numbers of workers on strike, and this tells us that in the very long run industrial conflict tends to become more common in advanced industrial society. Peculiarly though, the progress along the trend line is irregular and uneven, moving with great leaps forward and backward. One can, in fact, pick out three distinct types of variation in the trend of strikes over time. The first is the long-term tendency for both measures of strike activity to increase. The second sort of variation is that connected with strike waves, which seem to usher in or to mark the climax of distinctive periods of strike experience. The third is the very short-term, year-to-year fluctuation. This, it seems likely, will reflect particular short-term influences which probably simply affect the timing of strikes rather than their absolute level or extent.

Because most of the progress along the trend line is concentrated in a few years, that is, in strike waves, it seems probable that the really important factors are those which contribute to the development of

Figure 2.1: Number of Strikes in the United Kingdom, 1888-1974

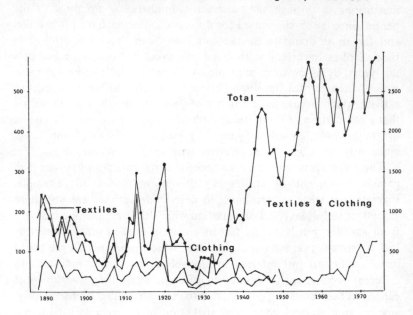

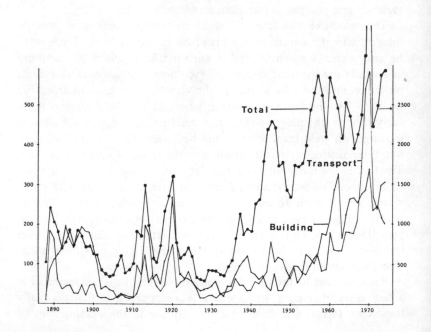

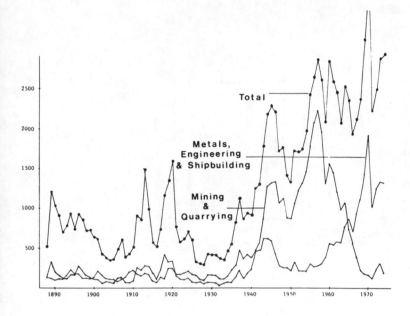

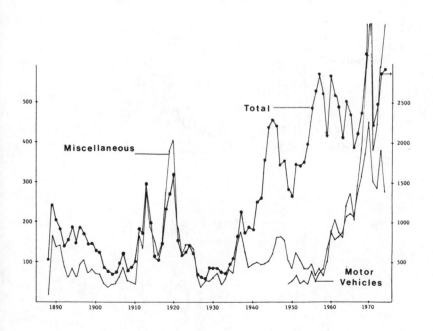

Figure 2.2: Number of Strikers (in thousands) in the United Kingdom, 1888-1974

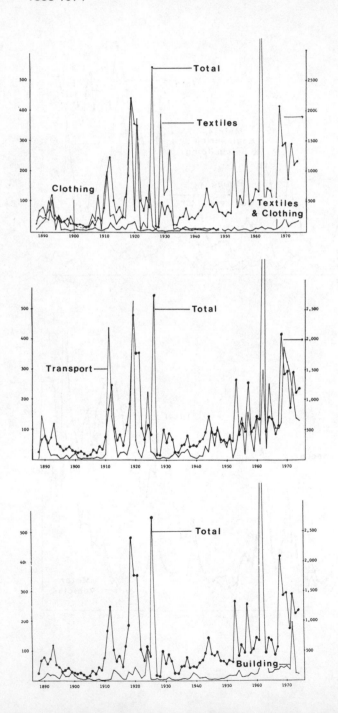

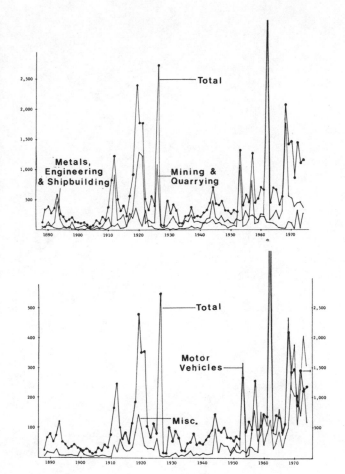

Figure 2.3: Trade Union Membership, 1880-1974 (in thousands)

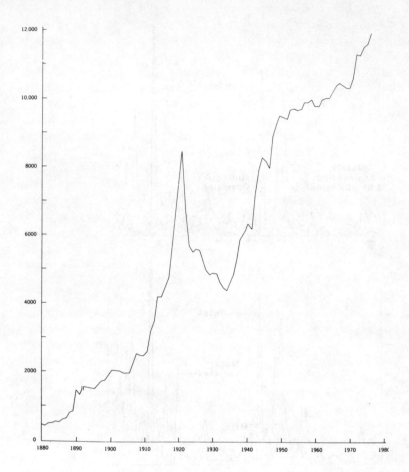

those waves. Such factors are likely to be of the sort which operate neither in the very short nor in the very long run, but somewhere in between. Long-term factors such as urbanisation or industrialisation are unlikely candidates, unless it can be shown that the pace of urban or economic growth is somehow orchestrated with the pattern of strikes. Equally unlikely are short-term fluctuations in the economy. Much more likely are trends in economic development which operate over one or two decades, or changes in workers' consciousness which, while perhaps resulting from a cumulation of short-term grievances, mature decisively, all of a sudden, and possibly in response to economic movements of a more intermediate duration.

In general, then, the time pattern of British strikes requires that a theory of conflict be historical in two different but related senses. First, explanations which stress change and development seem much more compatible with the facts than those whose emphasis is upon relatively stable social or technical structures. Presumably historical and structural factors interact, but the primacy must in this case be given to the former. Second, unilinear conceptions of the historical factors involved in strike determination should be likewise rejected in favour of some notion of uneven development.

Armed with these few insights, derived admittedly as much from *a priori* reasoning as from the analysis of data, it is nevertheless considerably easier to discern the weaknesses of competing theories of industrial conflict. As usual in this sort of research, there are almost as many theories of strikes as there have been studies, each successive author adding a slight new twist to previous arguments.[2] Nevertheless, most work falls into one of four distinct approaches. The first theory with which we shall deal is related closely to certain versions of modernisation theory; a second derives from work done in industrial sociology and focuses upon the differences among various types of workers; a third is the economic approach based on aspects of bargaining theory; and fourth, there is the political-organisational model proposed by Shorter and Tilly and developed by several of their students and collaborators.

Modernisation theory is essentially an over-arching model of the nature and historical development of industrial society, but it is not for that reason necessarily historical in the sense used here.[3] In positing a linear and universal trajectory to societal development, it can actually be said to be anti-historical; and it is largely for that reason that modernisation theory has been sharply and effectively criticised.[4] Applied to strikes, the thrust of the modernisation approach has been on the manner in which the early stages of industrialisation stimulate large-scale migration, hasten the destruction of old social networks and produce stresses and strains ('psychic dislocation') in individuals leading to protest or even rebellion. As Clark Kerr and his colleagues explained in the classic formulation of this view, 'One universal response to industrialisation . . . is protest on the part of the labour force as it is fitted into the new social structure.'[5] Strikes are thus seen as 'pathological, in that they represent the inarticulate expression of individual impulses . . .', and also as transitional.[6] They occur primarily during the period when workers are being 'fitted in' to the new system; greater social integration gradually decreases industrial conflict.

There are several variations on this same theme, but they all tend to imply that conflict should lessen in advanced industrial society. Ross and Hartmann, for instance, in their famous study predicted the 'withering away' of strikes as stable collective bargaining machinery evolved and as workers themselves matured.[7] Unfortunately for such argument, contemporary trends in strike activity utterly contradict the prognosis of constantly diminishing levels of conflict.[8] Indeed, were it not for the fact that the key assumption behind such notions − that strife is the product of dislocated, marginal or immature individuals: 'troublemakers' in another parlance − still informs popular and some academic accounts of strikes, the theory would be hardly worth criticising.[9]

Uniting all variants of strike analysis based on modernising assumptions is a certain common prescriptive tone. Strikes are seen as having only a very minor legitimate role in modern, democratic society. This normative sense clearly informs the main British version of the argument, in which a modest level of strikes is considered inevitable to the workings of the industrial relations system, but in which high strike rates are indices of severe dysfunction. Hugh Clegg and the late Allan Flanders have been this school's leading exponents.[10] The key concept in their system is the interrelationship between the institutional mechanisms for regulating industrial employment, and the problems institutions have to solve.[11] In their view, the incidence of strikes is essentially an indicator of the suitability of current bargaining techniques to the problems arising from employment. Given the constant technological change which affects modern industrial economies, some strike activity is a necessary lubricant absorbing the friction of an evolving system. It is when changes in technology, and, consequently, in the structure or level of industrial employment, outrun changes in the institutional framework of industrial relations that abnormally high strike rates occur.

The norm in advanced economies is for the machinery of industrial relations to be in relative harmony with the problems it confronts. The problem with Britain is that full employment and the spread of advanced processes have given increased power to workers at the point of production. The locus of important negotiations has thus shifted downward, and the traditional industrial relations system has become inadequate. The problem of unofficial strikes is due to Britain's fossilised institutional structure; hence the crucial necessity of reforming the institutions of collective bargaining.[12]

There are several blind-spots in this approach. It is based ideologically on thoroughly liberal assumptions: social conflict is omnipresent, but ultimately reconcilable; society is a balance of forces in constant equilibrium; even certain types of conflict, like strikes, serve to reinforce the equilibrium and integrate dissidents into the system; and the role of social theory is not to criticise, but to discover the friction points in the system, so as to guide the process of technical adjustment.[13] Part cause and part result of this bias, the Clegg-Flanders approach has a second conceptual flaw. It ignores workers' ability to think and to feel; more specifically, it neglects to mention that workers' feelings, attitudes, and abilities to express dissatisfaction with 'the industrial relations system' can change markedly over time, in response to many aspects of social and economic development. Consequently, their narrow institutionalism misses the impact of 'social pressures and aspirations' in strike movements, and reduces the study of industrial conflict to the analysis of bargaining structures and procedures. Such an approach is unlikely, given its assumptions, to provide a very satisfactory explanation of the historical fluctuations in strikes. To put it slightly differently, the peculiar rhythm of industrial strife, with its accent on discontinuity, is so unlike any notion of the development of industrial relations institutions, which is almost always continuous if not quite linear, and which generally proceeds by precedent, or by groping empiricism, rather than by innovation, that the Clegg-Flanders model is of little practical use in understanding the history of strikes.[14]

Neither the Clegg-Flanders approach nor any of the related concepts of strike determination lends itself readily to transformation into a quantitatively testable model. The modernisation perspective does of course impute a particular teleology to industrial relations systems which is obviously some way from completion, but one can always find reasons for postponing the millennium. Still, it is possible to test whether there is any correlation between strikes or strikers and the types of situations and people allegedly most prone to conflict. According to the theory, strikes should increase with migration and urbanisation and be highly correlated with crime, while the actual participants in strikes should more often than not be migrants or other marginal characters. In fact, such is not the case. As several studies have shown, protesters and strikers tend to be relatively stable, respectable persons well integrated in their respective community or occupational networks.[15] On both conceptual and empirical grounds, modernisation theory is unlikely to provide many useful insights into strikes.

The approach to strike behaviour which focuses primarily upon differences between types of workers might well be labelled 'structural' in that, according to this view, what differentiates one group of workers from another are the social structures of their communities and the technical structures of their environments at work. Again, the inspiration came from the work of Clark Kerr, this time writing with Abraham Siegel, in 'The Inter-Industry Propensity to Strike'.[16] The two argued that different types of workers have unequal strike propensities primarily because of variations in the communities in which they live. Coal-miners are their archetypal strike-prone workers because they live in one-industry towns with closely-knit social structures. They are isolated from other workers and, more importantly, from their social superiors. There are consequently few moderating influences within the community. This leads to an 'us/them' view of the world, and industrial conflict against the (often absentee) mineowner in such situations gains the sanction of the whole community. Conversely, workers living in socially and industrially integrated towns are allegedly less prone to strike, although some, like dockers, may form socially isolated enclaves within a more variegated environment and also become strike-prone. To some degree this theory deals with both the desire and the ability to strike. Living in solid communities can give workers the strength to strike, as well as the willingness. But clearly the emphasis is on how such communities shape workers' collective consciousness and their attitudes toward striking. That is certainly the way the theory has come to be interpreted and applied by more contemporary sociologists.

The Kerr-Siegel hypothesis provides the framework for David Lockwood's well-known essay on English workers, 'Sources of Variation in Working-Class Images of Society'.[17] Lockwood constructed a three-fold typology of deferential traditional, traditional proletarian, and modern privatised workers. Traditional proletarians are to be found in those very same industries that Kerr and Siegel designated as highly strike-prone, where men have both 'a high degree of job involvement and strong attachments to primary work groups that possess a considerable autonomy . . . ' These attachments also carry over into leisure-time associations in what Lockwood referred to as 'occupational communities'. Deferential workers, by contrast, work in jobs that involve close and frequent contact with superiors and discourage the formation of 'strong attachments to workers in a similar market situation'.[18] The residential patterns of such workers also serve to reinforce vertical rather than horizontal loyalties; indeed, often the very definition of the work situation of deferential workers involves a supervised and paternalistic living arrangement. The new breed of privatised workers are very different, and can allegedly be found in the newer, mass-produced industries like motor-car manufacture, in which high wages are said to compensate for lack of intrinsic work satisfaction. They live in new towns or developments and form there a 'population of strangers' with little or no 'communal sociability'; in consequence, they develop home-centred, consumption-oriented lifestyles and aspirations.

Documentation for the empirical usefulness of this typology was provided in the 'Affluent Worker' studies conducted by Goldthorpe, Lockwood and their co-workers in the 1960s. Most of the evidence concerned the social and political behaviour of 'affluent workers' from Luton, but one volume concentrated on their 'Industrial Attitudes and Behaviour'.[19] Here the implications of the typology for strikes were clarified: 'affluent workers' had little interest in their work or workmates other than pecuniary and were thus less likely to develop the solidarity and collective traditions necessary for sustained militancy. By implication, traditional proletarians had social ties that encouraged strikes and so struck much more often, while deferential workers had neither the wish nor the capacity to launch collective action. Strike behaviour is therefore a function of community structures and patterns of work organisation.

This approach has been extensively debated among British sociologists. Critics have argued repeatedly that the stress on community patterns and hence on 'prior orientations' to work leads to a neglect of the workplace and its impact on workers' attitudes.[20] But it is by no means clear that giving equal weight to what have been called the more 'proximate' influences at the point of production would make the approach any more satisfying to the historian. Indeed, the most telling objections to this theoretical perspective are of an historical nature and would apply even if it were broadened to take work environments more fully into account. As Richard Hyman has argued, even the most complex structural explanations nevertheless 'view human behaviour as mechanically determined by the social structure . . .', and see workers as blissfully ignorant of all but a narrow range of constant environmental structures, ignorant of economic and social changes outside the confines of the pit or the pub, as well as of politics.[21] Even wages are excluded from the range of influences, if one takes the argument to its logical conclusion.

In terms of fact, this typological approach also fails. It fails in the present because, as many researchers have demonstrated, all sorts of workers refuse to act and feel as their environments dictate. The 'affluent workers' at Luton, to take only the most extreme case, launched a miniature strike wave even before the volume explaining why they would avoid strikes was published. Other workers have been no more predictable.[22] The typology fails historically even more conspicuously because of the way the inter-industry propensity to strike has varied over time. Textile workers were the prototypical strike-prone workers of the nineteenth century, but strike rates in that industry fell to very low levels after 1932.[23] Miners, notorious for high strike rates at all times, were not noticeably more prone to strike than other workers before 1920, and since 1957 their level of activity has decreased markedly.[24] Likewise the dockers, whose reputation for militancy seems to have been largely a product of the years since 1945, or thereabouts.[25] Unfortunately, the connections between the turning points in the strike propensity of these or other industries and changes in social or occupational structure have not been thoroughly investigated, but as the structural determinants emphasised by Kerr and Siegel, Lockwood and others are generally conceived in static terms, subject only to slow, incremental changes, they seem uniquely inappropriate to explain the peculiarly uneven pattern of strikes in England.[26]

Neither the view of strikes based upon modernisation theory nor the structural approach so popular among industrial sociologists is capable of comprehending the historical dimension of strike activity. The models of the econometricians, however, seem at first glance more compatible with temporal variations. Their equations are ordinarily designed to explain fluctuations over time and are thus at least formally symmetrical to an historical approach. Still, it must be remembered that the economist's prime concern has been with the determination of wage and price levels and only in that connection with collective bargaining and strikes. Their concerns are narrow, and they view industrial conflict as the functional manifestation of breakdowns in wage bargaining. In the words of Sir John Hicks, 'the majority of strikes are the result of faulty negotiations'. Usually these faulty negotiations are due to inadequate knowledge or poor communications; conversely, 'adequate knowledge will always make a settlement possible'.[27] Ashenfelter and Johnson summarise: 'the basic function of the strike is as an equilibrating mechanism to square up the union membership's wage expectations with what the firm may be prepared to pay.'[28]

Explaining strikes therefore becomes primarily a problem of estimating how far workers' expectations are out of line with 'what the firm may be prepared to pay' at any given moment. The further workers' expectations have outrun management's ability to pay, the greater the likelihood of a strike. The difficulties in developing a proper quantitative 'expectations function', however, are legion. A comprehensive theory of workers' expectations would have to take account at least of all the possible influences with which industrial sociologists have been concerned, as well as the tactical strengths and weaknesses of trade unions and employers' organisations. But most such factors are not easily quantifiable, and economists have tended to focus more narrowly on previous rates of change of wages as shaping workers' current expectations. Even here there are problems. How rapidly do expectations respond to conditions? If, for example, five years of rising wages were followed by two years of falling ones, what would workers expect and demand for the next year? Would they demand a further decrease? This seems a bit unlikely, but what size of increase would they demand? It may be that the years of decline would have caused them to adjust their sights downwards, and thus to ask for a smaller increase. It seems equally likely that they might try in the next year to recoup their losses by making an unusually large claim. How long, in other words, and in what ways, do the effects of changing conditions work themselves out in changed expectations? The result predictably has been that the economists have devoted enormous time and energy to specifying the precise form of the expectations-achievement function to the exclusion in most cases of other potential influences.[29]

Still, the several econometric studies of British strikes which have included such functions have been surprisingly successful. The behavioural assumption involved is simple enough: the probability of a strike occurring increases as the gap between expectations and achievements widens. Most often the variable developed has been some sort of lagged moving average of rates of change of real wages over several years or quarters with more recent periods weighted more heavily. The results have been impressive. Studies of British strikes using such variables have generated equations accounting for 80-90 per cent of the yearly or quarterly variation in strike frequency.[30] The relevant estimations are presented in Chapter 4. Here it will suffice to note that the typical equation contains a prosperity variable whose coefficient is positive (unless the variable is unemployment), a rate of change of wages variable whose coefficient is negative, seasonal 'dummy' variables if quarterly data are used, trend and error terms.

Evaluation of these models is highly problematical. Conceptually, their narrow economic determinism is shocking to the historian's sense of causality. Wages are seen as the primary, if not the only concern of workers, and even this concern is shaped by the immediate, or very recent, economic situation. The conditions and pace of work, its regularity, and the trade union organisation it inspires, are all left out of the model, as well as any indicators of the overall economic and political climate. Were it not for the impressive statistical results, it would be tempting to reject the approach out of hand as conceptually naive and methodologically restricted — not to mention its bias in favour of employers.

Even the statistical results are subject to several qualifications. The model fits best in the period 1950-67. Applied to 1920-39 data, the fit is less good, and the major explanatory variable becomes a 'dummy' designed to capture the dampening after-effects of the General Strike, a rather *ad hoc* and in any case non-economic solution. Applied to the period since 1967, the model underpredicts significantly. Applied to the whole period from 1893 to 1970, there are serious problems of autocorrelation of residuals, and the standard error is very large. The precise statistical significance of these problems need not be entered into here, but they suggest two probable deficiencies in the econometric models. First, it is likely that the determinants of strikes are conceived much too narrowly to explain long-term patterns or, indeed, any patterns other than those prevailing during the circumscribed period 1950-67. On the other hand, it may also be — and this would be more in keeping with the argument of this book — that what appears in the economists' formulations as historical models are really incapable of comprehending the sorts of historical interactions which produce strikes. The weakness of economic models when applied to the data over the extended time span since 1893, for example, implies that the causes and hence also the meaning and significance of strikes shift over time.[31] More specifically, economic models are concerned entirely with annual fluctuations in strike rates, and seek to relate them to economic fluctuations in the short term. This procedure seems to miss those historical movements of medium duration which the peculiar historical pattern of strikes suggests may be critical. Finally, it is worth noting here that what success has been achieved has been limited to efforts at predicting the number of strikes; none of the models has been successful using the number of workers involved in conflicts or the number of days lost as a dependent variable.[32] They cannot, in particular, account for those periodic explosions of militancy, those strike waves which appear important in marking the transitions between distinctive historical patterns of strike behaviour and determination. Both of these weaknesses detract from the explanatory power of econometric models, but while the first might be remedied by the addition of new variables designed to measure other, non-economic factors, the second weakness is more fundamental to the methodology employed. It is for that reason more serious and theoretically significant.

All of the approaches surveyed to now have had a common focus — they concentrate their attention on measuring workers' desires and attitudes and are based on the (unspoken) assumption that these are translated without difficulty into strike action. Once this assumption is made explicit, it becomes immediately clear that it is highly questionable, since besides the desire there must also be the ability to carry out strikes with a reasonable chance of success. The great contribution of Charles Tilly and his associates is to have made explicit the hidden assumption upon which previous analyses have been based and to have placed the problem of workers' organisational strength at the centre of discussions of industrial conflict.[33]

Tilly *et al.* are reacting against two traditions in the study of industrial and social conflict which we have already discussed. The first they call the 'breakdown' approach, in which conflict is seen as peculiar to the early stages of industrialisation,[34] and resulting from impulsive action among the unorganised and unaffiliated; the second is the econometric approach with its narrow focus on wages. Tilly and his coworkers, in contrast, propose a model of strike determination that emphasises politics and organisation.

The most sustained attempt to apply this approach to an actual historical situation has been Shorter and Tilly's *Strikes in France, 1830-1968*. They see industrial conflict as basically political and intimately linked to broader societal struggles for power. Strikes both reflect and respond to shifts in the locus of political influence. Specifically, the nationalisation of social and political processes in France since the founding of the Third Republic has led to increased government intervention in industrial disputes and hence to their politicisation, as the actors in conflicts come to see the importance to the eventual outcome of influencing the government. Shorter and Tilly illustrate this argument by several facts from the history of French strikes: by the tendency for disputes to be timed to take advantage of political crises; by the frequent use of large-scale and very brief strikes as political demonstrations; by the attempts of both sides in conflicts to secure government intervention on their behalf, especially in the years 1890-1930; and by the general link between the major strike movements and the oscillating position of labour in the polity.

A similar argument can well be made for aspects of the strike history of Britain. The explosion of 1889 may well have been related to the dismal fortunes of Liberalism in the 1880s, and was in any case instrumental in convincing a section of the labour movement of the need for independent working-class political action. It was surely more than accidental that it was Ben Tillett, leader of the great dock strike of 1889, who two years after should have voiced the call for 'a distinctive Party with Labourism its religion and principle . . .', in order, as he put it, 'to bring about that common clannishness to enable us to turn the vote at election times'.[35] Political processes were intertwined with strikes at other moments as well. Certainly, the several great bouts of militancy between 1910 and 1926 cannot be disentangled from the general reorientation in British political allegiances occurring more or less simultaneously. Nor can the absence of a major strike wave during the 1930s be adequately explained without reference to the political demoralisation of Labour after the events of 1931-5. And, finally, it is evident that government efforts to regulate wages and incomes had a good deal to do with the transformation of industrial relations since 1967.

Nevertheless, as will be shown later, politics has been only one factor in the determination of industrial conflict in Britain. Economic change and shifts in the attitudes and consciousness of workers have also been important, and in most cases seem more basic. On the other hand, the Shorter-Tilly argument does not stand or fall on the ability to show direct linkages between political events and strikes. Rather, their focus upon political processes is part of a more general emphasis upon collective action, in which the balance of organisational resources determines the form and resolution of social conflict. Indeed, at the root of Shorter

and Tilly's view of strikes as political phenomena is the important
insight that strikes require organisation, and 'the existence of . . . organization . . . involves workers in the struggle for political power and
makes the strike available as a political weapon', whether they like it or
not. Because they reflect and sometimes alter the balance of organisational resources between workers, employers, and the state, 'strikes
have an important role in the struggle for power'. Thus, for Shorter and
Tilly the critical variable mediating between industrial conflict and
politics proper is organisation; and the translation by workers of exploitation and oppression into protest, of grievances into strikes, depends
primarily on workers' organisational strength, on their 'ability to act
collectively'.[36]

Shorter and Tilly would argue, therefore, that any attempt to
construct models of strikes in countries other than France must allow
for the influence of political and organisational variables. In their own
analysis, these take the form of variables measuring trade union membership, violent political conflicts, government crises, and the like.
Minimally, their theoretical perspective demands the addition of trade
union membership to the range of influences allowed into models by
the economists. Doing so does, in fact, improve the fit of models
predicting British strikes between 1893 and 1974. However, the improvement is only marginal, and the same statistical problems that
cast doubt upon purely economic formulations also trouble equations
incorporating both the economic and political-organisational approaches,
suggesting once more the difficulty of ever constructing successful
long-term models of strike determination. Still, the connection between
industrial conflict and trade unions is significant; and although the
statistical relation by itself says nothing about the direction of causation,
Shorter and Tilly themselves do offer a theory of the determinants of
union strength and structure which implies both the independence and
priority of organisational factors.[37]

Fundamentally, they see workers' ability to organise as a direct
function of the richness of the social, or 'associational' life they construct, and of the complexity of their social networks. This is detemined,
first of all, by the work structure and technologies of the jobs at which
people work and, second, by the type of community in which they
choose to live. Shorter and Tilly are explicit about the primacy of
'technological differences' in forging the 'organisational coherence' of
various groups of workers. They explain ' . . . if we have to say what
matters most over the years or across industries (in developing unions),
we would say technology'.[38] Skilled craft workers, with their personal

control over production and close and continuous interaction at the workplace, are in a position to develop strong unions. At the other end of the spectrum, machine-tenders in mass production industry, with little skill and few chances for social interaction on the job, find it most difficult to organise.[39] These differences in technology predispose workers both to different degrees and kinds of collective organisation. Craft workers would tend to generate small, strong localised unions with firm roots in the shop and high ratios of membership participation. Mass production workers would develop weak, national federations of highly bureaucratic but often politicised character, weak on the shop floor.[40] By implication, the general character of unionism will also change as technological change transforms one industry after another.

The sorts of communities in which workers live can also aid or hinder their capacity for collective action. Urbanisation, for example, has important (though opposite) short and long-term effects. In the short run, rapid urban growth means a high proportion of recent migrants, whose social relations rarely extend beyond kin, and who find organisation difficult. On the other hand, the general character of city life, which asserts itself in the long run, encourages a rich and diverse 'associational' life beyond kinship networks which tends to promote collective organisation.[41] So the ability to organise is determined by a whole range of factors connected with economic and urban growth, but the emphasis is upon technology.

Like Lockwood and Goldthorpe, then, Shorter and Tilly link different types of workers to parallel variations in collective organisation and by that route to strike behaviour as well. Where analysts like Lockwood stress community structure, however, Shorter and Tilly place the emphasis on technology. Because of this focus on technology they avoid the pitfall of too static a conception of working-class behaviour, and in the notion of technological change their model finds a source of continual dynamism. Their typology of artisanal, proletarian, and white-collar and service sector workers is thus both *sociological and historical*, and the history of strikes can for that reason be written in terms of the succession of leading industrial sectors in which first artisanal, then proletarian, and finally white-collar and scientific workers have been in turn the dominant types.

Perhaps the easiest way to understand Shorter and Tilly's approach in its complexity is to look at its application to the problem of French strike waves. As in Britain, the curve of strikes in France is distinguished by a series of exclamation marks (as Shorter and Tilly call them), which punctuate distinct phases of labour history. Of this phenomenon they offer an analysis in which 'politics and organization dovetail': the timing of strike waves is determined primarily 'by the timing of political crises'; while their 'structural features' reflect the structure of the labour force, the character and extent of prior organisation and certain structural aspects of French society as a whole. Behind the structural changes in strike waves are technological developments which 'operate in a rather *cyclical* fashion, going from artisanal to mechanical, then back again in the post-Second World War period to a modern adaptation of the classical artisan', as well as certain essentially linear social and political changes. Among these are the 'nationalisation' of politics and 'an increase in the scale of those institutions regulating working-class life'.[42]

The interaction of these forces is reflected in the various strike waves. To take but a few examples: explosions of militancy before 1890 were dominated by artisans and characteristically lacked national or even regional co-ordination, but were in each case correlated with other aspects of social and political unrest; beginning in 1870 but increasingly clearly from 1890, participation in strike waves revealed the growing importance of semi- and unskilled workers in mass production industries in French economic life. Each outburst from 1890 to 1920 involved larger numbers of such workers and consequently each was more centrally organised and ideologically charged. 1936 mobilised roughly similar groups of workers but was more widespread and involved particularly heavily operatives in the new industries (like automobile production) from the dynamic north-eastern half of the country. Since the Second World War, strikes have maintained their connection in time with political crises but have been marked by a growing involvement on the part of white-collar and science sector workers. This was especially the case in 1968, when the enhanced role of this new working class imparted a more decentralised and spontaneous tone to events than had been seen in many years.[43] There has been therefore an integral relation between union form and structure, the pattern of workers' associational networks, technology, political crisis and the timing and morphology of French strike waves. Indeed, the interlacing of the various strands of Shorter and Tilly's argument and the diverse aspects of these historical clusterings of conflicts is beautifully close and clear.

Nevertheless, the analysis of strike waves also reveals what is surely a real weakness in the political/organisational approach. For all the symmetry between the model and the physiogonomy of strikes, there is still no explanation of why strikes come in waves or why strike waves come when they do. These questions Shorter and Tilly intentionally bypass, suggesting simply and unsurprisingly that to 'understand what essential circumstances conjoin to produce a strike wave' would entail the inclusion of a large number of factors. Their aim is 'more modest', to demonstrate the links between politics and organisation and strikes. But is this enough? Doesn't the wave-like pattern of strikes have more significance in itself, beyond its usefulness in showing the evolution of the structure of collective action? Doesn't the periodicity of strike waves have additional meaning? Just to raise such questions is to suggest a set of answers and hence a criticism of Shorter and Tilly's work. The criticism at its most basic level is that Shorter and Tilly dissect strike waves to discover the structural contours of modern industrial society but ignore the occurrence of strike waves as itself an indication of social change. Their interests are in a sense more sociological than historical, history is the field on which the structural tendencies in modern society play themselves out, but has little meaning of its own.[44] One may take a different approach and argue that chronological patterns must be analysed in themselves in order to gain an understanding of the dynamics of societal development.[45]

The neglect of chronology makes Shorter and Tilly's analysis incomplete, and leaves one feeling that there is something more to the story. The gap in their analysis can be understood in both empirical and methodological terms. Empirically, they do not explain the facts of strike waves. Methodologically, their research strategy was obviously not designed to supply such explanation; specifically, it either excludes or does not utilise analytical tools to make sense of the dramatic temporal variation exhibited by strikes. In their theory of the technological determinants of organisation, for example, they have at hand a factor which could possibly explain this variation if only it could be shown that somehow the pace of technological change were synchronised with, and related to, outbursts of strikes. But Shorter and Tilly do not attempt such an analysis; their basic concerns lead them in other directions. They fail to overcome, therefore, the crucial weakness of most structural theories of the determinants of conflict — that is, their inability to comprehend historical change. We have already discussed that static and ahistorical bases of explanations of strikes based on aspects of community structure. But theories which focus on the work situation are not immune to similar problems. Many writers on British industrial relations, for example, have composed subtle analyses of situations where technological changes initiated by management have undermined the *status quo* in a particular plant or industry, and workers have responded with strike militancy.[46] The difficulty with such case studies is that they offer no mechanism with which to explain |the| simultaneity of eruptions in different industries. Are we to assume that all or most industries experience comparable technical change at approximately the same moment? This is of course possible, and there are those who would argue that technological innovations tend to cluster in much the same fashion as strikes.[47] But no one has as yet shown that the two types of clustering are in fact correlated, or that the impact of technological development on workers' attitudes and behaviour is direct and unmediated.[48]

Let us put the critique in more theoretical terms. Granting that strikes and organisation reflect the richness of workers' associational networks and that these are themselves functions of primarily technical but also community structures, the time pattern of strikes both in France and more clearly in England still suggests that the impact of structure on behaviour must be mediated by workers' attitudes and consciousness. Our criticism of the political/organisational model is analogous to Shorter and Tilly's criticism of previous models. They demanded that organisational strength be accorded an independent role in the determination of levels of conflict because organisation mediated between structure and behaviour. We would carry the argument one step further and insist that consciousness intervenes between structure on the one hand and organisation and behaviour on the other. By contrast, Shorter and Tilly dismiss the problem of assessing consciousness out of hand, asserting that 'such emotional qualities as worker "happiness" or "contentment", if in fact they vary over the years or from one kind of technology to another, are of little importance in explaining conflict. What counts is people's desire and ability to act collectively.'[49]

In sum, therefore, the model developed by Shorter and Tilly provides an extremely useful corrective to previous approaches by demanding that separate attention be given to the political and organisational resources available to both sides in industrial relations. They also proffer a theory of the structural determinants of organisational strength that is perceptive and in many cases persuasive. Still, their formulations lack any mechanism with which to explain the odd time pattern exhibited by both strikes and union growth, or any factor to mediate between structure and behaviour. By leaving out the subjective dimension, they telescope and oversimplify the complicated process by which the structural features of industrial society come to inform collective action.

In the end, none of the approaches derived from current social science models suffices to comprehend accurately the specifics of strike history in Britain. This analysis should not be construed in entirely negative terms, however. Our critical findings can be recast positively into guidelines for a more historical theory of strikes. A new theory must be above all multi-dimensional, encompassing factors that affect the attitudes and desires of workers and those that affect their ability to translate consciousness into action. The conception of how workers' attitudes are determined must also be broadened to allow for influences beyond the workplace and community and for the possibility that workers respond to less proximate political and economic movements. Most importantly, a better theory must be dynamic, capable of dealing with continuous change in all of the factors affecting industrial conflict. It must have at its centre therefore some mechanism for incessant change, a factor whose impact can somehow be synchronised with the outbreak of strike waves and related to the qualitative changes in strikes and strike determination which these outbursts seem to mark.

By elaborating on and refining these criteria it should be possible to deduce the contours of a satisfactory theory of strikes, but the route would be circuitous and altogether too time-consuming. Let us instead propose as an hypothesis that the core of a new theory of strikes would consist in the recognition that the uneven character of economic growth lies behind the comparable unevenness of industrial conflict. Economic growth must be seen as proceeding through a variety of qualitatively distinct stages which successively impose new contexts upon all of the actors in the industrial relations system. Growth is never simply quantitative but also qualitative, and each period is different in character from what went before or will come after. The perpetual dynamism of industrial society throws up new industries and new processes with successive phases of growth, and these alter as well as the constellation of economic movements accompanying each trend period. The effect upon workers of this uneven pattern is to confront them with a different complex of problems and grievances at each major shift and to stimulate a 're-making' of their consciousness and forms of collective organisation every two or three decades. Strike waves thus appear as periodic and concrete manifestations of the new attitudes and novel strategies produced by the impact of 'long waves' of economic growth upon the working class.

Why economic development should periodise itself into a series of distinct phases is by no means clear. What is clear is that recent conventional economic analysis has focused too narrowly on either short-term fluctuations or long-term growth and paid too little attention to such fluctuations of intermediate duration. One must turn for guidance therefore to figures who are distinctly outside the mainstream of economic theory, perhaps the most useful of whom is Kondratiev.[50] His theory of 'long waves' of 40 to 50 years — 20 to 25 years of expansion followed by 20 to 25 years of slow growth or contradiction — may well provide the starting point for understanding the interaction between prosperity and depression and the technical and structural evolution of industrial economies. But it is *only* a starting point, for what is most necessary is not an analysis of the exact periodicity of the movement of various economic indicators but a study of the nature of economic advance in successive phases of growth.[51] Each stage of development seems to be characterised by different leading sectors, by distinctive technologies, by shifting entrepreneurial styles, by alterations in plant size and layout, by differences in the composition of the labour force, its precise occupational mix, and its conditions of life. In short, we need a social history focusing on qualitative aspects of economic growth.

Fixing upon the impact of different phases of growth on strikes recommends itself for several reasons. First, it enables us to deal with both the desire and ability to strike simultaneously. Strike waves appear to come toward the end of either phase of a 'long wave' during a short-term upswing. In England the major explosions since the 1880s have occurred in 1889-90, 1910-13, 1919-20, 1957-62 and 1968-72. 1889-90, for example, were relatively prosperous years which allowed the expression of grievances built up over the course of the Great Depression of 1873-96. The pre-First World War outburst likewise came during a tight labour market but was primarily a response to diverse grievances, concerning prices, working conditions and so on, built up during the previous 15 years of 'boom'. Similar connections between trend periods of economic development and the timing of upsurges in strikes can be found in each succeeding period. But the connections in fact run deeper than mere timing. It is possible also to discover correlations between particular problems faced by workers in successive periods, the demands and slogans typical of each outburst, and the forms of union organisation generated to press for their achievement. Turning again to 1889-90, it seems obvious that the push for general unionism and the demand for shorter hours were both in their way attempts to cope with the unemployment so characteristic of the previous fifteen years. Each strike wave was also associated with break-throughs in union structure and strategy and led to substantial, at times truly dramatic, increases in membership. So both strikes and unionisation are reflections of a broader learning process on the part of workers stimulated by the effects of different phases of economic development. A common dynamism rooted in economic change informs conflict and organisation, and affects both the desire and the ability of workers to execute collective action.

Such are the main outlines of the argument we shall try to substantiate in the following pages. It will be elaborated and specified more precisely in the next chapter on the history of British strike waves, and subsequent chapters will attempt a more rigorous application to the facts of strike history. What deserved emphasis here, however, is that the hypothesis we have proposed is designed to overcome the inherent limitations of competing social science models by utilising the time pattern of strikes to shape the contours of its explanation; and it is our conviction that only by creating a model with a dynamic historical dimension can one make sense out of the peculiarly uneven pattern of industrial conflict in modern industrial society.

It is fitting that we should close with a brief methodological note. The critique conducted in the preceding pages utilised a strategy based on the notion of *symmetry*, a term used several times above. The spatial or geometric metaphor was chosen deliberately in order to suggest that explanations should be fundamentally symmetrical to the problems to be solved. Long-term questions deserve long-term answers, short-term ones short-term answers. Non linear or irregular patterns must therefore be explained by reference to forces operative on a comparable time scale or to a combination of forces such that their interaction can explain temporal irregularity. By the same logic, cross-cultural phenomena should be analysed in cross-cultural and comparative terms.

No doubt David Fischer and others would find in this notion of symmetry a classic instance of the fallacy of identity, which assumes 'that a cause must somehow resemble its effect'.[52] Nevertheless, it seems clear that what historians have to offer to other social scientists is primarily their sense of chronological time, and the timing of events broadly conceived provides us with a unique criterion to apply to the theories and explanations generated by our colleagues in these other fields. It should be possible, moreover, to press the insights gained from a study of the time pattern of events into the historically dynamic theories needed to replace the static or simplistically linear ones so popular today. This, it seems, is what Eric Hobsbawm had in mind when he reminded us that when, as has recently occurred, 'nonhistorical social scientists have begun to ask properly historical questions, and to ask historians for answers, it is because they themselves have none'.[53] Recognition of this is the essential precondition for inter-disciplinary history.

Notes

1. This is a relatively common failing among historians who seek to apply insights gleaned from other social sciences. On this problem, see the remarks by E.J. Hobsbawm, 'From Social History to the History of Society', *Daedalus*, C (1971), pp. 20-45.

2. The most comprehensive bibliography on studies of British strikes is that contained in R. Hyman, *Strikes* (London, 1972).

3. A brief but useful summary of modernisation theory can be obtained from C.E. Black, *The Dynamics of Modernization* (New York, 1966).

4. Two very useful critical evaluations of modernisation theory are D. Tipps, 'Modernization Theory and the Comparative Study of Societies', *Comparative Studies in Society and History*, XV (1973), pp. 199-226; and H.-U. Wehler, *Modernisierungstheorie ünd Geschichte* (Göttingen, 1975).

5. C. Kerr, F. Harbison, J. Dunlop and C. Meyers, 'The Labour Problem in Economic Development', *International Labour Review*, LXXII (1955), pp. 13-14.

6. D. Snyder, 'Determinants of Industrial Conflict: Historical Models of Strikes in France, Italy, and the United States' (unpublished Ph.D. dissertation, University of Michigan, 1974), p. 31.

7. A. Ross and P. Hartmann, *Changing Patterns of Industrial Conflict* (New York, 1960).

8. See, for example, D. Hibbs, 'Industrial Conflict in Advanced Industrial Societies', Center for International Studies, MIT, 1974.

9. J. Amsden and S. Brier argue in 'Coal Miners on Strike: The Transformation of Strike Demands and the Formation of a National Union', *Journal of Interdisciplinary History*, VII (1977), pp. 583-616, that Peter Stearns' discussion of the maturation of strike demands in Europe from 1890 to 1914 embodies such a perspective. For the original argument, see Stearns, 'Measuring the Evolution of Strike Movements', *International Review of Social History*, IX (1974), pp. 1-27.

10. See H. Clegg, *The System of Industrial Relations in Great Britain* (Oxford, 1970); and A. Flanders, *Management and Unions: The Theory and Reform of Industrial Relations* (London, 1970).

11. Flanders, *Management and Unions*, pp. 83-128; and Clegg, *The System of Industrial Relations*, pp. 314-42.

12. See Clegg, *The System of Industrial Relations, passim*.

13. The liberal bias in much of the work of British industrial relations specialists has provoked sharp disputes within the field itself. See, for example, A. Fox, 'Industrial Relations: A Social Critique of Pluralism', in J. Child (ed.), *Man and Organisation* (London, 1973); H. Clegg, 'Pluralism in Industrial Relations', *British Journal of Industrial Relations*, XIII (1975), pp. 309-16; and R. Hyman and I. Brough, *Social Values and Industrial Relations* (Oxford, 1975).

14. On the other hand it must be pointed out that Clegg and others who share his perspective have produced an enormously useful body of literature from which a good deal can be learned.

15. On this point, see Charles, Louise and Richard Tilly, *The Rebellious Century* (Cambridge, Mass., 1975), and the works cited there.

16. C. Kerr and A. Siegel, 'The Inter-Industry Propensity to Strike', in

42   Theories of Industrial Conflict

A. Kornhauser, R. Dubin and A. Ross (eds.), *Industrial Conflict* (New York, 1954), pp. 189-212. Actually the lineage of this concept can be traced back still further to J.T. Dunlop's seminal piece, 'The Development of Labor Organization: A Theoretical Framework', in R.A. Lester and J. Shister (eds.), *Insights into Labor Issues* (New York, 1948), pp. 163-93.

17. D. Lockwood, 'Sources of Variation in Working-Class Images of Society', *Sociological Review*, XIV (1966), pp. 249-67, reprinted in M. Bulmer (ed.), *Working-Class Images of Society* (London, 1975).

18. Lockwood, in Bulmer, *Working-Class Images*, pp. 17-20.

19. J.H. Goldthorpe *et al., The Affluent Worker: Industrial Attitudes and Behaviour* (Cambridge, 1968).

20. See especially C.T. Whelan, 'Orientations to Work: Some Theoretical and Methodological Problems', *British Journal of Industrial Relations*, XIV (1976), pp. 142-58; and G. Mackenzie, 'The "Affluent Worker" Study: An Evaluation and Critique', in F. Parkin (ed.), *The Social Analysis of Class Structure* (London, 1974), pp. 237-56; and most recently, P.K. Edwards, 'A Critique of the Kerr-Siegel Hypothesis of Strikes and the Isolated Mass: A Study in the Falsification of Sociological Knowledge', *Sociological Review*, XXV (1977), pp. 551-74.

21. Hyman, *Strikes*, p. 67.

22. See the various articles in Bulmer, *Working-Class Images of Society*.

23. H.A. Turner, *The Trend of Strikes* (Leeds, 1963), pp. 4-5.

24. R.S. Moore's *Pitmen, Preachers and Politics* (Cambridge, 1974) is a useful antidote to stereotyped views of miners' behaviour. See also C. Storm-Clark, 'The Miners, 1870-1970: A Test Case for Oral History', *Victorian Studies*, XV (1971), pp. 49-74, on the consolidation of miners' occupational communities in the early twentieth century.

25. D.F. Wilson, *Dockers: The Impact of Industrial Change* (London, 1972), esp. pp. 44-58.

26. An argument could well be developed linking the stabilisation of social and community structures to the extremely high strike rates of some industries like mining and dockwork. Rigid, closed systems of social relations preserve traditions of militancy and nurture grievances which would subside in ordinary circumstances. Still, the original generation of militancy and a sense of grievance does not seem directly related to community structures in Britain. On this point, see Ch. 7 below.

27. J.R. Hicks, *The Theory of Wages* (New York, 1948), pp. 146-7.

28. O. Ashenfelter and G. Johnson, 'Bargaining Theory, Trade Unions, and Strike Activity', *American Economic Review*, LIX (1969), pp. 35-49.

29. The most elaborate attempt using English data is D. Sapsford, 'The United Kingdom's Industrial Disputes (1893-1971): A Study in the Economics of Industrial Unrest' (M. Phil. thesis, University of Leicester, 1973); and 'A Time Series Analysis of U.K. Industrial Disputes', *Industrial Relations*, XIV (1975), pp. 242-9. For an attempt using comparative data, see Hibbs, *'Industrial Conflict'*.

30. See J. Pencavel, 'An Investigation into Industrial Strike Activity in Britain', *Economica*, XXXVII (1970), pp. 239-56; and J.C. Shorey, 'A Quantitative Analysis of Strike Activity in the United Kingdom: With Reference to the Time Pattern and to Inter-Industry Differences' (Ph.D. dissertation, LSE, 1974), and 'Time Series Analysis of Strike Frequency', *British Journal of Industrial Relations*, XV (1977), pp. 63-75, for a more accessible formulation. Cf. also R. Bean and D. Peel, 'Business Activity, Labour Organization and Industrial Disputes in the U.K., 1893-1938', *Business History*, XVIII (1976), pp. 205-11, for an econometric approach in which economic variables proved of limited value.

31. David Snyder has reported a similar problem with economic models when applied to long-term data from France, Italy and the US. See his 'Institutional

Setting and Industrial Conflict', *American Sociological Review*, XL (1975), pp. 259-78.

32. Thus Sapsford explains in one article how his statistical manipulations only work on the number of strikes. He writes that only strike frequency 'was chosen for detailed . . . analysis for two reasons: (1) This variable is the one most independent of its previous values, thus making it especially sensitive to changes in the conditions causing strikes. (2) It is not subject to such erratic fluctuations as days lost and workers involved.' See Sapsford, 'A Time Series Analysis of U.K. Industrial Disputes', *Industrial Relations*, XIV (1975), pp. 242-9. Since the proof of these two claims is simply the failure of standard statistical techniques to make sense of the intractable data of strikers and days lost, the argument is essentially circular.

33. E. Shorter and C. Tilly, *Strikes in France, 1830-1968* (Cambridge, 1974) is the most important and detailed statement of the argument. But see also Tilly, Tilly and Tilly, *The Rebellious Century*, and Snyder, 'Institutional Setting and Industrial Conflict'.

The following critical evaluation of the political/organisational model was the subject of a very fruitful discussion at a session of the annual meeting of the Social Science History Association in Ann Arbor, Michigan, 21-2 October 1977. The major point made here (and there) is that Shorter and Tilly's approach, while extremely helpful and insightful, does not place sufficient emphasis upon changes in attitudes and consciousness in mediating between economic and technical development, organisation, and industrial militancy. Professor Joan Scott has argued in response that because subjective factors cannot be measured – only behaviour can be – it is implicitly recognised in the latter's formulations concerning strike behaviour and the decision to join unions themselves; consequently, the theory developed in this chapter does not differ substantively from Shorter and Tilly's model. The problem, however, is not one of measurement, but of theoretical completeness. The difficulty of finding quantifiable surrogates for consciousness is quite real, but can be overcome or mitigated by a number of research strategies, several of which are employed in subsequent chapters. Still, Scott is correct in suggesting that the two approaches are far from incompatible.

34. This is obviously what we have been discussing as the modernisation approach.

35. B. Tillett, to the Bradford Labour Council, 4 May 1891, reprinted in *The Clarion*, 24 September 1909.

36. Shorter and Tilly, *Strikes in France*, p. 10.

37. The point to be stressed here is that the primacy of organisation in relation to strikes derives only from the fact that Shorter and Tilly offer an autonomous theory of union growth. It has not been established statistically in their work, nor has it been possible to ascribe priority using British data. We tried to do so, for example, by lagging the variables measuring organisational strength behind strikes to test if these might not correlate better than unlagged variables. They did not; nor have other attempts to determine the direction of causation produced clear results. Thus, R. Bean and D.A. Peel, 'Business Activity, Labour Organization and Industrial Disputes in the U.K., 1892-1938', *Business History*, XVIII (1976), pp. 205-11, have found a strong positive relation between aggregate union growth and strike levels, but K. Armstrong, D. Bowers, and B. Burkitt, 'The Measurement of Trade Union Bargaining Power', *British Journal of Industrial Relations*, XV (1977), pp. 91-100, have found no such relation in their disaggregated study.

It is also necessary, if Shorter and Tilly's argument is to be accepted, to show that the determinants of trade union membership are not simply economic – if they were, then economic variables could be substituted in Shorter and Tilly's equations and models for organisational ones. This is what the econometricians in fact argue, and their position has no doubt been buttressed by the findings of

G.S. Bain and F. Elsheikh, *Union Growth and the Business Cycle: An Econometric Analysis* (Oxford, 1976).

38. Shorter and Tilly, *Strikes in France*, p. 187.

39. Ibid., pp. 175, 184.

40. See the graphic presentation, ibid., p. 175.

41. Ibid., pp. 271-80.

42. Ibid., pp. 104-6.

43. Ibid., p. 107ff.

44. It seems to me that Shorter and Tilly's intense concern for the 'shapes' of strikes clearly reveals this predisposition.

45. For a more elaborate argument on the importance of chronological time and its uses for historians, see P. Vilar, 'Histoire Marxiste, histoire en construction. Essai de dialogue avec Althusser', *Annales E.S.C.*, XXVIII (Jan.-Feb. 1973), pp. 165-98.

46. See, for instance, the case studies discussed in J.E.T. Eldridge, *Industrial Disputes* (London, 1968): and also A. Lane and K. Roberts, *Strike at Pilkington's* (London, 1971).

47. E.J. Hobsbawm makes this connection in his essay on 'Economic Fluctuations and Some Social Movements since 1800', in *Labouring Men* (Garden City, 1967), p. 169. Thus he writes, 'Perhaps the most important factor making for discontinuous social movements is the tendency of innovations themselves to cluster; a phenomenon we need not investigate further here.' Just why further investigation was unnecessary is not quite clear.

48. The argument being advanced here is not that technology makes no difference to strikes, but that the linkage is more complicated than extant models allow for.

49. Shorter and Tilly, *Strikes in France*, p. 12.

50. See N.D. Kondratieff, 'The Long Waves in Economic Life', *Review of Economic Statistics*, XVII (1935), pp. 105-15. Near the opposite political pole among economists and economic historians one can also find concern for 'long waves'. See, for example, W.W. Rostow, 'Kondratieff, Schumpeter, and Kuznets: Trend Periods Revisited', *Journal of Economic History*, XXXV (1975), pp. 719-53.

51. See G. Garvy, 'Kondatrieff's Theory of Long Cycles', *Review of Economic Statistics*, XXV (1943), pp. 203-20.

52. David H. Fischer, *Historians' Fallacies* (New York, 1970), p. 177.

53. Hobsbawm, 'From Social History to the History of Society', p. 26.

3 THE PECULIAR PATTERN OF BRITISH STRIKES

The absence of a strong historical tradition in the study of strikes, so evident from our critique of current social science models, is in some ways surprising. Since its inception back in the interwar decades, the very best workers in the academic study of industrial relations have acknowledged the need for an historical perspective. There has been a genuine feeling, as John Dunlop has explained, that labour organisation must be viewed in 'its total environment, regarding that environment as the technological processes, the market structure, the community institutions, and the value judgements of the society'.[1] Put rather more theoretically, it has been argued that even though 'trade unions (and strikes) are structurally determined', and 'conflict is permanent, endemic, pervasive' in capitalist society, one must nevertheless explain how it is that trade unions are formed and strikes launched at specific times. It is necessary to discern the sequence of events that causes workers to 'realize the primary importance of production relationships and ... their positions of inferiority in those relationships'.[2] History in short is the arena where structurally-determined necessities are actualised. The project of history is thus to discover the specific mediations between structure and behaviour; conversely, it is only by tracing linkages backward from behaviour that one can discover structure itself.

To comprehend the system of industrial relations and the role of strikes within it therefore requires historical analysis. But where do we begin? Ideally, the narrative should commence with the early stages of the industrial revolution, and trace from there the process by which strikes gradually replaced food riots and similar crowd actions as the dominant form of conflict. Charting this evolution in detail is, unfortunately, beyond the limits and possibilities of this study, but a few summary observations can be made based on the existing literature.[3] The first is that, for a long time, modern strikes and pre-modern collective actions seem to have coexisted and, at times, merged into one another. Form and content were especially confused, with old weapons like secret societies and mass physical violence being adapted for industrial uses, as in machine-breaking and in the oath-swearing and elaborate rituals surrounding early unionism, or with new tactics, such as the strike, being utilised for much more than industrial aims. Strikes of artisans and labourers, for example, were a prominent component in the Wilkite agitation, and spokesmen for reform from the 1790s to the 1840s can be found advocating strikes as tactics in the political struggle with increasing frequency, culminating in Benbow's famous call for a general strike and in the abortive Plug Riots of 1842. Riots and crowd violence, on the other hand, accompanied strike movements throughout the nineteenth century, as in Blackburn in 1878, where textile operatives rioted in classic fashion as part of a bitter dispute over wage reductions.[4] One reason, no doubt, why riots continued for so long was that they were often only responses to police provocation at public gatherings – as with the unemployed riots of the 1880s in London or at Manningham Mills in 1891, or to employers' attempts to import blackleg labour, as in many conflicts on the docks – rather than a preferred style of popular protest. The basic trend, of course, was for strikes to grow and for riots to fade into the background as the nineteenth century wore on, becoming confined increasingly to marginal, non-urban areas, to small one-industry towns, or to particular industries, like mining and docking. Still, the trend was a long time working itself out.

It is clear, then, that strikes became differentiated from earlier forms of collective action only slowly, and even in the twentieth century the separation has been at certain moments precarious. And yet, the transition from archaic and backward-looking to modern and forward-looking patterns of action was real enough overall. It is not that any single mode of protest ever predominated absolutely, but that one has tended to become more, and others less important over time. This inevitably complicates any effort at locating a precise moment of transition in forms of collective action; so it should come as no surprise to learn that several quite different estimates of the turning point compete in the literature. Charles Tilly seems to feel that 'the shift from reactive to proactive ... collective action on the part of ordinary people' occurred mainly in the years 1828-34, the days of the great Reform movement. Focusing more narrowly upon strikes, both Richard Price and Eric Hobsbawm argue that working people learned 'the rules of the game' in the market economy during the second half of the nineteenth century, abandoning the futile demand for control of productive processes in favour of monetary compensations. This (enforced) willingness to bargain away control and, by implication, intrinsic work satisfaction is presumably the key precondition for the transition from old to new types of struggle, for the adoption of the characteristically modern strike over wages. Certainly Peter Stearns thinks so; and he finds this 'maturation' in working-class attitudes, and hence in strike demands, largely completed by 1914.[5]

This confusion and disagreement over the timing of the shift in modes of protest suggest again the complexity of the process. Nevertheless, there is some consensus that the strike became the 'natural' response to distress in England some time between 1850 and 1900. To this author the break appears sharpest before and after 1870: the movement leading to the Second Reform Act in 1867 was conducted without substantial industrial action, while the prosperous years immediately following 1870 witnessed England's first major strike wave. The latter was cut short, to be sure, by the slump beginning in 1873, and its gains largely eroded by the 1880s, but the period 1871-3 does seem to have seen the decisive acceptance of the strike weapon by Britain's working population.

Sadly, the data from which this book is constructed do not become available for almost two decades after this first modern explosion of militancy, and rigorous analysis can only begin in 1888-9. However, the dynamism of social protest did not diminish once the transition from old to new forms was accomplished. Rather, the statistical history of strikes since 1888 is as exciting and as discontinuous as was the process by which industrialism first transformed the shapes and patterns of social conflict between 1770 and 1870.

The dimensions of the discontinuity of modern industrial strife are indicated by the graphic representation of strike data presented earlier in Figures 2.1 and 2.2. They illustrated that the most salient aspect of the evolution of British strike activity has been its distinctive and uneven time pattern. Movements in various industries have been generally in the same direction and of at least comparable magnitude, as if orchestrated to one basic rhythm. That rhythm itself is unique: periodic explosions of militancy, or strike waves, have predominated over the long-term trajectory and short-term fluctuations. Progress along the trend line of both measures of strike activity was not steady and linear, but concentrated, ' "jumpy" and discontinuous'.[6] The history of strikes appears as a series of great leaps or 'explosions' which climax or initiate particular periods of industrial struggle. Strike waves also serve as quantitative indicators of qualitative changes in the relations between workers and employers. Figure 2.3 depicted the growth of trade union membership, and it showed how strike waves mark off distinctively different stages in the organisational development of the labour movement. Any explanation of the history of industrial conflict must first of all make sense of these dramatic acts in the evolution of the British system of industrial relations.

Six strike waves have occurred in England since 1880: 1889-92, 1910-13, 1918-21, 1926, 1957-62, and 1968-72. These beginning and end points are admittedly arbitrary and approximate. One could argue, for example, that the wave which began in 1889 lasted longer, ending only with the mining strike of 1893, or with the defeat of the engineers in 1897-8. The period 1910 to 1926 could be considered one long wave instead of three, or 1957-72 one instead of two. One could well point also to the bitter struggles which marked the final days of the Heath government as prolonging the last wave to February 1974. Such indeterminacy is largely inevitable in any attempt at periodisation. We shall endeavour to show that, while possessing certain generic similarities, each of these particular waves differs sufficiently from the others to merit independent classification and analysis. In any case, there is little reason to doubt the basic contention about the wave-like pattern of strike history, or the general selection of years; and the validity of the explanation to be offered will not be affected greatly if the limits are shifted slightly one way or another.

Strike waves can be distinguished from other sections of the curve of strike activity by several features other than sheer size. Most obvious is their scope and range – they touch a much more varied cross-section of the working population than industrial conflict normally does. Of course, participation is far from equal, but it is extremely widespread. Strike waves are marked also by an almost surprising rate of success. Initially at least they roll on gaining momentum from one victory to another until, certain major advances secured, a firm stand by government or industry, coupled often with a serious economic slump, breaks the flow. This success itself is connected with two further interrelated aspects of strike waves – their apparent spontaneity and their innovative character. In reality, little that occurs in the history of labour is genuinely and completely spontaneous, but strike waves appear so because they spring from the occasional and massive intervention of the rank-and-file into the affairs of labour-management relations. They are profoundly democratic movements which ordinarily develop as much in opposition to entrenched labour leaders as to employers or the state. This insurgent quality is in turn linked to the creativity of strike waves. New strategies and forms of organisation based on novel ideological orientations characterise each eruption and largely account for the resistance offered by union leaderships to the initiatives from below.

This innovative function common to all strike waves also helps to distinguish one wave from another. Each explosion of militancy seems to have been associated with shifts in the attitudes and consciousness of workers and in organising tactics and union structure. Charting the changes in the perceptions of the inarticulate bulk of the working class is naturally extremely difficult. The clusters of issues raised in succeeding strike waves provide no real guide because the demands have been concerned overwhelmingly with wages — for the obvious reason that such demands are more easily formulated and specified than the vaguer and more subterranean discontents which may possibly be fuelling militancy. Nevertheless, the slogans and justifications attached to upsurges in strike action have differed substantially and indicate their distinctiveness. A brief description of the circumstances of each strike wave will suffice to demonstrate these similarities and differences.

From 1888 to 1892, the process of gathering and publishing strike statistics was gradually refined and made more comprehensive, so information for these early years is somewhat tentative. It is difficult therefore to gauge the precise magnitude of the explosion of industrial conflict that began in 1889. Sidney and Beatrice Webb did a tally of the numbers of separate strikes listed in *The Times* between 1876 and 1889, and these show a four-fold increase in 1889 over the average of the preceding five years.[7] The official statistics record that the number of strikes more than doubled from 517 in 1888 to 1,211 in 1889, and remained at comparable levels for the next two years. The number of workers involved in these disputes rose from around 120,000 in 1888 to something above 337,000 in 1889 and over 393,000 in 1890. The number dipped to 267,000 in 1891, but rebounded to 357,000 in 1892.

The industrial distribution of strikes and of workers affected between 1888 and 1892 was remarkably dispersed. This explosion affected both skilled and unskilled, workers organised in old unions like the engineers and the builders and in 'new' unions like the dockers and (it can be argued) the miners. The railwaymen — still too weak to undertake the co-ordinated and large-scale stoppages which the nature of the industry demanded, and also possibly still held in check by a liberal, 'respectable' outlook — were the only major exception to the general militancy. A clear indication of the widespread character of the movement is that the average strike included just over 350 workers. Considering the impact that such enormous strikes as the seamen's and dockers' in 1889 and the miners' strike and cotton lockouts of 1892 had on this figure, it is extremely low. Most of the action appears to have been small-scale and localised. This period, moreover, antedated the creation or consolidation of the major industrial federations, so it seems reasonable to assume that whatever co-ordination and communication developed among various groups of workers did so informally and through pre-existing, informal social networks. Unions, which by all accounts grew most either during or after the strikes, apparently played a minor role in initiating the struggles.

The issues of the strikes were what one would expect, and claims for wage increases were consistently predominant. Still, they were often accompanied by demands for shorter hours or trade union recognition, evidence of concerns that transcend the size of the pay packet. As the years passed, however, the economic climate worsened and the proportion of strikes fought against proposed wage reductions increased. Also, the number of strikes concerned with union rights and recognition jumped drastically in 1890 and stayed high to 1892, a sign of the beginning of that employers' counter-offensive against the unions which would culminate in the Taff Vale decision handed down in 1901.[8] There was, however, little indication in the results of strikes in these years of the employers' routs soon to come. Workers were extremely successful in achieving their stated aims in strikes. They lost outright only 27 per cent of all conflicts involving less than 23 per cent of those concerned — figures suggestive of a greater effectiveness of large strikes. The employers, it seems, were taken by surprise by the elemental outburst of working-class activism and, finding themselves very poorly organised, were forced to grant numerous concessions. As quickly as possible, they began the reaction which first became visible in 1890, but the high proportion of compromise settlements in 1891-2 shows that it was as yet not entirely successful.

With increased conflict came also breakthroughs in union organisation and strategy and corresponding shifts in workers' attitudes. Almost 800,000 new members were enrolled in unions affiliated to the Trades Unions Congress between 1887 and 1892. Depression and defeat halted growth in the early nineties, but membership never again declined below a million and a half. But the changes were not merely quantitative: 1889-92 also saw the first serious and successful attempts to form unions among the unskilled; it witnessed, too, the rejection of sliding scales, the demand for an eight-hour day, the first substantial recruitment of women into the (cotton) trade unions, and the spread of new ideas on organisation and tactics among engineers, railwaymen and others. In sum, the strike wave of 1889-92 marked the beginning of a whole new phase of labour history.[9]

Unions were forced on the defensive sometime after 1890 and strikes became less productive and more of a liability. The defeat of the engineers in 1898 had a profoundly depressing effect throughout the world of labour, and Taff Vale seemed to betoken yet another dismal decade. Eventually, though, workers regained the initiative and launched a strike wave of unprecedented size accompanied by unaccustomed bitterness and violence. This second outburst is generally referred to as the 'Labour Unrest' and began in 1910, when 385,000 employees took part in 531 strikes. The number of strikes rose to 903 in 1911 – more than twice the level of 1909 – then dropped minimally to 857 in 1912 before jumping again to 1,497 in 1913. The number of strikers followed a somewhat different pattern: increasing to 831,000 in 1911 and still further to 1,233,000 in 1912, then falling to a modest 516,000 in 1913. The two measures of strike activity thus seem to alternate, with a year of large confrontations in major industries being followed by (and probably stimulating) more widespread but limited action in less important parts of the economy.

Like 1889-92, the prewar movement ultimately touched most groups of workers, the dispersion actually broadening in 1913 as the numbers involved declined. Again, however, the impact was uneven and certain anomalies appear. In metal and engineering, for example, the number of strikes rose dramatically, but strikers did not increase proportionally. This apparently reflects the peculiar internal dynamics of the engineering union, where widespread rank-and-file militancy was frustrated by a confused and chaotic leadership – as then prevailed in the Amalgamated Society of Engineers (ASE) – which prevented the translation of membership enthusiasm into large-scale action.[10] The building industry was also under-represented in the totals of strikers, as were those countless minor industries which the Board of Trade labelled 'miscellaneous'. Numerically, therefore, this strike wave was dominated by semi- or unskilled labour organised, or just being organised, in industrial or general unions, i.e., miners, textile operatives, dockers and railwaymen. Hence the size of the typical strike increased to 780 persons, double that of 1889-92.

The demands which surfaced in 1910-13 again concerned mainly wages, although the issue of union recognition also brought many onto picket lines. Whatever the issue, the workers enjoyed considerable success. Less than 14 per cent of all strikers experienced defeat in these years. The predominance of the less skilled workforces in the major industries in the strike wave also left its mark on the ideological and strategic innovations that accompanied it. The 'Labour Unrest' aided the founding or consolidation of the great federated unions in transport, and brought sharp increases in union density in textiles and mining.

This strategic impetus toward bigger and stronger organisation reached its climax with the founding of the Triple Alliance of unions in mining, in transport, and on the railways. Surrounding all such efforts was a surge of sentiment in favour of broader and more effective forms of labour solidarity as the only effective tactic against the combinations of the employers and the apparent duplicities of the state. There is, to be sure, still a good deal of debate as to how deeply syndicalist ideology infected the average worker, but there can be little doubt that something of its spirit affected a good many. As H.G. Wells argued, 'The worker now is beginning to strike for unprecedented ends — against the system, against the fundamental conditions of labour, to strike for no ends at all, perplexingly and disconcertingly. The old fashioned strike was a method of bargaining, clumsy and violent perhaps, but bargaining still; the new-fashioned strike is far less of a haggle, far more of a display of temper.'[11] Just as the 'new unionism' of 1889-92 represented a fundamental break with the ideas and strategies of the 'seventies and 'eighties, the explosion of 1910-13 represented a new stage in the consolidation of class loyalties and antagonisms.

The effect of the First World War on strikes was contradictory: at first, it dampened militancy and caused a decrease in conflict, but gradually this gave way to a still deeper unrest. Thus the relationship between the pre- and postwar strike waves is complex. The postwar militancy was in many ways the last act of the 'Labour Unrest', yet it was also conditioned by the political and economic transformations stimulated by the war. In any case, 1919 saw new highs in the frequency and extent of strikes. The number of strikes hit 1,607 in 1920, while that of strikers peaked in 1919 at almost 2½ million. The pattern of participation closely paralleled that of 1910-13, except for the fact that the engineers and builders took a greater part, the dockers a lesser one. Miners, textile workers, and railwaymen again played leading roles.

Once more the demands centred on the question of wages, though by 1921 most workers were involved in negotiated, compromise settlements. As early as 1920 the employers began chalking up increasing numbers of clear-cut victories in small strikes. From the summer of 1920, with unemployment rising swiftly and spectacularly, the tide began to turn against the workers. During 1921, with the postwar boom decidedly over, textile workers and miners were forced to accept decreases in wages, and in 1922 the engineering lockout was a complete victory for the employers. Still, certain organisational advances were achieved in 1918-22 that were never to be reversed. The formation of the Amalgamated Engineering Union and of the Transport and General Workers' Union streamlined and strengthened unionisation in their respective industries enormously, while the establishment of the General Council of the TUC created the machinery (if not necessarily the willingness) to co-ordinate joint activity among the entire labour movement. On a quite different level, the organisation of shop stewards which came out of the war were conceded an official role in the conduct of workplace industrial relations by the Engineering Employers' Federation. It also seems clear that the upsurge of industrial militancy after the war went hand in hand with the transformation of working-class political consciousness which allowed the Labour Party to replace the Liberals as the second party in the country. None of these gains, it may be assumed, were sufficient compensation for the disasters experienced by large sections of the working population during the interwar decades, but they were gains nonetheless.[12]

By 1922, then, the postwar militancy had been thoroughly checked, and workers all over England were on the defensive against employers whose positions were bolstered by the mounting unemployment of the early twenties. Defeat was capped by ignominious capitulation in the General Strike of 1926 which, it now seems clear, the Baldwin Government deliberately provoked. From the beginning, the General Strike had little in common with previous strike waves, which were much more clearly offensive efforts by the rank-and-file. In 1926 almost all of the militancy was focused on support of the miners; neither before, during, nor after the General Strike did any significant group of other workers feel confident enough to press their own grievances — and these were many — to the point of striking. If one subtracts the General Strike and the great coal stoppage, there were only 321 strikes involving just under 95,000 workers in 1926. So, the General Strike is perhaps best understood as a serious after-shock of the eruptions of 1918-21 and the lockouts and wage cuts of 1922-5, rather than as a strike wave in its own right.[13]

The real significance of the General Strike was that it served to bring in an extremely long period of industrial peace.[14] Between 1926 and the mid-1950s, workers seemed to put aside the strike weapon in all but a few cases — e.g., textile workers in 1929-32, dockers in the late 1940s, and of course the coalminers, who waged guerrilla war in the pits from 1927 to about 1957. But the mid-1950s saw the beginnings of a series of quite important changes. From 1955 or 1956, strikes and strikers in engineering, especially in the motor industry, began a rise which continued until the 1970s. So, too, did strikes in the construction industry; and workers in miscellaneous industries and in transport and communication began striking more frequently from 1959-60. At the same time, the level of strikes and strikers in mining fell dramatically from 2,226 strikes involving 249,000 workers in 1957 to 993 strikes involving 129,000 workers in 1963. These changes, coming together between 1955 and 1960, led to the emergence of a new and distinctive pattern in the 1960s, in which the small, short and unofficial strike in modern sectors like engineering came to represent the typical British strike.[15] This is also reflected in the divergence of the two main indices of strike activity: between 1957 and 1963 the number of separate strikes outside mining increased 62 per cent, from 665 to 1,075, while the number of strikers rose only 36 per cent, from 240,000 to 327,000. Thus in the strike wave of 1957-62 the average strike involved less than 510 workers, compared with over 780 in 1910-13 and 1,400 in 1918-21 – and even these figures are inflated by the inclusion of national engineering stoppages in 1957 and 1962.

The industrial dispersion differed from that of earlier strike waves in the decline of strikes in mining, their virtual disappearance in textiles and clothing, and their flowering in metal and engineering. The growth of the modern engineering sector, where the advanced division of labour and interdependency of productive processes enable small work groups to bring large production units to a standstill, allowed the short, small and unofficial strike to come into its own. These strikes appear to have grown largely out of tensions at the point of production rather than from the breakdown of national wage bargaining. In each of the years 1957-62, less than half of the disputes were concerned explicitly with wages. Similarly, if one leaves out the years of the national engineering strikes, in none of those years did the percentage of workers on strike over wages top 57 per cent.

Typically, the demands pressed during a strike wave are a poor indicator of its ideological character, but in this case they are more suggestive. The apparent lack of interest in higher wages was paralleled by an enhanced concern for job security, which was reflected in an increase in conflicts over shop rules, manning regulations and, most obviously, redundancy. It has even been pointed out that in at least one of those few areas where wage struggles predominated between 1957 and 1962, motor-car manufacture, the real problem was a sense of insecurity fostered by the stop-go pattern of economic growth.[16] This focus on employment stability can probably be traced back to the 1930s, but whatever its origins, it seems to have produced in the late 1950s a desire among workers to re-establish a modicum of control over the process of production. This was done through an impressive elaboration of shop stewards' and workplace organisations – the main strategic innovation of this particular strike wave.

It might be argued that the strike waves of 1957-62 and 1968-72 really constituted a single, long wave; it is undoubtedly true that strikes and strikers in some industries continued to move upwards throughout the period. (See Figures 2.1 and 2.2) But there were several important differences between the two movements. The scale of strikes grew, as large strikes became more frequent. Though the average size of strikes increased by just about ten workers from 1957-62 to 1968-72, if 1957, 1962, and 1968 are all excluded as years of national engineering strikes, the average jumped from 230 to over 450 workers per strike. This was the product of two distinct but related developments: the growing concern among workers over inflation and consequent large strikes over wages, and the spread of wage militancy along with unionisation beyond the major industries to almost all sections of the manual, and many sections of the non-manual, working class.[17]

Three sets of statistics illustrate these trends. The industrial dispersion of strikes broadens. Compared to the earlier postwar outburst, the later one involved many more workers in transport and communications and 'miscellaneous' industries (both of which include a large number of public employees), and even in such traditional employments as textiles, clothing and construction. Second, the question of wages motivated increasing numbers of strikers. In each year between 1968 and 1972 more than half the strikes dealt with wages, and such conflicts involved at least 57 per cent of the strikers in each year. Third, these years witnessed a revitalisation of union growth. Up to 1962, membership had been growing slowly, from, for example, 9,829,000 in 1957 to 9,887,000 in 1962, an increase of only 58,000 or a mere 0.6 per cent. But the strike explosion of 1968-72 was accompanied by a jump in unionisation from 10,189,000 members in 1968 to 11,341,000 in 1972, an increase of 1,152,000 or 11.3 per cent. The advance in organisation was not merely quantitative, however. Membership grew absolutely because it spread laterally to previously unorganised groups of white-collar and service sector employees. Such an extension, moreover, would seem to have been impossible without some comparable transformation in the social attitudes and perceptions of these new recruits to trade unionism, and what little survey data is available presently seems to point in this direction. Thus, ideological and strategic innovations were again linked to a dramatic explosion of strike militancy.

Curiously, the uneven and wave-like pattern of strikes and union growth has elicited little comment and less analysis from British labour historians. Henry Pelling, for example, focuses in his *History of British Trade Unionism* on 'the slow but steady growth of trade unionism', ignoring the obvious fact of discontinuity. He smugly ascribes this style of development, especially the 'continuity of particular unions', to 'the evolutionary character of our political history'.[18] A.E. Musson takes virtually the same position, and the works of the leading students of industrial relations — such as Professor Clegg and others of what has been called the 'Oxford School' — share a similar perspective. They prefer to dwell upon the gradual elaboration and adaptation of bargaining and conciliation machinery rather than on the waves of unrest which provoked the search for such institutions.[19]

Many reasons could no doubt be adduced for this neglect of strike waves, and among them we should certainly have to rank political and ideological motives fairly high. It seems that historians are frequently more comfortable with notions of persistence and continuity rather than those of change and discontinuity. As Pierre Vilar has argued, 'To the historian, the temptation to search for stabilities is an ideological temptation, founded upon the anguish of change.'[20] It is obvious, however, that any serious social historian dealing with the modern world must be prepared to place change and development at the centre of his research. The oddly fitful and jerky pattern of strikes is, after all, merely symptomatic of the generally dynamic, uneven and often apparently unpredictable character of history since the industrial revolution; and it should be as susceptible to analysis as any other part of the story.

Analysis must commence, therefore, with that handful of scholars who have at least recognised the non linear development of strikes and unions. These include Shorter and Tilly, John Dunlop and Eric Hobsbawm. Shorter and Tilly's argument was discussed in some detail in the previous chapter, and it is concerned with strike waves insofar as their timing reveals the role of politics in stimulating conflict and their structural features reflect the evolution of the labour force. Applied to Britain, their approach highlights one or two interesting relationships. Participation in strike waves, for example, clearly reveals the general organisational and structural development of the British working class. The historic organising efforts in transport, the predominance and then decline of staple industries like coal and textiles in the economy and in the working class, and the rise of the service sector since 1945 are all reflected in the statistics. But when this much has been said, there still remains the question of why strikes have come in waves, and just what each wave signifies. Shorter and Tilly's approach seems ill-equipped to provide that sort of explanation.[21]

Dunlop asserted as early as 1948 that useful labour history must begin by acknowledging that 'The evolution of social institutions does not take place at uniform rates. The process is more like waves eating away at the base of a cliff, which eventually crashes into the sea.' The metaphor may be flawed, but its use constituted a recognition that union growth had until then occurred in several distinct spurts of two types. One kind of dramatic increase took place in wartime, when tight labour markets shifted the balance of tactical advantage sharply in the workers' direction. The second sort of advance he labelled as periods of 'fundamental unrest' and 'basic dissatisfaction with the performance of the economic system and the society as a whole'. These Dunlop linked to the downswings of Kondratiev cycles: each 'major upheaval came at the bottom of the period of bad times in the long wave', and each represented an accumulation of grievances.[22]

Hobsbawm's analysis is roughly similar to that of Dunlop. He begins by noting that the sparks with which to trigger an explosion of militancy are 'readily available in the trade cycle, or in political events'. The problem, however, 'is whether the whole labour situation is sufficiently inflammable to ignite'. Hobsbawm provides no formula for explaining just how such situations arise but he does suggest that strike waves 'appear to have been hatched in periods when important groups of workers became less well-off'. By this he appears to be referring to that way in which what he calls 'qualitatively different phases of economic evolution' – but which others know as Kondratiev waves – lead to a build-up of grievances and thus provide the material which fuels strike waves.[23]

The main difficulty with Dunlop's and Hobsbawm's formulations is that both seem to imply that there must be some actual deterioration in workers' living conditions to create a combustible mixture. In fact, explosions of strikes in Britain are as likely to have occurred during the upswings of long waves – e.g., the upheavals of 1910-13, 1919-20, and 1957-62 – as during prolonged slumps. Still, the connection between trend periods of economic development and strike waves may well hold whether the trend is up or down. We would therefore hypothesise the following pattern of causation behind the phenomenon of strike waves. Economic growth is a permanent problematic in history, a perpetually disruptive force. In each period, it proceeds through an expansion or alteration of methods of production and distribution which transforms previous patterns and, in the first instance, negatively affects certain aspects of workers' lives. Workers need time to adjust, to grasp what is happening to them, and to develop the ideas and tactics with which to cope with the new problems. The unequal division of power in industrial society probably guarantees that most often it is the employers who initiate and the workers who react. Usually changes in the character and quality of economic life make themselves felt first in employers' policy, but only gradually in workers' consciousness and attitudes, and still more slowly in their collective actions. There is, therefore, a time lag during which a new set of attitudes and expectations is developed; then, given a favourable economic or political conjuncture, workers translate this new consciousness into strike action. There is no need, in such a theory, to postulate an absolute decline in standards of living, as Hobsbawm seems to imply; it is only necessary that the new tasks of economic growth have some negative and disruptive impact on workers' daily lives. Let us look briefly at the six strike waves to see whether this hypothesis illuminates the British experience.

The strike wave of 1889-92 fits extremely well.[24] Certain recent arguments notwithstanding, the Great Depression of 1873-96 brought, along with higher real wages, also a troubled feeling of insecurity to many groups of workers.[25] It was no accident that the 1880s witnessed a remarkable intellectual ferment, a revolt against *laissez-faire* and other liberal doctrines, the growth of socialism as an idea, and widespread agitation among the unemployed.[26] It appears that the experience of the decade or so before 1889 worked a transformation in the outlook of many workers which waited only upon a revival to turn itself into a wave of strikes and organisation.

The origins of the outburst preceding the First World War were somewhat more complex. The Great Depression had initiated, or at least called atttention to, a profound transformation in the character of economic advance which continued into the boom of 1896-1914. Increasing international competition and a slowing down in the rate of productivity increase created a new mood among British businessmen, and led to a worsening in the industrial relations climate. At more or less the same moment, employers took the first critical steps toward self-organisation — founding the Engineering Employers' Federation in 1896 — launched their legal — from Temperton v. Russell in 1893 to Taff Vale in 1901 — and extra-legal — especially the funding of the

'Free Labour' movement – offensive against the trade unions, and began turning their 'thoughts toward [increasing] labour efficiency'.[27]

There is reason to think that their simultaneity caused these movements towards tougher bargaining and towards greater productivity to cancel each other out. Employers apparently saw workers' attempts to enforce customary notions of a 'fair day's work for a fair day's pay' as a key barrier to innovation, so breaking the power of the unions became in their minds the precondition of technical and economic advance. Hence the famous Engineering Lockout of 1897 over 'managerial rights'. Many workers, especially in engineering, responded by trying to restrict output and to resist innovations, insisting on established manning and apprenticeship ratios and obstructing the introduction of piece-work. From 1897 or 1898, total productivity virtually stagnated, increasing just 5.5 per cent from 1898 to 1910, or less than 0.5 per cent per year. Many factors were involved in this technological retardation, as other writers have pointed out, but the timing is at least indicative of some connection between industrial relations and productivity.[28]

Whatever the precise nature of that relationship, one thing is clear: almost all workers *perceived* some deterioration and intensification in their work between 1895 and 1914, and most felt that contemporary developments in industrial concentration and management strategy were working to their disadvantage.[29] To this accumulated sense of grievance over conditions on the job must be added the specific course of prices, wages, and unemployment after 1900. After a period of stability from 1900 to 1905, prices rose by 7.6 per cent between 1906 and 1911. Nominal wages failed to keep pace, and real wages therefore decreased by 4.6 per cent in the same years.[30] The short, but severe, recession of 1908-9, as reflected in Figure 3.1 on unemployment, made the inflation even harder to bear.[31] Even without invoking that widening of 'orbits of [social] comparison' which Phelps Brown claims occurred in this period, we have here more than enough inflammable material to account for the fiery outburst of 1910-13.[32]

The period after the First World War was equally conducive to the spread of unrest. It followed on the previous strike wave very closely, probably because the problems workers confronted before and after the war were so similar that there was no time lag necessary for them to adjust their attitudes and strategies. The chief economic problem was no doubt the course of prices during the war, which led to a marked decline in real wage rates until 1917.[33] Many obtained higher earnings nevertheless, but to do so worked much longer hours. Another factor was the further drastic intensification of work and the quickened pace of innovation.[34] No doubt political factors played a part as well. To many workers going on strike appeared as the only way to obtain the promised 'land fit for heroes to live in', especially after the 'Coupon Election' of 1918 returned a parliament which many felt did not really reflect the temper of the nation.[35]

After the immediate postwar militancy, the situation becomes less clear. The General Strike of 1926 can best be explained as part of the aftermath of 1918-21 rather than as a strike wave in its own right. Still, one would have expected an outburst in the 1930s, as in France and the US during that brief revival which separated the two troughs of the Depression. The deep and prolonged slump of the 1930s certainly altered workers' attitudes. As John Saville has argued, it caused the fear and hatred of unemployment to be burned deeply into the collective consciousness of almost every working-class family,[36] and this was translated into political terms no later than the election of 1945. Indeed, it appears that during the 1930s many of the attitudes traditionally associated with the respectable artisan, such as pride in the possession of necessary skills and in one's work or an unwillingness to go on the dole, were seriously weakened. The decay of apprenticeship, described with such bitterness in *Love on the Dole*, and the prolonged spells of idleness tore away from workers many of the accoutrements of respectability.[37]

Why, given all this, were there so few strikes? First, there were the after-effects of the General Strike, which served to discredit industrial militancy and thus, in a curious way, to bolster the power of the trade union leadership. Their power, which was consistently used to prevent militancy, was also strengthened by the reforms in the structure of the TUC during the 1920s, and by the use of the bloc vote.[38] On the other hand, the long depression eroded the bases of workshop organisation. Only in times of prosperity have workers been able to develop the independent rank-and-file organisation with which to resist the influence of the national union leaders. It is also possible that the policies of the Communist Party of Great Britain, with its extremely sectarian thrust in the 1920s and early 1930s and its almost exclusive concern with foreign policy after 1935, prevented rank-and-file militants from affecting union policy to any great extent.[39] These difficulties were intensified by Britain's peculiarly localised economic recovery, which was based on the development of new industries in different areas.[40] In might be expected that in these fluid, new industrial environments it would take a few years for workers to develop

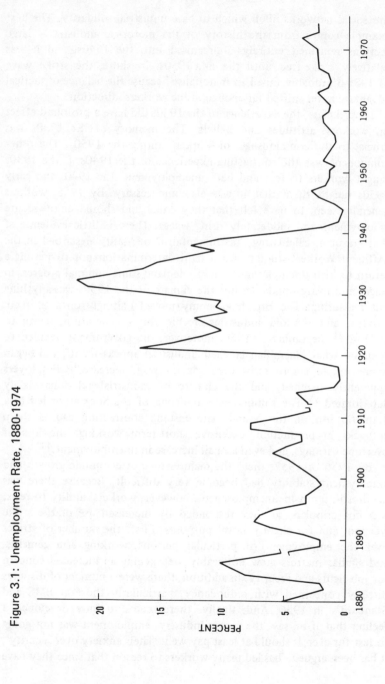

Figure 3.1: Unemployment Rate, 1880-1974

the social networks upon which to base industrial solidarity. The best example comes from the history of the motor-car industry — large sections remained entirely unorganised into the 1940s, and it was relatively strike-free until the mid-1950s. In short, the strike wave of 1935-6 probably failed to materialise because the balance of tactical advantage never shifted far enough in the workers' direction.

Nevertheless, the experience of the 1930s did have a profound effect on workers' attitudes and beliefs. The memory of the 1930s was crucial to the consciousness of workers during the 1950s. The other component was the contrasting experience of the 1940s. If the 1930s taught workers to fear and hate unemployment, the 1940s and early 1950s taught them that it was also unnecessary. By 1955, workers generally seem to have felt that they could and should enjoy secure employment and moderately rising wages. There is little evidence of that grasping, calculating, 'instrumentalist' mentality described in the 'Affluent Worker' studies, just a hard determination not to permit a return to high unemployment and to demand some minimal progress in wages and living standards. But the climate of the 1950s was anything but reassuring. The British economy moved haltingly on a 'stop-go' pattern, and the old industries, feeble for a generation, began to collapse.[41] Beginning in 1956, moreover, the government decided to abandon what Macmillan labelled 'industrial appeasement', and began urging employers to resist demands for wage increase.[42] Employers apparently listened, and the climate of industrial relations visibly deteriorated.[43] The simultaneous bungling of the Suez affair led to a dramatic run on the pound. The ensuing contraction caused sharp cutbacks in production, extensive short-term working, the loss of overtime earnings, and even a small increase in unemployment.[44]

By 1956 or 1957, then, the maintenance of economic growth and employment stability had become very difficult. Because there was no drastic jump in unemployment, however, workers' ability to resist was not crippled, so they responded by increased use of the strike weapon, and for slightly novel purposes. First, the number of strikes over the employment of particular persons, working arrangements, and similar matters grew noticeably, betokening an increased concern for job rights and security. In addition, there were a number of disputes directly concerned with redundancy, particularly those at BMC and Standard's in 1956. And, finally, there seems to have developed a feeling that if in, say, the motor industry, employment was not going to last for ever, it should at least pay well. 'Their anxiety over security', it has been argued, 'has led many workers to reason that since they have no way of knowing how long either their high boom-time earnings or their jobs will last, their best policy is simply to go all out for what they can get while the companies' profits are high.'[45]

On balance the workers won their battle of 1957-62. They raised wages, enforced the public commitment to full employment, and extracted from the Labour Government the Redundancy Payments Act of 1965.[46] In the process they also fashioned a new shop stewards' movement which subsequently exerted substantial leftward pressure in major unions like the Engineers and the Transport and General Workers' Union (TGWU). But, again, the character of economic growth changed as new trends set in. By the mid- or late 1960s, inflation had emerged as the key problem affecting both workers and employers, and the defence of living standards replaced the maintenance of employment as workers' major concern. This seems to have been the basis of the wave of strikes and unionisation which occurred between 1968 and 1972. The actions of government in challenging the unions — for instance, the Labour Government's attempt to put *In Place of Strife* into legislation and the Heath Government's Industrial Relations Bill — probably also played a part, but at root these actions were also concerned with slowing down the rate of pay increase as a means of curbing inflation. One commentator has suggested in addition that there was another widening of 'orbits of comparison' in the late 1960s,[47] while another important study has shown that the high rates of inflation dramatically worsened the problem of pay differentials.[48] Whatever the interaction between these various factors, it is obvious that the late 1960s brought a set of economic problems that produced a new and different strike wave.

It would be premature to claim that this quick survey has done any more than simply lay the groundwork for a definitive demonstration of the relationship between 'long swings' and strike waves. Still, the evidence presented to this point does put the existence of a wave-like pattern of strike history beyond reasonable doubt. Equally clear is the significance of these explosions, most starkly indicated by the close link between the quantitative indices of conflict and what is known about the timing of qualitative changes in the development of the labour movement. What requires more scrutiny are the modes of interaction between the trend periods of economic history and the periodic outbursts of industrial militancy. Several statistical and 'letristic' strategies will be employed in subsequent chapters to confirm and flesh out this connection. At this stage, however, it might be most helpful to dwell briefly on how to conceptualise the mediations and reciprocal influences.

The notion that strikes respond to different phases of growth is not entirely original with us – indeed, it possesses a distinguished lineage. But previous writers have been unable to complete the connection, and their arguments have generally remained tentative and suggestive rather than convincing. There have been three reasons for this lacuna in labour historiography. In the first place, both Hobsbawm and Dunlop in their earlier formulations seemed to feel that the impact of long waves was confined only to upheavals occurring during downswings, and so could account only with difficulty for workers' tendency to strike in prosperity with equal ferocity and greater frequency. A more successful analysis must recognise that periods of upswing can intensify the sense of grievance by raising expectations or by highlighting other problems which are equally conducive to remedy through strike action. A second obstacle to a better understanding of the relationship between conjuncture and conflict has been the habit among modern economists to eschew the study of fluctuations of medium or long duration in favour of a focus of either long-term problems of growth or shorter business cycles. For guidance on the qualitatively different stages of economic history, it will be necessary to turn to figures like Kondratiev or the very early or very late Walt Rostow, and even then there is much work left to do.

The third difficulty stems from the nature of the relationship itself. It has been suggested that particular periods of economic change transform the climate of industrial relations by altering employer attitudes and policies and by presenting workers with new sets of problems. There is ordinarily, however, a gap between the onset of a new phase of growth and workers' collective reactions to it, a period during which workers' consciousness adapts and new strategies and organisational forms are generated. Generally, strike waves occur only when such processes are well underway, and during a favourable economic (though occasionally political) moment.[49] In some ways, such a time lag is only to be expected – the learning process of social classes always takes what seems a long time.[50] Still, its existence means that the impact of conjuncture upon strikes is mediated and indirect, and makes documentation of the interaction considerably more complicated. Because of the time lag, it is both necessary and difficult to specify the mechanisms and paths by which economic trends make their way via economic policies and problems through workers' shifting attitudes and organisational responses to produce novel forms of strike behaviour. Theoretically, there may be detours and blockages at each stage, and a comprehensive analysis must be able to anticipate these as well as to discover the ultimate reflection of economics in strike waves.

One route by which this mediation might occur immediately suggests itself, and that would be the process by which successive generations of workers translate their key experiences and insights into programmes within the labour movement. Phelps Brown, for example, has offered an explanation of the strikes and pay explosion of 1968-72 which points to a generational view of the unique rhythm of strikes. He argues that by 1968 the number of workers who had had no direct, personal experience of depression, and whose social outlooks were shaped entirely during a period of full employment and prosperity, reached a 'critical mass' and caused the sky-rocketing expectations that lay at the root of the ensuing unrest.[51] This is an attractive notion, and it has been applied with notable success to several questions in social and political history.[52] But it is not entirely unproblematical. A thorough testing of it would require the compilation of an enormous range of data on the age structure of leadership groups and possibly also the entire workforce in various industries over time, rates of migration into and out of rural and urban areas as well as specific occupations, and so on, little of which is readily available. More important, however, than the insufficiency of the data are the difficulties involved in defining and locating generations. Mannheim argued years ago that generations are not simply or even primarily biological groups, but also share certain experiences and problems. For him, generational differences arise only when social change causes aspects of traditional culture and conventional behaviour to become outdated and questionable. A generation is thus defined by its problems and enemies or, as Mannheim put it, 'any two generations following one another always fight different opponents, both within and without'. Historically, then, tracing the coming to age of generations involves essentially the chronicle of the successive inventories of problems and experiences which unite particular generations. So even if change within the labour movement is synchronised with the accession to positions of influence of new cohorts of activists, the way to analyse the succession is not demographically, but by explaining the ensemble of issues which each sets out to resolve, and by narrating their (essentially) political battles.[53]

Still, the problem of generational succession is particularly apposite in the history of labour because, as V.L. Allen has told us, 'trade unions are patently not initiators'. They 'have always been sluggish in their assessment of circumstances', and leaders usually cling to worn-out slogans and antiquated policies.[54] It is precisely this that makes generational change so crucial — only with the emergence of a new crop of militants younger and more ready to challenge currently entrenched leaderships can the necessary strategic and ideological innovations take hold on a basis broad enough to revitalise labour as a whole. Hence the question of generations merges with that of internal struggle within unions and other working-class forums. Royden Harrison has reminded us that every 'serious student of the Labour Movement knows that internal conflict is as much the law of its development as is the struggle against the enemies'.[55] Unfortunately, he left unspecified how the forces involved in these conflicts are arrayed against one another and how the battles are actually conducted.

These considerations on the problems of generations and of change within unions now allow us to reformulate our argument with greater specificity and with more intervening variables between long waves and strikes. Our first approximation began by positing that the distinguishing features of different stages of economic growth alter consciousness and stimulate organisation and strikes. From the preceding discussion, it seems likely as well that the carriers of the new attitudes and orientations are younger generations, and that before organisational forms adapt to changed circumstances, internecine battles must be fought and resolved. Indeed, it may be assumed that for much of the history of labour in Britain a rendering of its internal squabbles will be equivalent to a record of the confrontations of succeeding generations of workers and of the influence that changing economic parameters exert on trade union policy and structure. This expanded version of the theory implies an extremely complicated process underlying the manifestations of conflict in strike waves. Several additional links have been inserted in the causal chain. Unfortunately, the complexity and subtlety added make definitive proof more elusive, and in the chapters that follow it will not be possible to touch upon all aspects of strike determination. This is due to limitations both of data and of space. At times, therefore, we shall take special note of the formative economic or social influences upon the outlooks of generations of workers. At still other points, the focus will be upon the difficulties entailed in translating attitudes into policies and actions, while occasionally attention will centre on the insurgent quality of the ideas and strategies manifest during strike waves. Still, it is critical to keep in mind all the stages in the process in order to avoid oversimplification and crude concepts of historical causation.

Two further issues of terminological nature may be clarified at this point as well. They involve such usages as 'working class', 'workers' attitudes', 'consciousness', and the like. Ambiguity and controversy surround each of these, and necessitate some discussion of the meanings intended here. It should be obvious — but it is still worth making the point explicitly — that our insistence upon the crucial role of qualitatively different stages of economic development in producing strike wave commits us to a dynamic and relatively fluid view of the working class itself. The very same economic movements that impose new contexts upon working-class collective activity also serve to re-shape and restructure the social formation itself.

Still greater difficulties attend our emphasis upon the role played by working people's attitudes and consciousness in the development of strike movements. Consciousness is an extremely difficult thing to write about, and practically impossible to measure. The problem is further complicated because the common-sense use of the term often merges imperceptibly into the concept of class consciousness. The latter confusion is unfortunate, for it is quite clear the 'class consciousness' is frequently invoked in a crude, one-dimensional and reified fashion: workers are more or less class conscious; their consciousness is embryonic or immature, or it is false or genuine. The lack of subtlety in such usages appalls.

And yet, it would be a still greater sin to omit workers' perceptions and attitudes from the history of industrial conflict in order to avoid the simplistic distortions that have beset the analysis of consciousness in the past. Moreover, the practical difficulty of distinguishing consciousness from behaviour is no compelling objection to making the attempt. Obviously the two are inseparable, but we believe that it is possible to reveal the discrete and distinct contribution of workers' developing understanding to their industrial behaviour by showing how the content — in terms of demands, organising strategy and tactics — of this militancy responds to the economic and political context in which they find themselves. To the extent that strike waves can be shown to differ qualitatively from one another, to be informed by the specific nature of the problems confronting workers in successive stages of development, to that extent we shall be describing the shifting social and strategic consciousness of working people. Hopefully, this will become clearer in the chapters that follow.

Notes

1. J.T. Dunlop, 'The Development of Labor Organization: A Theoretical Framework', in R. Lester and J. Shister (eds.), *Insights in Labor Issues* (New York, 1948), p. 189.

2. V.L. Allen, *The Sociology of Industrial Relations* (London, 1971), p. 34.

3. The history of collective action before and during the industrial revolution has been the subject of much recent study. See, in particular, E.P. Thompson, 'The Moral Economy of the English Crowd in the 18th Century', *Past and Present*, no. 50 (Feb., 1971), pp. 76-136, and 'Patrician Society, Plebeian Culture', *Journal of Social History*, VI (1974), pp. 382-405, and, of course, *The Making of the English Working Class* (New York, 1963); E.C. Black, *The Association: British Extraparliamentary Political Action* (Cambridge, Mass., 1963); John Bohstedt, 'Riots in England, with Special Reference to Devonshire' (unpublished Ph.D. dissertation, Harvard University, 1972); G. Rudé, *The Crowd in History* (New York, 1964); W.J. Shelton, *English Hunger and Industrial Disorders* (London, 1973); J. Stevenson, 'Food Riots in England, 1792-1818', in J. Stevenson and R. Quinault (eds.), *Popular Protest and Public Disorder* (London, 1974); E.J. Hobsbawm, *Primitive Rebels* (Manchester, 1959), and *Labouring Men* (Garden City, NY, 1967), esp. the essays on 'The Machine Breakers' and 'Labour Traditions', and Hobsbawm and Rudé, *Captain Swing* (New York, 1968), on the period up through 1832. The historiography of the Chartist era is still richer, but it is generally lacking in theory. See the classic collection by Asa Briggs (ed.), *Chartist Studies* (London, 1959), for an excellent introduction, and the most recent survey, J.T. Ward, *Chartism* (London, 1973), for additional references. P. Hollis, *Class and Conflict in Nineteenth-century England, 1815-1850* (London, 1973), is a particularly good collection of documents on these transitional years; and John Foster, *Class Struggle and the Industrial Revolution* (London, 1974), is a stimulating and controversial case study. Of more theoretical interest is I. Prothero, 'William Benbow and the Concept of the "General Strike" ', *Past and Present*, no. 63 (1974), pp. 132-71. Events of the 1850s and 1860s are less thoroughly studied, but see, among others, that curious though informative publication of the National Association for the Promotion of Social Science, *Trades' Societies and Strikes* (London, 1860); also W.H. Fraser, *Trade Unions and Society: The Struggle for Acceptance* (London, 1974); T. Tholfsen, *Working Class Radicalism in Mid-Victorian England* (New York, 1977); and R. Harrison, *Before the Socialists* (London, 1965). Two brief overviews of some value on the evolution of protest in Britain are H.J. Perkin, *The Origins of Modern English Society* (London, 1969), pp. 340-7; and V.G. Kiernan, 'Patterns of Protest in English History', in R. Benewick and T. Smith (eds.), *Direct Action and Democratic Politics* (London, 1972), pp. 25-48.

4. G.C. Miller, *Blackburn, Evolution of a Town* (Blackburn, 1951).

5. Charles Tilly and R.A. Schweitzer, 'Contentious Gatherings in Britain, 1828-1834: Provisional Plans for Enumeration and Coding', Center for Research on Social Organization, University of Michigan, Working Paper no. 163 (September 1977); E.J. Hobsbawm, 'Custom, Wages, and Work-load', in *Labouring Men*, pp. 405-35; Richard Price, 'Learning the Rules of the Game: The Crisis of the mid-Victorian Working Class', paper presented to the Conference on British Studies, New York, November 1976; and P. Stearns, 'Measuring the Evolution of Strike Movements', *International Review of Social History*, XIX (1974), pp. 1-27.

6. E.J. Hobsbawm, 'Economic Fluctuations and some Social Movements since 1800', in *Labouring Men*, p. 149. Hobsbawm has suggested that this rhythm is common in the history of social movements throughout Europe. The comparability of patterns of conflict in various countries since 1850 is indeed striking, and constitutes an important support for our focus upon the role of medium-term economic movements, which ordinarily transcend national boundaries, over

peculiarities of national development in the determination of conflict. Nevertheless, national differences are of sufficient magnitude as to make the telling of the common story of conflict immensely complicated and well beyond the scope of this book. For more comparative treatments, see D.A. Hibbs, 'On the Political Economy of Long-Run Trends in Strike Activity', *British Journal of Political Science*, VIII (1978), pp. 153-75, and *Strikes: The Political Economy of Industrial Conflict in Western Industrial Societies* (Princeton, forthcoming); and C. Crouch and A. Pizzorno (eds.), *The Resurgence of Class Conflict in Western Europe* (London, 1978).

7. The Webbs counted the following references to strikes in the *Times*:

YEAR	NO.	YEAR	NO.	YEAR	NO.
1876	17	1881	20	1886	24
1877	23	1882	14	1887	27
1878	38	1883	26	1888	37
1879	72	1884	31	1889	111
1880	46	1885	20		

See S. and B. Webb, *The History of Trade Unionism* (New York, 1920), p. 347n. Obviously, the Webbs counted only an infinitesimal proportion of strikes in these years, but the trends are nonetheless evident.

8. John Saville, 'Trade Unions and Free Labour: The Background of the Taff Vale Decision', in A. Briggs and J. Saville (eds.), *Essays in Labour History*, rev. (London, 1967), pp. 317-50; and R. Brown, 'The Temperton v. Russell Case (1893): The Beginning of the Legal Offensive against the Unions', *Bulletin of Economic Research*, XXIII (1971), pp. 50-66.

9. See, on the engineers, Jefferys, *The Story of the Engineers, 1880-1945* (London, 1946), pp. 98, 111-17; on the railwaymen, G. Alderman, 'The Railway Companies and the Growth of Trade Unionism in the Late Nineteenth and Early Twentieth Centuries', *Historical Journal*, XIV (1971), pp. 131-2, and P.S. Gupta, 'Railway Trade Unions, in Britain, c. 1880-1920', *Economic History Review*, XIX (1966), pp. 128-9. More generally, D.W. Crowley, 'The Origins of the Revolt of the British Labour Movement from Liberalism, 1875-1906' (unpublished Ph.D. dissertation, University of London, 1952), is quite useful.

10. Jefferys, *The Story of the Engineers*, pp. 167-73.

11. H.G. Wells, *The Labour Unrest* (London, 1913), cited in Knowles, *Strikes*, p. 4; and R. Holton, *British Syndicalism* (London, 1976), *passim*.

12. See A. Bullock, *The Life and Times of Ernest Bevin*, vol. I (London, 1960), pp. 180-220 on the T&GWU; see Jefferys, *The Story of the Engineers*, pp. 192-226 on the AEU; on the TUC, see V.L. Allen, 'The Re-Organization of the Trades Union Congress, 1918-1927', *British Journal of Sociology*, XI (1960), pp. 24-43; and on the recognition of the shop stewards, see Eric Wigham, *The Power to Manage: A History of the Engineering Employers' Federation* (London, 1973), pp. 99-101. On the political transformation, see D. Butler and D. Stokes, *Political Change in Britain* (New York, 1969), pp. 254-63; and Ross McKibbin, *The Evolution of the Labour Party, 1910-24* (Oxford, 1975).

13. On the general strike of 1926 see P. Renshaw, *The General Strike* (London, 1975); G.A. Phillips, *The General Strike* (London, 1976); and A. Mason, 'The Government and the General Strike', *International Review of Social History*, XV (1969), pp. 1-21.

The purpose here is to distinguish the General Strike from other strike waves, not to minimise its importance as an event in itself — an event which stimulated an amazing amount of grass-roots activity, and shaped the opinions of hundreds of thousands of working people for a long time to come. For a brief account of the extent of local activity in those nine days in May, 1926, see Emile Burns, *The General Strike May 1926: Trades Councils in Action* (London, 1926, reprinted 1975).

14. H.A. Clegg, 'Some Consequences of the General Strike', *Transactions of the Manchester Statistical Society* (1953-4).

15. Thus, between 1960 and 1962 over 97 per cent of all strikes were unofficial (*see British Labour Statistics, Yearbook 1972* (London, 1975), Table 149). The first person to really sort out these developments was H.A. Turner, in his *The Trend of Strikes* (Leeds, 1963). See also Michael Silver, 'Recent British Strike Trends: A Factual Analysis', *British Journal of Industrial Relations*, XI (1973), pp. 66-104. On the shop stewards' organisation that lay behind this, see W.E.J. McCarthy and S.R. Parker, *Shop Stewards and Workshop Relations*, Research Papers 10, Royal Commission on Trade Unions & Employers Organizations (London, 1968).

16. See H.A. Turner, G. Clack and G. Roberts, *Labour Relations in the Motor Industry* (London, 1967), esp. pp. 82-3.

17. J.W. Durcan and W.E.J. McCarthy, 'What is happening to strikes?' *New Society* (2 Nov. 1972), pp. 267-9; and J. Hughes, 'Patterns of Trade Union Growth', in M. Barratt Brown and K. Coates (eds.), *Trade Union Register 3* (Nottingham, 1973), pp. 47-59.

18. Henry Pelling, *A History of British Trade Unionism*, 2nd ed. (London, 1972), p. 283. In the same vein, see Pelling's chapter on 'The Labour Unrest' in his *Popular Politics and Society in Late Victorian Britain* (London, 1968), pp. 147-64; also A.E.P. Duffy, 'New Unionism in Britain, 1889-1890; A Reappraisal', *Economic History Review*, XIV (1961), pp. 306-19; and G.A. Phillips, 'The Triple Industrial Alliance in 1914', *Economic History Review*, XXIV (1971), pp. 55-67.

19. A.E. Musson's *Trade Union and Social History* (London, 1974) clearly exhibits this perspective. See also the essays in A. Flanders and H.A. Clegg (eds.), *The System of Industrial Relations in Great Britain* (Oxford, 1954), with the exception of Asa Briggs' introductory piece. See also E. Brunner, 'The Origins of Industrial Peace: The Case of the Boot and Shoe Industry', *Oxford Economic Papers*, N.S., I (1949), pp. 247-59; and A.J. Odber, 'The Origins of Industrial Peace: The Manufactured Iron Trade of the North of England', *Oxford Economic Papers*, N.S., III (1951), pp. 202-20.

20. P. Vilar, 'Marxist History, A History in the Making: Towards a Dialogue with Althusser', *New Left Review*, no. 80 (1973), pp. 65-106.

21. Charles Tilly and Edward Shorter, 'Les Vagues des grèves en France, 1890-1968', in *Annales. Économies, Sociétés, Civilisations, XXVIII* (1973), pp. 857-87, and *Strikes in France, 1830-1968* (Cambridge, 1974), pp. 104-46.

22. Dunlop, 'The Development of Labor Organisation', pp. 189-93.

23. Hobsbawm, *Labouring Men*, pp. 149-84. On the nature and definition of Kondratiev waves, one should begin with his own article on 'Die langen Wellen der Konjunktur', *Archiv für Sozialwissenschaft und Sozialpolitik*, LVI (1926), pp. 573-609, a shortened version of which appeared as 'The Long Waves in Economic Life', in the *Review of Economic Statistics*, XVII (1935), pp. 105-15.

The precise nature of the relationship between Kondratiev waves and different stages in economic growth is still being debated. See G. Garvy, 'Kondratieff's Theory of Long Cycles', *Review of Economic Statistics*, XXV (1943), pp. 203-20, for some Soviet views on the question; and W.W. Rostow, 'Kondratieff, Schumpeter, and Kuznets: 'Trend Periods Revisited', *Journal of Economic History*, XXXV (1975), pp. 719-54, for a more recent interpretation.

24. The brief survey undertaken in the remainder of this chapter on the connection between stages of economic history and strike waves is intended only as a preview. A more extended treatment will be found in Chapters 5 and 6.

25. S.B. Saul, *The Myth of the Great Depression* (London, 1969). In addition, see the Second Report of the Royal Commission . . . into the Depression of Trade and Industry. Appendix D. Answers received from Associations representing the interests of the Working Classes to the questions addressed to them. *British Parliamentary Papers*, 1886, XXII (Cmd. 4715-I), pp. 3-98.

26. There is really no good up-to-date survey of this period. A useful introduction is Helen M. Lynd, *England in the Eighteen-Eighties* (London, 1968).

27. Cf. Wigham, *Power to Manage*, pp. 29-62; Brown, 'Temperton v. Russell', and Saville, 'Trade Unions and Free Labour'; and E.J. Hobsbawm, 'Custom, Wages and Work-load in Nineteenth-Century Industry', in *Labouring Men*, p. 421.

28. Productivity calculated from Table 20 of C.H. Feinstein, *National Income, Expenditure, and Output of the United Kingdom, 1855-1965* (Cambridge, 1971). The debate over the causes of lagging productivity in prewar Britain is by no means settled. For a useful overview of the problem, see E.H. Phelps Brown with M.H. Browne, *A Century of Pay* (London, 1968), pp. 174-95. D.N. McCloskey and L.G. Sandburg review the more recent literature in 'From Damnation to Redemption: Judgments on the Late Victorian Entrepreneur', *Explorations in Economic History*, IX (1971), pp. 89-108. My reading of the recent Aldcroft/ McCloskey exchange is that the late 1890s probably represents the crucial turning point. Cf. D.H. Aldcroft, 'McCloskey on Victorian Growth', *Economic History Review*, XXVII (1974), pp. 271-4, and McCloskey, 'Victorian Growth: A Rejoinder', pp. 275-7. In our discussion, we depart specifically from the interpretation of A.L. Levine, *Industrial Retardation in Britain* (London, 1967). Levine counts the number of strikes concerned more or less explicitly with restriction of output (e.g., manning ratios, apprenticeship, etc.) and combining the results with the statements of union leaders, concludes that labour resistance did not retard innovation. This seems to me wrong. As Peter Stearns has pointed out in his *Lives of Labor* (New York, 1975), pp. 308-10, it is extremely difficult for workers to mount potentially winning strikes on such issues, so data on strike causes is at best inconclusive, possibly even irrelevant, for this question. And who would expect union leaders to acknowledge that their members were restricting output, even if they were? Of course, employers' arguments about the lack of enthusiasm of their employees, or of the widespread practice of 'ca-canny', are no more reliable. As Mark Blaug has said, 'In what age would it not be possible to collect complaints from the upper classes about the laziness of workers?' See M. Blaug, 'The Myth of the Old Poor Law and the Making of the New', in M.W. Flinn and T.C. Smout (eds.), *Essays in Social History* (Oxford, 1974), p. 144.

29. P. Stearns, *Lives of Labor*, Part II; and also 'The Unskilled and Industrialization. A Transformation of Consciousness', *Archiv für Sozialgeschichte*, XVI (1976), pp. 249-83.

30. Based on an index of real wages constructed from price and wage data taken from Tables 11-13 and 87-94 in *British Labour Statistics: Historical Abstract, 1886-1968* (London, 1971).

31. Thus, while prices rose from 100 in 1906 to 107 in 1910 (1900 = 100), many hundreds of thousands of workers were forced to accept wage reductions. In 1908, for instance, over 141,000 workers struck against proposed wage decreases.

32. Henry Phelps Brown, 'A Non-Monetarist View of the Pay Explosion', *Three Banks Review*, no. 105 (March, 1975), pp. 6-7.

33. The index referred to above, which is admittedly less accurate for the war years, shows that real wages went from 62.0 in 1914 to 55.9 in 1915, 51.8 in 1916, 51.2 in 1917, and 56.3 in 1918. (January, 1956 = 100). So the war, while bringing full employment by 1915, and presumably boosting actual earnings for some (via overtime, piece-rates, and 'lieu rates') must have meant severe hardships for many workers, especially those in non-strategic industries.

34. See James Hinton, *The First Shop Stewards Movement* (London, 1973) for an excellent discussion of this process in the munitions industries.

35. For a useful discussion, which is only occasionally fanciful, of the political climate of the period, see the Directorate of Intelligence's 'A Survey of Revolutionary Feeling During the Year 1919', PRO, CAB 24/96 CP 462.

36. John Saville, 'May Day 1937', in A. Briggs and J. Saville (eds.), *Essays in Labour History* (London, 1977). Professor Saville was kind enough to communicate some of his findings to me prior to publication.

37. This point is reflected in many of the social surveys of the period; one of the best is *Men Without Work*, by Pilgrim Trust (Cambridge, 1938).

38. See Saville, 'May Day, 1937'.

39. On Communist Party policy in the 1920s, see the interesting discussion by James Hinton and Richard Hyman, *Trade Unions and Revolution: The Industrial Politics of the Early British Communist Party* (London, 1975).

40. D. Landes, *The Unbound Prometheus* (Cambridge, 1969), pp. 393-7; and H.W. Richardson, *Economic Recovery in Britain, 1932-1939* (London, 1967), *passim*.

41. See S. Pollard, *The Development of the British Economy, 1914-1967*, 2nd ed. (New York, 1969), pp. 412-31, 468-84.

42. Harold Macmillan, *Riding the Storm* (London, 1971), p. 346.

43. Very little has been written on this crucial turning point in British labour and social history. For starters, see Hugh Clegg and Rex Adams, *The Employers' Challenge* (Oxford, 1957). Probably the best discussion, however, is in Wigham, *The Power to Manage*, p. 178ff.

44. The period 1956-9 was a prolonged recession. In motor vehicles, a good index of the general health of the economy, average weekly hours worked declined by 3.3 per cent between April 1955 and October 1956 and did not substantially recover until 1959. Employment in motor vehicle manufacture dropped 6 per cent between 1955 and 1957, and regained the 1955 level only in 1959. Overall industrial production, which had grown by 17.9 per cent between 1952 and 1955, increased by just under 1 per cent from 1955 to 1959. See *British Labour Statistics, Historical Abstract*, Tables 44 and 204; C.H. Feinstein, *National Income*, Table 51; Turner, Clack, Roberts, Labour Relations in the Motor Industry (London, 1967), p. 103.

45. Turner, Clack and Roberts, *Labour Relations*, pp. 82-3.

46. Cf. Dorothy Wedderburn, 'Redundancy', in D. Pym (ed.), *Industrial Society: Social Sciences in Management* (Harmondsworth, 1968), pp. 65-81.

47. Phelps Brown, 'A Non-Monetarist View', pp. 17-20.

48. D. Jackson, H.A. Turner and F. Wilkinson, *Do Trade Unions Cause Inflation?* 2nd ed. (London, 1975), pp. 89-95.

49. In England, prosperity has been more closely related to the outbreak of strike waves than political crises. Thus, between 1893 and 1974 the correlation between the percentage of workers unemployed and strike activity was -.59, which is significant at the .001 level. This is consistent with the results of the three major econometric studies by Pencavel, Shorey and Sapsford, all of which find strong associations between some measure of economic activity and industrial conflict.

Still, the link between business upswing and outbursts of militancy is subject to various interpretations other than that which stresses simply the balance of tactical advantage. Michelle Perrot, *Les ouvriers en grève* (Paris, 1974), for example, suggests that the quickness with which workers normally took the opportunity offered by prosperity shows their aggressiveness and prior consciousness and extent of organisation. W.G. Runciman, *Relative Deprivation and Social Justice* (London, 1966), p. 60, argues on the other hand that booms stimulate new attitudes and heighten dissatisfaction – hence, 'to emphasize that prosperity is a necessary permissive condition of many expressions of discontent is only to emphasize the importance for the sense of relative deprivation of what are seen to to be the limits of feasibility'. I do not feel these different perspectives to be either incompatible or mutually exclusive.

50. Thus, the time lag between the beginning of a new phase of economic growth and workers' political and strategic response also appears to affect periods earlier than that dealt with here. Royden Harrison, for example, has noted that improvements in workers' economic circumstances preceded the emergence of a tame and moderate working class movement by several years during the third quarter of the nineteenth century. He argues, 'It is the socio-economic characteristics of 1850-1873 which underpin the political developments of 1861-1881.' See R. Harrison, *Before the Socialists* (London, 1965), p. 4.

51. Phelps Brown, 'A Non-Monetarist View', pp. 19-20.

52. Cf., for instance, Robert F. Wheeler, 'German Labor and the Comintern: A Problem of Generations', *Journal of Social History*, VII (Spring, 1974), pp. 304-21.

53. K. Mannheim, 'On the Problem of Generations', in *Essays in the Sociology of Knowledge* (London, 1954).

54. V.L. Allen, *The Sociology of Industrial Relations*, p. 47.

55. Harrison, *Before the Socialists*, p. 42.

4 TOWARDS AN HISTORICAL MODEL OF STRIKE ACTIVITY

By combining a critical review of current social science theories of industrial conflict with a brief consideration of the main contours of British strikes in the past, it has proved possible to fashion the outlines of a model more historical in approach. The hypothesis developed here rests on three assertions: (1) strikes change in their incidence, form, meaning and context over time; (2) the nature of these transformations is intimately linked to the evolution of the market economy, (3) which is itself best conceptualised in terms of distinct and qualitatively different stages rather than as a linear progression. Add to these the mediating roles assigned to consciousness and organisation, and the argument is essentially complete — and fortunately it can be expressed verbally, without the aid of diagrams full of boxes, arrows and path coefficients. Alterations in the pattern and pace of economic growth impose various sets of problems and opportunities upon working people, who gradually adapt their ideas and strategies before launching a wave of strikes and organisation designed quite explicitly to cope with the new situation.

The task now is to flesh out this theory with more systematic evidence. As a first step, it is necessary to deduce some testable empirical propositions from the general hypothesis. The first and most obvious is that simple, long-term models of British strikes, which specify fixed and stable interactions and a constant pattern of causation, should *not* work. The historical variability of industrial conflict should doom any such attempt to major instabilities and inconsistencies.[1]

By the same logic, we should meet with greater success in devising models encompassing a more modest span of experience. If one can delineate with some precision the boundaries of the different stages of economic history, then it should be possible to predict patterns of strike activity within specific periods or in the transitions from one era to another. Just what form such medium-term models take will depend, of course, upon the exact nature of the impact of economic trends at particular times, upon how they are felt and perceived, and upon the strategic prospects for economic and political mobilisation. Irrespective of the specific correlates of militancy at any given time, the very blocking of years should reveal the overriding impact of successive phases of economic change.[2]

74

Most of this chapter will be concerned with developing and testing a long-term model of strike activity. When it becomes clear that no such model is satisfactory, the first half of the argument will have been proven correct. In the process, we shall introduce much of the basic statistical work upon which this book is built, and attempt briefly to familiarise the reader with the methods employed. Following this, we shall begin to develop more successful medium-term models by determining the turning points that mark off different stages of economic growth. The actual specification of these models will occur in the two subsequent chapters.

A successful long-term model of strike determination would presumably take its cue from previous attempts at the quantitative analysis of industrial conflict, and should embody aspects of the theories embedded in earlier statistical projects. The primary group of researchers working with British strike data has consisted of economists, and, naturally enough, their assumptions have been essentially economic.[3] The results of this type of research have ordinarily been rather ambiguous and have usually failed to fulfil the expectations of those who conceived and executed it. Table 4.1 summarises the findings of the four major econometric studies of British strikes.

A brief excursion into methodology is necessary for the interpretation of these and subsequent results. Multiple regression procedures produce an equation with four or five basic explanatory statistics: R^2, the coefficient of determination; B, the coefficient(s) of the predictor variable(s), or Beta, the standardised coefficient(s) of the predictor variable(s); the Durbin-Watson statistic, the standard test for serial autocorrelation of residuals; and the Standard Error of Estimate. The meaning of the last is self-evident; the others are not. R^2, which ranges from 0.0 to 1.0, is the major statistic which summarises the predictive power of the equation. An R^2 of .80 means that 80 per cent of the variance (a statistical measure of the variation, or spread, of a variable) is 'explained by' a given set of variables. The regression coefficient 'B' refers to the amount, in units (e.g., strikes, thousands of strikers, etc.) by which the value of the dependent variable would change in response to a change of one unit of the predictor variable. Beta coefficients, or 'weights', refer to the amount, in terms of standard deviations, by which the value of the dependent variable would change in response to a change of one standard deviation in the predictor variable. The rank order of Beta coefficients is often used to measure the relative importance of independent variables in causing changes in the dependent variable, although this applies strictly only

Table 4.1: Statistical Studies of British Strikes: Summary and Results

Author	Measure of Strikes and Dates Covered	Primary* Determinants(±)	Coefficient of Determination (R^2)	Problems of Autocorrelation
Pencavel (1970)	Non-mining strikes 1950-67	Seasonality, Unemployment (−), *Lagged Rate of Change of Real Wages (Expectations Function)* (−), Rate of Profits (+), Time (+)	.87	None
Shorey (1974)	Non-mining strikes 1950-67	Seasonality, *Prosperity (+)*, Lagged Rate of Change of Money Wages (−), Lagged Rate of Change of Prices (+), Previous Year's Strike Level (+)	.89	None
Shorey (1974)	Non-mining strikes 1920-39	Unemployment (−), Rate of Change of Money Wages (−), Price Level (+), *After-effects of General Strike (−)*, Previous Year's Strike Level (+), Time (+)	.86	None
Sapsford (1975)	All strikes 1893-1966	*Wholesale Prices (+)*, Rate of Change of Wholesale Prices (+)	.71	Major
Bean & Peel (1976)	All strikes 1893-1938	Business Activity (+), Profits (−), Rate of Change of Real Wages (+), *Rate of Growth of Trade Union Membership (+)*, Unionisation (+), Previous Year's Strike Level (+)	.77	None

* By primary, we simply mean all statistically significant determinants. The most important variable in each model is italicised.

to situations in which the independent variables themselves are uncorrelated, so it must be done cautiously.

The Durbin-Watson statistic serves as a check on these other measures when applied to time series data, and it is very important. It tests, whether there is a substantial correlation between residuals considered in case order. Residuals are the differences between observed values of the dependent variable and values predicted by an equation. The Durbin-Watson statistic tells us whether there is a discernible pattern in the dependent variable which is unexplained by the variables in the equation. Most standard textbooks on econometric methods contain tables for the interpretation of Durbin-Watson statistics at 5 per cent and 1 per cent levels, but such precision is not necessary here. We will interpret it somewhat more loosely. The statistic always takes a value between 0 and 4; 2 is the ideal value, indicating no autocorrelation. A minus 4 would be added to all values over 2; the resulting values are interpreted the same as positive values between 0 and 2, except that one is now testing for a negative correlation of residuals. Durbin-Watson statistics between 1.4 and 2.0 will be taken in this study to indicate a lack of significant autocorrelation problems; values between 1.1 and 1.4 will be considered inconclusive; and values below 1.1 as revealing significant problems of autocorrelation. When substantial problems of autocorrelation exist, the model is seriously deficient.

Judged by the coefficients of determination alone, these economic models all appear quite succesful. Closer analysis, however, reveals some difficulties. A purely economic model works well only for a relatively brief period, from 1950 to 1967. For earlier years, the economic variables must be supplemented, almost supplanted in fact, by organisational variables. When extended forward beyond 1967, on the other hand, the economic model underpredicts strike activity substantially.

Nor can the equations generated for the period before 1938 be generalised to cover a long span of years. Shorey's equation for the interwar years is completely idiosyncratic: the 'dummy' variable capturing the after-effects of the General Strike of 1926 contributes a very high proportion of the explained variance. Bean and Peel's solution, by contrast, took even them by surprise – they expected economic activity to be the most important predictor of strikes – and, as we shall see shortly, such a model does not perform well over the long run. Moreover, they offer no theoretical justification for their chosen time span; it seems to have been simply accidental.

Despite apparent success, then, the most elaborate econometric analysis can only offer short-term answers to the question of strike determination. Especially significant are the serious autocorrelation problems attending Sapsford's long-term model. We too attempted to estimate a primarily economic model of strike determination and encountered the same problem. It does indeed seem that economic theories of strikes cannot generate an equation that adequately predicts the level of strikes over the broad sweep of time from the 1890s to the 1970s.

Lastly, it must be noted that all of these efforts had to do only with the explanation of the number of strikes – the number of strikers and of days lost were both ignored. A case can well be made for not considering the time lost from strikes because it tells us less about the nature of the conflict *per se* than about the impact in narrow economic terms. But surely the number of workers involved in disputes is an important indicator of their social force. Most previous authors have rationalised ignoring this measure by claiming that for some mystical reason the pattern of participation in strikes does not respond to economic movements, but the argument is circular and unacceptable.[4] There is, of course, a practical difficulty – the number of strikers can be greatly influenced by one or two national strikes affecting a whole industry, as in 1893, 1912, 1921, 1957, 1962 and 1968. However, it seems to us that the occurrence of big strikes is neither accidental nor random. The particular moment of their outbreak may indeed be fortuitous, but the very fact of it should reflect something more basic about workers' attitudes. Thus while the number of strikers in any one year may not accurately reflect the sentiments prevailing at the base of the labour movement during a particular period, an average of strikers over several years should. This suggests that one of several available smoothing techniques could be utilised to produce a variable more capable of being explained. That the economists have not done this is a further reflection of the narrowness of their concerns and the limited applicability of their findings.

Besides the economic approach, the most impressive theory of industrial conflict encountered in our review of the literature was the political-organisational model proposed by Charles Tilly and his various associates. The work of Bean and Peel suggests that such an approach might in fact do well for Britain. To test for this possibility, we estimated equations incorporating in simple fashion both economic and organisational influences for the number of non-mining strikes and for a three-year moving average of non-mining strikers (which we found to be the most satisfying means of smoothing the data on strikers). The variables used were gross domestic product, the rate of change of real wages, trade union membership, and time. The results were generally satisfactory — we explained 80 per cent and 51 per cent of the variance in the two measures — except for the high degree of residual autocorrelation.[5] Again, the statistical evidence seems to point to a series of discontinuities in strikes and their causes that make it impossible to assimilate them to any stable model.

Still, it might be objected that a fair test of the hypothesis of constant determination of industrial conflict requires that a more extensive and comprehensive range of influences be allowed into the model. In order to rule out this possibility, we performed step-wise regression with nineteen different variables to generate the best long-term model of strike determination of which we are capable. The variables were developed in such a way as to provide statistical surrogates for just about every factor which various writers have proposed as influences upon strikes.[6] Let us review the variables and the rationale behind each.

Economic Variables

— Gross Domestic Product (GDP), as an indicator of the general state of the economy and the labour market.
— Unemployment Rate (U_t), as an alternative indicator of the state of the labour market.
— Rate of change of Real Wages ($\dot{R}_t$), calculated as the percentage change of the real wage index from June to June. This is, in a sense, an expectations function with a lag of about two quarters. However, it can also be viewed as another measure of prosperity.
— Rate of change of Real Wages lagged one year ($\dot{R}_{t-1}$). A relatively unambiguous expectations function, with a lag of about six quarters.
— Cost of Living Index (P_t), on the theory that workers operate under a 'money illusion', and would be more moved to strike by price levels than real wage levels. A Money Wage Index could be substituted here with little harm, since money wages and cost of living correlate .90 or better throughout our period.
— Rate of Change of Cost of Living ($\dot{P}_t$), to get more directly at the impact of inflation or deflation.
— Rate of Productivity Increase ($\dot{P}$rod), as a possible though very rough indicator of the relationship between technological change, workers' attitudes, and strikes. Several other indices of technical change or the pace of work — like numbers of industrial accidents, or rates of capital

formation — were considered for possible use, but data problems led to the selection of the rate of productivity increase.

Political Variables

— Labour Government in Power (LG), a 'dummy' variable (1=yes, 0=no) used to test whether the presence of representatives of labour at the head of government affects strikes. Some have hypothesised a positive relationship: workers' expectations rise with the coming to power of a friendly regime; others a negative one: unionists are reluctant to embarrass 'their people' while in office. This variable should help decide which, if either, hypothesis is correct.

— Conservative Government in Power (CG), analogous to Labour Government variable and aimed at testing the impact of a Conservative administration. (Includes Lloyd George Coalition after 1918).

— Liberal Government in Power (LIBG). Included to try to throw light on the possible value of numerous suggestions made by various writers about a) the direct impact of the Liberals on strikes; b) the special role of the Liberals in integrating the working classes into the political system; or c) the role of labour in the decline of the Liberals.

— Wartime-Coalition Government (W-TG), as a measure of the effects of wartime appeals for national unity on the willingness to strike.

— Election Year (EY), to show whether, as has been maintained, workers press their claims at moments of political instability, or alternatively, whether strikes decrease during election years because all parties try to woo labour with promises of reform, or — in the case of a party in power — with actual economic concessions.

— Number of Conservative MPs (Cons), included in order to gauge shifts in the general political climate, which may take place without actually producing a change in the party in office. Numbers of Labour or Liberal MPs were also considered as possible indicators, but their peculiar interaction — the replacement of one by the other, and consequent transformation of both — made this inadvisable. An attempt was also made to use criminal statistics to measure the general political climate, but their interpretation proved highly problematical.[7]

— Repressive Legislation in Force (RL). This refers specifically to the period when the Taff Vale judgement had yet to be reversed by parliament, and to the duration of the Trade Disputes and Trade Union Act of 1927.[8] The effect of the Osborne Judgement (1910-13) was excluded because it did not directly affect the industrial behaviour of unions. The period 1946-51, when Order 1305 which banned strikes during the war was still in operation, is also excluded because the attitude of the unions toward the government and Order 1305 was not sharply antagonistic, in stark contrast to the unions' attitude toward Taff Vale and the punitive Act of 1927.

Organisational or Emulation Variables

– Trade Union Membership (TUM), to test the argument that organisational strength is the key prerequisite to strike action.
– Trade Union Growth (TUG), the rate of change of membership, to be used an as alternative or supplement to the absolute level of union membership.[9]
– Number of Strikers in Mining and Quarrying lagged one year ($SRSMQ_{t-1}$), on the theory that many workers are strongly influenced by the fate of the miners, who have allegedly played a 'vanguard' role in the labour movement.
– Number of Strikes in All Industries except Mining lagged one year $STSNOM_{t-1}$), a variant on the previous measure. Both of these variables assume an internal dynamic in the history of strikes. A positive coefficient on either of these variables would suggest that workers were influenced by broadly-based shifts in attitudes throughout the working class, and would lend considerable support to the contention about the importance of strike waves.

Trend Variable

– Time (T), included to represent trend. It should be noted, however, that even when a trend term is included in an equation and it is not acting as a 'suppressor, it has no necessary substantive meaning. It is simply a stand-in for some long-term, but unspecified, variable or combination of variables.

Equations were developed using this exhaustive list of possible predictors for the number of strikes and a three-year moving average of strikers in all industries, in all except mining, and in mining (and quarrying) itself. No more than seven variables were allowed in any one equation.[10] Even with all these variables, however, a truly satisfactory and comprehensive model for the period 1893-1974 continued to elude us. Nevertheless, some of the results were suggestive, and merit detailed examination. The estimations are set out in Tables 4.2-4.4.

When all industries are considered together, as in Table 4.2, the results are poor. For strikes, prosperity (GDP) appears to be the most important long-term stimulant. Rising rates of real wage increase,

Table 4.2: Determinants of Strike Activity in All Industries, 1893-1974

Equation	Dependent Variable	Beta coefficients on:							R^2	D-W	SEE
		GDP	$\dot{R}_t$	$\dot{R}_{t-1}$	U_t	LG	RL	T			
4.2.1	STS	.74	.10	.14	-.19		-.18		.88	1.02	320.0
4.2.2	STS	.43	.10	.13	-.25	-.10	-.19	.35	.90	1.14	298.1

		Beta coefficients on:						R^2	D-W	SEE
		P_t	$\dot{P}rod$	$SRSMQ_{t-1}$	RL	Cons EY	T			
4.2.3	SRS(3)	.66	-.23	.35	-.24		-.22	.63	.93	303.0
4.2.4	SRS(3)	.68	-.23	.33	-.33	.18	-.22	.65	.98	295.9

Notes: STS = Number of strikes in all industries; SRS (3) = 3 year moving average of strikers in all industries. For the meanings of other symbols used here, see the list of variables presented above.

Table 4.3: Determinants of Strike Activity in All Industries except Mining and Quarrying, 1893-1974

Equation	Dependent Variable	Beta coefficients on:							R^2	D-W	SEE
		GDP	U_t	TUG	$STSNOM_{t-1}$	$SRSMQ_{t-1}$	RL	T			
4.3.1	STSNOM	.82		.17	.53	.11		-.43	.89	.184	230.2
4.3.2	STSNOM	1.07	.17	.22	.47	.11	-.10	-.57	.90	1.86	217.8

Equation	Dependent Variable	Beta coefficients on:					R^2	D-W	SEE
		$\dot{P}_t$	$STSNOM_{t-1}$	RL	EY	Cons			
4.3.3	SRS(3)NOM	.61	.16	.32	-.18	.17	.63	.89	258.9

Notes: STSNOM = Number of non-mining strikes; SRS(3)NOM = 3-year moving average of non-mining strikers

Table 4.4: Determinants of Strike Activity in Mining and Quarrying, 1893-1974

Equation	Dependent Variable	Beta coefficients on:					R^2	D-W	SEE
		$\dot{P}_t$	TUM	U_t	LG	$STSNOM_{t-1}$			
4.4.1	STSMQ	-.37	.62	-.43	-.17		.53	.31	389.8
4.4.2	STSMQ	-.31	.94	-.47	-.17	-.59	.74	.81	288.3

		Beta coefficients on:								
		GDP	$\dot{P}_t$	$\dot{R}_t$	Ṗrod	TUM	$SRSMQ_{t-1}$			
4.4.3	SRS(3)MQ	-.13	.25	.26	-.25		.76	.75	1.51	95.1
4.4.4	SRS(3)MQ	-.57	.22	.23	-.21	.49	.65	.78	1.40	88.2

		Beta coefficients on:									
		GDP	$\dot{R}_{t-1}$	U_t	TUM	LIBG	Cons	T			
4.4.5	SRS(3)MQ	-.22	.17	.42	3.16	.36	.25	-2.62	.77	1.21	91.1

Notes: STSMQ= the number of strikes in mining and quarrying industries; SRS(3)MQ= the three-year moving average of strikers in mining and quarrying.

which presumably signify both prosperity and heightened expectations, also contribute positively. There is, in addition, a clear, unexplained trend toward more strikes, as indicated by the coefficient on T. Unemployment, repressive legislation, and a Labour government all tend to depress strikes somewhat. The low Durbin-Watson statistics, however, tell us that significant short- or medium-term patterns are operative, but that they have not been tapped by any of the nineteen variables.

So also with Equations 4.2.3 and 4.2.4 on the number of strikers, whose Durbin-Watson statistics are even worse. Still, the variables included in these equations are indeed interesting. High prices seem crucial in bringing large numbers of workers out on strike, while elections and times when repressive legislation is in force serve to deter them from striking. It appears also that miners do play something of a 'vanguard' role: there is a clear emulation effect. The impact of productivity on strikes is also extremely interesting. On the basis of some theories, periods of rapid technical change ought to produce stress and strains leading to strikes. This is not the case; the opposite appears to be true. Periods of declining, or more likely, stagnating or slowly growing productivity are associated with high levels of striking. The direction of causation is by no means clear; whether extensive striking cripples innovation or whether lack of innovation and consequent sluggish growth lead to a slackened pace of economic advance and thus to strikes, or whether both simply reflect an underlying poor climate of industrial relations cannot be determined at this stage, but all of the possibilities are intriguing.

When mining and quarrying are left out of the equations (Table 4.3), the results improve somewhat, especially for strikes. Most important, the Durbin-Watson statistics are very good, suggesting that there are no clearly discernible patterns being missed by the model. Prosperity (GDP) again plays the critical role. Time appears to enter as a suppressor on this index of prosperity, and thus has no substantive importance.[11] Repressive legislation again depresses strikes, union growth increases them. Surprisingly, unemployment in this instance seems to boost the number of strikes. Can this be true, in view of the way unemployment has decreased strikes according to other equations? We believe so. One must remember that unemployment enters the equation only after prosperity and the rate of trade union growth. We are dealing only with the net effect of rising unemployment, holding these other factors constant. The positive impact of unemployment can perhaps be interpreted as suggesting that as long as the economy stays relatively prosperous (and by implication unemployment stays below certain limits) and trade unions can still grow, rising unemployment would produce an increase in militancy. Conversely, once the dampening effect of high unemployment on strikes via its effect on workers' ability to strike is accounted for (as measured by the organisational variables), it actually enhances the willingness to strike. Such effects would be consistent with what we have said about the effects of the 1930s on workers' attitudes, and about the strike wave of 1957-62. It also may apply to the early 1970s.

It is not at all difficult to interpret the positive coefficient on trade union growth (TUG). Shorter and Tilly are obviously on the mark in arguing that organisation mediates between grievance and collective action. More significant and surprising, however, is the combined positive impact of the two variables representing the previous year's strike experience. The strike movement clearly has a dynamic and momentum of its own. The strike itself is thus part of the learning processes of the working class, a means by which new attitudes and strategies come to infect increasingly broader segments of the labouring population. This phenomenon constitutes a very definite confirmation of the significance of strike waves. Of course, it does not explain why strike waves come and go as they do. Indeed, a single equation containing variables suggesting an internal logic to strikes, and, by implication, to changes in workers' attitudes, does not of itself constitute an explanation of that logic. Nevertheless, it is not without significance that, in the midst of numerous models with obvious deficiencies, the one equation that satisfies all statistical criteria and explains 90 per cent of the variance should embody relationships most in line with our argument.

Unfortunately, serious problems of autocorrelation remain in the equation for strikers in non-mining industries (Equation 4.3.3). There is once again an emulation effect, and repressive legislation and an election year push the numbers in the expected direction, but the rate of inflation seems to be the most powerful influence bringing workers out on strike. Strangely, the number of Conservative MPs also increases the number of strikers, apparently reflecting the tendency of large Conservative majorities to press electoral advantage to the point of confrontation.

Explaining the equations for mining and quarrying (Table 4.4) is more problematical. This is undoubtedly due to the drastic transformation of industrial relations in mining beginning in the late 1950s.[12] Just when strikes in other industries were starting their dramatic rise around 1957, miners' strikes began to drop off – hence the high, negative coefficient of the rate of inflation, and the abysmally low Durbin-Watson statistics, showing again the importance of some strong undetected influence. On the other hand, the preponderant importance of trade union strength, the dampening effects of unemployment and of a Labour government are more what one would expect of the miners. Unemployment apparently lowers the level of militancy that even the miners can sustain. Miners, moreover, are known for their firm commitment to the Labour Party; the fact that the Conservatives ruled the country during most of the bitterly catastrophic interwar period has firmly wedded most of them to the Labour Party.

The equations for the number of strikers in mining are still more difficult to fathom. The best predictor of the three-year moving average of strikers is the number of strikers in the preceding year. Unfortunately, the three-year average always includes the year before, so the high coefficient on $SRSMQ_{t-1}$ partly reflects its correlation with itself. For this reason three different equations have been presented for the number of mining strikers, one of which excludes the lagged number of mining strikers from the predictor list. The level of trade union membership is consistently the most important influence. Conservative strength again increases the number of strikers, as does a Liberal government. The economic variables move in contradictory fashion. The negative effect of GDP probably reflects the experience since 1957, while the positive effects of inflation and rates of wage change are in line with previous results. In this case (Equation 4.4.5), the positive coefficient on unemployment is ambiguous: it is probably another index of the peculiar, recent decrease in mining militancy, but it may also reflect the big disputes in mining during periods of high or rising unemployment, as in 1893, 1921, 1926, 1972 and 1974. Periods of unemployment appear to restrict the number of separate disputes in mining, and produce instead broad, concentrated battles. In any case, the Durbin-Watson statistics for the equations predicting strikers are much higher than those for equations predicting strikes in mining, so while the predictive power of the equations is low, what is being missed is at least not something obvious and simple.

Many of the relationships suggested by these estimations will be explored in detail in later chapters. What stands out at this point is the general intractability of the time series on strike activity – they will not be forced into simple and stable models covering an extended span of years. For this reason, it has not been possible to develop a satisfactory set of predictors for the two major measures of strike activity along the lines suggested by any of the extant theories of strike determination. Moreover, even the one successful equation we did generate told us only that strikes come in waves and possess an internal dynamic, without providing any enlightenment as to the external correlates of such movements. The historical variability of strike patterns thus resists any such straightjacketing, and forces us to reaffirm that industrial conflict has changed dramatically in the course of modern British history.

The first proposition derived from our theory — that long-term models of strikes should be difficult, if not impossible, to construct — is thus strongly confirmed. The second prediction from the hypothesis remains to be proven: that medium-term models should be far more successful. These models will be developed in the course of the next two chapters, which also review in detail the linkages between economic movements, consciousness and organisation, and conflict. The creation of such models, however, requires a preliminary grouping of years so as to correspond to distinct phases of economic growth or to specified combinations of trend periods in order that the economic impact can be properly controlled for and analysed. As a first step, then, it is necessary to discuss briefly the periodisation of economic history.

Picking out trends in economic development is a complicated business, beset by theoretical and empirical difficulties, and most schemas have fared rather poorly — remember Walt Rostow's 'stages'?[13] The principal practical obstacle to a useful periodisation is that movement of the various indices of economic activity — prices, wages, employment, and production — are not always in the same or correlated directions. To take but the most obvious case, prices for a long time fluctuated directly with production and employment and inversely with wages; since the Second World War, this connection has ceased to hold. Nor have trends in production and employment correlated as closely as one might expect. As a result, it is impossible to use the same set of indicators to delineate each succeeding phase of growth. The theoretical analogue of this empirical problem is that without a theory of economic growth it is hard to understand its stages, and the theory of growth may well be the weakest link in contemporary economics.

Theoretical and empirical contradictions also plague the older work of Kondratiev and Schumpeter. Kondratiev claimed to have discovered long waves in economic life of 40-50 years duration; 20-25 years of rising prices and prosperity followed by 2-2½ decades of slow growth, declining or stable prices. Schumpeter accepted Kondratiev's claim, and appended an explanation primarily in terms of technology. The upswings in the long waves were linked to the diffusion of novel technologies, the downswings to the exhaustion of a given set of innovations. Neither Kondratiev's original contribution nor Schumpeter's revision have gone unchallenged: both leave many aspects of economic behaviour unexplained and, perhaps more important, it has proved difficult to apply Kondratiev's scheme to the historical experience since 1945.[14] Nevertheless, the argument has produced a profitable consensus upon a few points of great relevance here.

First, the confrontation has forced recognition of the unevenness of economic development. Rather than conceiving of economic growth as an essentially linear path of continual advance, it has become clear that there are, at the very least, sharp inflections along the trend line of development. The debate has also revealed the fitfulness of technological innovation — great breakthroughs in technology do tend to cluster, and their impact is often violent and dramatic. More generally, this emphasis upon uneven development, sharp twists and turns, explosive innovations, and the like, has led at least a few scholars to conclude that there are indeed qualitatively different stages of economic evolution, each one characterised by a different set of wage, price and production trends, technologies, leading sectors, market structures and consumption patterns, management styles and forms of economic organisation. In short, growth is not a mere matter of the movement of quantitative indicators, it is also a question of structural shifts in the parameters of economic activity. As George Garvy concluded in his evaluation of Kondratiev's theory, the best solution to its difficulties would be to 'substitute for the hypothesis of long periodic swings the study of the successive stages of our present economic system . . .'[15]

Granting the qualitative distinctiveness of each phase of growth, however, only compounds the empirical problems. For if our concern is as much with structural change as with aggregate movements, the existing indices are even less adequate. Nevertheless, there is considerable if scattered evidence suggesting that the pace of structural advance is ordinarily syncopated with the general level of prosperity. So, it seems reasonable for present purposes to utilise the most commonly accepted benchmarks in economic history to guide our analysis of structural and conjunctural evolution. These are fairly well established, and suggest five clear trend periods since the late nineteenth century:

the years of the so-called Great Depression, 1873-96, a controversial but nonetheless coherent era; the long Edwardian boom, beginning in 1896 and continuing to either 1913 or 1920, depending upon whether or not one includes the war; 1920-39, the dismal interwar era; the postwar economic revival, commencing, depending upon one's taste, in 1939 or 1947 and lasting until the late 1960s; and, last, the current phase of slow, halting growth, dating from about 1967 or 1968. There have been, to be sure, several additional turning points of some importance, for example, 1929-32 or 1956-8, but they do not seem quite as significant over the long run as those we have picked out.[16]

Basing our investigations on this rough chronology will at least provide the contours within which to investigate more thoroughly the structural and qualititative aspects of economic transformation in Britain, and particularly the impact of such changes upon the daily life — at home, at work and in the market — of the British working class. Only when we have ascertained these subtle aspects of economic development can we accurately assess the contribution of economics to industrial unrest.

Notes

1. The testing of this prediction will be done using standard, least squares multiple regression. On these techniques, see H.M. Blalock, *Social Statistics*, 2nd ed. (New York, 1972); and J. Johnston, *Econometric Methods*, 2nd ed. (New York, 1972).

2. Much of this will become clear in this and the two subsequent chapters. In arguing for the grouping of years covered in a model as a key to its significance, we are implicitly downplaying the importance of the variables entered into predicting equations in favour of its general closeness of fit, as measured by R^2. The reasoning is that the truly important influence may be that which gives coherence to the strike experience of a particular time rather than that which correlates in the short run with strike fluctuations. A somewhat similar argument has been used by David Snyder, who claims the primacy of organisational factors in determining conflict even in periods when, because organisation is stable, purely economic factors correlate more closely with variations in strike activity. See Snyder, 'Determinants of Industrial Conflict' (unpublished Ph.D. dissertation, University of Michigan, 1974).

3. The studies included are: J.H. Pencavel, 'An Investigation into Industrial Strike Activity in Britain', *Economica*, XXXVII (1970), pp. 239-56; John C. Shorey, 'A Quantitative Analysis of Strike Activity in the United Kingdom' (Ph.D. dissertation, LSE, 1974); and 'Time Series Analysis of Strike Frequency', *British Journal of Industrial Relations*, XV (1977), pp. 63-75; R. Bean and D. Peel, 'Business Activity, Labour Organisation and Industrial Disputes in the U.K., 1892-1938', *Business History*, XVIII (1976), pp. 205-11; D. Sapsford, 'A Time Series Analysis of U.K. Industrial Disputes', *Industrial Relations*, XIV (1975), pp. 242-9. More detailed discussion of Sapsford's attempt to specify a long-term

model is contained in D. Sapsford, 'The United Kingdom's Industrial Disputes (1893-1971): A Study in the Economics of Industrial Unrest' (M. Phil. thesis, (University of Leicester, 1973).

4. See Chapter 2, note 32, above for Sapsford's attempt to handle this issue. More recently, Bean and Peel, 'Business Activity' have argued . . . similarly that 'strike frequency . . . is the most appropriate independent variable to use in the estimating equation because it is the one most independent of its previous values, thus making it especially sensitive to economic influences and cyclical fluctuations' (p. 206). In fact, there has been no satisfactory study dealing with this issue, and, on *priori* grounds, there is no reason to assume that the number of workers on strike in a given year is any less independent of its previous values than the number of strikes.

5. The Durbin-Watson statistics were .91 for the equation predicting the number of non-mining strikes and .74 for that predicting the 3-year average of non-mining strikers.

6. In developing these variables, we made some use of the theoretical sections of the works cited above by Shorter and Tilly, *Strikes in France*; Pencavel, 'An Investigation into Industrial Strike Activity'; Shorey, 'A Quantitative Analysis'; and Sapsford, 'The United Kingdom's Industrial Disputes'. Extensive use was also made of Douglas A. Hibbs, 'Industrial Conflict in Advanced Industrial Societies' (Center for International Studies, Massachusetts Institute of Technology, 1974); and D. Snyder, 'Determinants of Industrial Conflict' (Ph D. dissertation, University of Michigan, 1974), pp. 104-38.

7. On the problems attendant upon the analysis of criminal statistics, see V. Gatrell and T.B. Hadden, 'Criminal Statistics and their Interpretation', in E.A. Wrigley (ed.), *Nineteenth-Century Society* (Cambridge, 1972), pp. 336-96. They show that to 1892 protest and crime seem to alternate, and that criminality seems more connected with economic fluctuations than with the political climate and governmental repression. In any case, it is difficult if not impossible to distinguish arrests linked to various forms of protest activity with any degree of confidence. Thus they admit that ' . . . while explicitly political or semi-political responses [of this kind] may be the most dramatic, they are quantitatively the least important recorded indices of discontent,' (pp. 371-2). It seems that various external factors make criminal statistics of limited use either as measures of protest or repressiveness.

8. Of course, the 1927 Act was not really enforced, but it nevertheless symbolised the climate of the period. See M.C. Shefftz, 'The Trade Disputes and Trade Unions Act of 1927: the Aftermath of the General Strike', *Review of Politics*, XXIX (1967), pp. 387-406; and Alan Anderson, 'The Labour Laws and the Cabinet Legislative Committee of 1927-1929', *Bulletin of the Society for the Study of Labour History*, 23 (Autumn 1971), pp. 37-54.

9. A case can be made for including both the level and the rate of growth of trade union membership in the same equations to capture the effects of their interaction. It may be, for example, that the impact of the rate of growth on strikes is operative only after certain absolute levels have been reached. Before these, it may not have much influence. The reverse is also possible, of course. Cf. A.B. Hines, 'Trade Unions and Wage Inflation in the United Kingdom, 1893-1961', *Review of Economic Studies* (1964), pp. 221-52.

10. No variable was allowed into an equation, even if there were less than seven already in, unless it a) made an independent contribution to R^2 significant at the 5% level, as indicated by its F-ratio; or b) added more than .005 to the R^2 of the equation in combination with the other variables. The seven variable

limit, incidentally, did not exclude any variable which satisfied either of these criteria.

11. On the problem of suppressor variables in multiple regression, see R.B. Darlington, 'Multiple Regression in Psychological Research and Practice', *Psychological Bulletin*, LXIX (1968), pp. 161-82; and Snyder, 'Determinants of Industrial Conflict', p. 211.

12. See H. Clegg, *The System of Industrial Relations in Great Britain* (Oxford, 1970), pp. 325-7.

13. W.W. Rostow, *The Stages of Economic Growth* (Cambridge, 1960). Cf., more recently, his article, 'Kondratieff, Schumpeter, and Kuznets: Trend Periods Revisited', *Journal of Economic History*, XXXV (1975), pp. 719-54.

14. N.D. Kondratieff, 'The Long Waves in Economic Life', *Review of Economic Statistics*, XVII (1935), pp. 105-15, an abridged version of 'Die langen Wellen der Konjunktur', *Archiv fur Sozialwissenshaft ünd Sozialpolitik*, LVI (1926), pp. 573-609; J. Schumpeter, *Business Cycles* (New York, 1939). Two recent attempts to rehabilitate and apply the argument are G. Barraclough, 'The End of An Era', *New York Review of Books*, XXI, II (27 June 1974), pp. 14-20; and E. Mandel, *Late Capitalism* (Atlantic Highlands, NJ, 1976). The difficulty in utilizing Kondratiev's approach for the years since 1945 can be seen in the disparate periodisations offered by Barraclough and Rostow.

15. G. Garvy's 'Kondatrieff's Theory of Long Cycles', *Review of Economic Statistics*, XXV (1943), pp. 203-20. See also E.J. Hobsbawm, *Labouring Men* (Garden City, NY, 1964), where he refers to Kondratiev's alleged cycles as 'qualitatively different phases of economic evolution' (p. 175).

16. The data upon which this periodisation is based are reviewed more thoroughly in J. Cronin, 'Strikes in Britain, 1888-1944' (Ph.D. dissertation, Brandeis University, 1976), pp. 300-17. Much of the relevant information is presented in Appendix B. For similar periodisation, see E.J. Hobsbawm, *Industry and Empire* (Harmondsworth, 1968), pp. 314-15. Some of the controversies concerning the nature of economic change in these periods are reviewed in Chs. 5 and 6.

5 THREE GREAT LEAPS — 1889-90, 1910-13 and 1919-20

The shape of the British labour movement was basically set between 1889 and 1920. This primary mobilisation of the working class proceeded through three turbulent explosions of strike militancy and persistent and profound social turmoil. The years encompassing this process provide the ideal setting in which to demonstrate the connections between economic movements, worker consciousness and organisation, and strikes. They include strike waves produced by two distinct periods of economic development — the outburst of the 'new unionism' came during the so-called Great Depression, while the unrest of 1910-13 and just after the war responded to the numerous problems created by the Edwardian boom, the 'Indian summer' of British capitalism.

Delineating the temporal boundaries of trend periods is easier than discovering their effects upon workers, though this is what gives content to strike movements. Traditionally, workers have troubled themselves primarily over three things: wages, employment and the character of work. The various available times series of economic indicators provide information on the first two; the last, the quality and organisation of work, is still for the most part *terra incognita* for labour historians, and one can only refer to some general and rather badly documented developments. The statistics on the demands raised during conflicts show a consistent concern with such questions as manning requirements, apprenticeship ratios and other work-related questions, but there is no discernible trend toward either an increase or diminution in the importance workers attached to such issues.[1] Nevertheless, abundant testimony points to an intensified sense of work place alienation, especially after the turn of the century. Before this, neither wages nor work seem to have been of paramount importance, but rather the questions of insecurity and unemployment.

Wage trends can be measured with some precision for these years, and there is no question but that real wages rose during the Great Depression of 1873-96.[2] The index reveals a jump of about 38 per cent from 1880 to 1896. Wood's estimates showed a comparable increase of 38 per cent for the whole period from 1873 to 1896.[3] Undoubtedly the greater part of this increase was due to falling prices, because money wages actually decreased. But it is also clear that money rates did not decrease continuously. In fact, most of the decrease occurred in the late 1870s causing real wages to stagnate; from 1880 money wage rates were reasonably stable. From the early 1880s, union membership, which had plummeted after 1873, also recovered. For those in work, then, things were in some sense getting better: real wages were higher, and for the first time in a slump, many workers were able also to resist employers' demands for longer hours.[4]

Still, the primary impact of the period seems to have been to stimulate a feeling of insecurity, and hence of resentment. The responses of local trade union representatives to a survey conducted by the Royal Commission on the Depression of Trade and Industry of 1886 contains numerous examples to this effect. The replies are remarkably candid, their authenticity demonstrated by the diversity of opinion and a certain inarticulate honesty. When asked if conditions were depressed in 1886, virtually all replied 'yes'. When asked about the prospects of trade, the answers were more varied. Some unions, especially representatives of well-placed engineers, answered optimistically, predicting a revival in the near future. More often, the answers were decidedly pessimistic, confessions of doubt and confusion. Booth, of the Power Loom Weavers' Association at Ashton-under-Lyne, described the course of trade as, 'irregular, a push for a time and over again. Cannot say what it will be in the immediate future.' Thomas, of the Aberdare branch of the Amalgamated Society of Boot and Shoe Makers, also found trade 'Irregular', but was still less sanguine about its prospects: 'We do not know what is in future, only wishing to see better times.'[5] The weakness of union organisation seems to have prevented many direct expressions of anger during the worst years of unemployment, but it is hard not to agree with Robert Knight of the Boilermakers, who in 1886 noted 'a depth of grief and trouble the full revelation of which, we believe, cannot be indefinitely postponed'.[6]

This insecurity affected different groups of workers to varying degrees, depending on the ease of entry into the trade, and whether or not wages fell with prices. Upon general and unskilled labourers, like dockers, the depression bore severely. Men temporarily out of work in other trades drifted to the waterfront or into similar occupations, considerably worsening the chances of anyone getting employment in these open trades. For others the manifestations of hardship differed. Sliding scales prevailed in several industries, most prominently among the miners. If these were allowed to operate as they had in the past, workers would reap none of the benefits of declining prices, and they would still feel the bite of unemployment. Such was the case with the miners, and the result was a growing determination to abolish sliding

scales throughout the coalfields — a determination made into a principle of organisation of the Miners' Federation of Great Britain, formed
in 1888.[7] Customarily, wages in the Lancashire cotton industry also
fluctuated with the price of cotton, but wage decreases are particularly
tough to take when unemployment threatens. Thus textile operatives
resisted proposed reductions by militant strikes in 1878 and 1885.
The strikes failed, and the reductions were enforced, but the strength
of the resistance, which led to serious rioting in several towns during
1878, probably deterred employers from demanding reductions com-
mensurate with the fall in prices. More importantly, the defeats led to
qualititative changes in the form of organisation among cotton workers,
as even the most backward came to see the need for closer union federations and for the recruitment of women into labour organisations.[8]

The form, ideology, and locus in militancy during the period of
'New Unionism' all testify eloquently to the nature of workers' problems in these years. It is true that in practice and over time the
distinction between 'old' and 'new' unionism was blurred, but the
banners under which the battles of 1888-93 were fought and the
ideas that animated the activist militants who spread the strike movement to countless smaller groups of workers, were reflections of the
major contemporary grievances. The demand for eight hours is the
clearest, but the efforts to bring all unskilled workers, even agricultural
labourers, into general unions were equally motivated by a desire to
combat insecurity. In textiles, mining, engineering and especially on
the railways, new and more inclusive organising strategies were adopted.

The story of the emergence of demands for the abolition of sliding
scales and for an eight-hour day, and of the recognition of the value
of general unions, is too long to recount here. But such an exercise
would demonstrate well the slow process by which workers adapt their
ideas and organisations to cope with new problems, how the time lag
between the beginning of a new period of economic development and a
strike wave is overcome. Almost with the inception of the slump, and
certainly by the late 1870s, voices were raised on each of these issues,
especially on the issue of sliding scales. The temporary revival of trade
in the early 1880s slowed the ferment, but renewed depression in the
mid-1880s spread and deepened it. In these years there occurred what
the Webbs termed a 'working on minds' which were 'awakened by an
industrial contraction of exceptional character'.[9] This second 'contraction' led to greater concern with unemployment, and the eight-hours
movement gathered speed from just this conjuncture of circumstance
c. 1883. At first reactions to the new ideas were mixed, but by the

early 1890s the demand for a shorter work day was backed by just about every major trade union. Sharp and pointed criticisms of the exclusive and lethargic character of the 'old unions' also date from the onset of the mid-1880s depression. Again, support was not immediately forthcoming, but by the 1890s the principles of 'new' and general unionism and of class solidarity had obtained at least a verbal acquiescence from most union leaders.[10]

The connection between economics and strikes was therefore relatively straightforward during the Great Depression. Between 1896 and 1920 the links are less obvious, in part because the economic history of those years is as yet so poorly conceptualised. Prices stabilised along with wages from the mid-1890s to about 1905. After that, prices moved upward while wages lagged, so that real wages fell. Unemployment was much less than in the preceding period, although 1908 and 1909 were bad years, with unemployment probably topping 9 per cent, and the building industry was depressed throughout the boom. In terms of prices, wages and employment, it was a classic Kondratiev upswing. Both Kondratiev and later Schumpeter explained the upswing, or at least associated it, with major innovations, yet most writers have discussed the period as one of slow productivity growth, more or less barren of innovation or creative entrepreneurship in Britain.

The alleged lack of innovation between 1895 and 1913 has often served as the crux of explanations of Britain's poor growth performance in relation to that of the USA, Germany, and even France. One authority has argued recently that England's relative retardation is best explained by 'the lack of "immense new technological inventions" upon which to base new industries'.[11] 'By 1900,' according to another, 'the application of steam to power and transport, and of steel to equipment, had been largely worked through. New techniques, in electricity, chemicals, the man-made fibres, and the internal combustion engine with its applications to transport, were being developed, but mostly as yet were only at the stage of the pilot plant: their impact would not be massive until after the First World War.'[12] The same writer also credits a 'change in the will and power of organised labour to resist management ...' with holding down productivity, but stresses too the lack of innovation and consequent absence of a new leading sector as the major retarding factor.[13] A close look at several statistics, however, forces us to question and qualify this view. The application of steel, for example, was by no means complete by the mid-1890s, when productivity was checked. In fact, British steel production increased by 135 per cent between 1895 and 1913.[14] Nor was steam power thoroughly applied within industry by 1895. In fact, the largest increase in its use occurred between 1880 and 1907, just when productivity began to decline.[15] Moreover, the industrial power of steam was being supplemented by electricity, use of which increased phenomenally from 1895 to 1920. By 1912, electric motors were supplying fully 25 per cent of the energy in manufacturing and mining.[16]

Presumably, these improvements and advances could have been greater and would have had to be so to turn the embryonic new industries into leading sectors of growth; it seems that they were applied more broadly and efficiently in both the US and Germany. What has to be explained, then, is not so much technical backwardness *per se*, but rather the slowness with which the entire economy responded to the new opportunities for growth and investment in steel, electrical engineering, chemicals and the like. Several reasons have been adduced, and most often the burden has been placed on the alleged decline in British entrepreneurial zeal.[17] More relevant, probably, were the structure and international position of the British economy. Despite progress in retailing and some increase in middle and lower middle class consumption, the home market remained circumscribed and made exports critical to the overall performance of the economic system. The role of exports in the generation of GNP actually increased in these years.[18] In addition, growing competition from abroad, particularly from Germany and America, prevented Britain from expanding its new industries in either European or North American markets. Instead, the empire provided soft and dependable outlets for traditional products and goods. Thus, empire customers absorbed a vast amount and a growing percentage of exports, particularly in the post-1900 boom. Finally, the well-developed foreign capital market helped to siphon funds from home to foreign investments, especially after 1900.[19] Of course, this may have simply reflected current profit possibilities, but these themselves were not unrelated to structural aspects of the economy.

The contradictions in Britain's economic performance had important effects on labour. The first point to be made is that the concern of today's economic historians for Britain's decline relative to other countries is but a reflection of contemporary opinion around 1900.[20] Much of the opinion was hysterical in tone and even racialist in content, but the sense that British industry was lagging was widespread among the employing and middle classes. *The Times'* well-known series on 'ca-canny' was but one manifestation. The effect seems to have been a worsening in relations between workers and employers. As James

Jefferys pointed out in his pioneering study of the engineers, 'foreign competition' became the bogey with which to fight the unions, and its role was a major strut in the argument of the employers during the great lockout of 1897.[21] Thus, the economic difficulties of the period formed the background to that offensive against the unions epitomised by Taff Vale and (at a later date) the Osborne judgement.

Despite all this, production grew substantially, and the combination of rising output and stagnating productivity point to a pattern of long hours – that is, much overtime – and increased pressure for production. This must have made an impact on the daily lives of workers. D.W. Crowley noted some time ago the response of English employers to foreign competition: 'too often Britain remained behind other nations in technical progress, with conservative management apparently trying to make up the leeway of their competitors by sheer driving at a faster pace.'[22] The 'agony of intense work was most keenly felt in branches of engineering and by some unskilled workers,' according to Peter Stearns, but 'its reports come from almost every industry.'[23] To some extent, the reports may testify to a new attitude on the part of labour, a more thorough 'learning of the rules of the game', rather than a real intensification of work. In these years, 'workers began to demand what the traffic would bear and, where they had any choice, to measure effort by payment.'[24] But employers were learning also, and in this same period work measurement and the use of piece rates made rapid headway.[25]

Indeed, the very weakness of the performance of the new industries like steel, chemicals and electricity meant that growth would still centre in the old trades and in activities concerned with transport and distribution. Structural transformation was manifest therefore in unexpected places and forms. In textiles, for example, the size of plant and capital requirements of firms increased notably, and the old pattern of recruiting managers and owners from the skilled workers disintegrated.[26] In mining, too, the scale of operations grew and with it the role of joint stock companies. Many miners testified to a new distance from the workers and a new hardness on the part of owners and operators. On the railways and the docks, ownership also concentrated and work patterns were rationalised. It appears that unskilled as well as skilled experienced the accelerated technical changes and changes in work routines of the Edwardian economy adversely. If one must generalise, however, it can be said that the key structural tendency was toward an increase in the ranks and in the social importance of the semi-skilled, and a decline of both the casual and the skilled craft traditions of the mid-Victorian economy.[27] In strategic terms, the mix was explosive, because skilled workers were antagonised and aggrieved but retained a good deal of collective strength, while unskilled workers achieved a new ability to transform long-standing grievances into organised militancy. The rise of the semi-skilled also served to mute the contrasts between the 'labour aristocracy' of skilled workers and the rest of the working class. And, finally, the unique pattern of urbanisation ushered in by the growth of mass public transport served to remove the middle classes into their prized suburban locations distant and isolated from the lower classes, and to bring workers together either in the inner ring of industrial suburbs or the core areas of the cities. In these increasingly homogeneous residential environments, working people founded and built solid communities of mutual support, which often became the centres of trade union and political organising.[28]

One specific result of these trends was a growing tension at the workplace, leading to a stalemate in terms of productivity. Hence the curious paradox that these years 'witnessed a minor revolution in the [engineering] workshop, contrasting sharply with the relative absence of technical change between 1850 and 1890', but productivity in much of engineering actually declined.[29] Similar problems occurred throughout the economy.

Still, translating discontent over the quality of work into concrete demands or slogans is notoriously difficult. To be sure, complaints were voiced: by warehousemen in 1896, Swansea dockers in 1912, London dockers much earlier, construction workers in 1908, boot and shoe makers throughout the 1890s, and by cotton operatives continually.[30] The main result seems to have been a general social polarisation, an intensification of class antagonism. To this end the offensive against the unions, the strengthened organisation of the employers, and the struggle over work all combined to produce a deep sense of grievance, a sense which was only increased by the failure of wages to keep pace with inflation after 1905. The peculiar course of economic growth seems to have generated such a welter of problems and frustrations from 1896 to 1913 that discontent came gradually to focus not on specific evils and localised enemies but on the performance of the entire system.

One should therefore not expect to find too close or direct a correspondence between the problems faced by workers and the articulated aims of the strike wave of 1910-13. Yet the very inchoateness of this upsurge itself reveals the connection. George Dangerfield was doubtless subject to frequent rhetorical excesses, but his *Strange*

Death of Liberal England contains some crucial insights. He felt, without really explaining why, that 'the deepest impulse in the great strike movement of 1910-14 was an unconscious one, an enormous energy pressing up from the depths of the soul . . . In this way the instinctive tactics of the syndicalists and the instinctive desires of the workers came together.'[31] Though we would prefer to replace such terms as 'instinctive' and 'unconscious' with a more concrete discussion of class relations, the meaning is clear, and Dangerfield captures well the sense of contemporary comment. G.R. Askwith's tone was less dramatic, but the famous arbitrator was equally surprised and frightened by the new spirit which gripped the rank and file. The events of 1910-11 had shown workers 'that their strength is greatly increased by united activity'. He feared that in the future, 'action is likely to be more sudden than heretofore', and warned against ignoring 'the grave danger of united action.' More significant still, he confessed at one point that 'nobody could understand the rapid and alarming spread of many of the strikes, which took the leaders of men themselves by surprise'.[32]

The fundamental strategic innovation of 1910-14 was the 'sympathetic strike'. Known before but seldom utilised, it revealed and served the new desire to counter employers' strength with broad working class unity, as concretised, for example, in the Triple Alliance.[33] Coupled with this syndicalist sentiment were attempts to establish one hundred per cent unionisation and to eliminate non-union labour wherever possible. These thrusts did not explicitly speak to the pressures at the workplace, or even to declining real wages, but did reflect the growing sense of class antagonism which permeated and united all the more specific complaints and demands. The new methods were also a calculated repudiation of the contemporary labour leadership in Parliament and in the unions, whose torpor and timidity reflected not so much the processes of *embourgeoisement* or bureaucratisation – these were to come later, with the war – as they did a sad and compromising weakness.[34]

It seems reasonable to argue that the diffuse and spontaneous, but surprisingly bitter tone of the 'Labour Unrest' was the result of the general dissatisfaction prevailing at the base of industry. The demands were for wages or union recognition, and no doubt they were seriously meant, but what troubled most observers was the tendency of workers to strike first, and frame their demands later. Askwith, the Government's industrial troubleshooter, often found his first task was to reduce the militant slogans and vague grievances expressed by strikes into coherent demands. The desire to fight, the 'strike fever', affected many thousands of workers outside the network of union organisation, and union leaders worked overtime to draw up lists of demands within which to capture the men's sense of grievance.[35] In this way, the confused and difficult position of the British economy found its reflection in workers' collective actions.

Multivariate analysis of strike data tends to confirm this picture. Because the impact of the half 'long wave' of 1896-1913 was so pervasive and varied, no single measure of economic trends predicts strike rates at all well. Instead, the balance of organisational resources in terms of labour legislation, political party and union strength plays a much greater role. Still, the success of the equations explaining strikes in these years suggests that militancy apparently does follow stable patterns during successive trend periods. Let us look more closely.

Tables 5.1-5.3 present the best fitting equations for 1893-1913, and they generally pass the basic statistical tests with ease. In most cases, R^2 is above .90, the Durbin-Watson statistic is above 1.50 (and is never lower than an inconclusive 1.18), and the Standard Error is reasonably low. Difficulties arise only over the precise interpretation of the coefficients on the different included variables.

Equation 5.1.1, in which the dependent variable is the number of strikes in all industries between 1893 and 1913, is a case in point. Here only one economic variable is included, the rate of price change, and its sign is opposite to what one would have expected. This apparently reflects the fact that the years of rapid price increase, 1906-10, formed the background, rather than the occasion, for the explosion of 1910-13. This does not mean that the rise was not an important cause or at least precondition, of 1910-13, but it does suggest that the linkage between the resentment over inflation and strikes was indirect; that other factors mediated between them. Similarly, two of the other included variables, the 'dummy' for a Liberal Government, and the lagged number of non-mining strikes, pose problems of interpretation. The latter seems mainly to be pointing to the wave-like character of strikes with which we are familiar, but does little to explain it. The Liberal Government 'dummy', despite its low coefficient, is also pointing to a verifiable fact, the presence of a Liberal administration during the prewar outburst of strikes. But is this symptomatic of a real causal relationship, or simply an idiosyncratic description of the particular circumstances of 1910-13? There probably is some real-world effect being hinted at here: namely a tendency for workers before the First World War, recognising their organisational and therefore industrial weakness, to

Table 5.1: Determinants of Strike Activity, All Industries, 1893-1913

Equation	Dependent Variable	Beta coefficients on:					R^2	D–W	SEE
		$\dot{P}_t$	$SRSMQ_{t-1}$	$STSNOM_{t-1}$	TUG	LIBG			
5.1.1	STS	−.22	.28	.54	.48	.09	.94	2.13	79.0

Equation	Dependent Variable	Beta coefficients on:						R^2	D–W	SEE
		GDP	TUM	$SRSMQ_{t-1}$	CG	LIBG	Cons			
5.1.2	SRS(3)	−.09	.82	−.34	−.37	1.15	1.34	.95	1.91	65.7
5.1.3	SRS(3)	.18	.40		−.30	1.10	1.21	.90	1.72	87.9

Notes: The symbols used in all of the equations presented in the tables of this chapter carry the same meanings as in the tables and in the variables list in the last chapter. We shall therefore dispense with 'Notes' in the rest of the tables of this and the following chapter.

Table 5.2: Determinants of Strike Activity, All Industries except Mining and Quarrying, 1893-1913

		Beta coefficients on:								
Equation	Dependent Variable	GDP	$\dot{P}_t$	$\dot{R}_t$	TUG	$SRSMQ_{t-1}$	$STSNOM_{t-1}$	R^2	D–W	SEE
5.2.1	STSNOM			.18	.44	.30	.47	.94	1.76	73.8
5.2.2	STSNOM	–.11	–.11		.55	.33	.46	.93	2.20	77.2

		Beta coefficients on:									
Equation	Dependent Variable	TUM	$SRSMQ_{t-1}$	LIBG	CG	RL	Cons	T	R^2	D–W	SEE
5.2.3	SRS(3)NOM	.36	–.48	1.17	–.36	–.36	1.65	.56	.96	2.22	30.9
5.2.4	SRS(3)NOM	.85	–.48	1.35		–.29	1.39		.92	1.27	40.7

Table 5.3: Determinants of Strike Activity, Mining and Quarrying, 1893-1913

Equation	Dependent Variable	Beta coefficients on:				RL	R^2	D–W	SEE
		$\dot{P}_t$	$\dot{R}_t$	$\dot{U}_t$	$SRSMQ_{t-1}$				
5.3.1	STSMQ	−.85	−.77	−.14	.46	−.40	.49	1.71	34.1

		Beta coefficients on:						R^2	D–W	SEE
		GDP	$\dot{U}_t$	$\dot{Prod}$	$SRSMQ_{t-1}$	$STSNOM_{t-1}$	TUM			
5.3.2	SRS(3)MQ	−1.37		.22	−.18		2.03	.86	1.18	53.6
5.3.3	SRS(3)MQ	−2.23	.22	.33	−.32	−.44	2.80	.91	1.57	45.2
5.3.4	SRS(3)MQ	−1.77		.28	−.25	−.24	2.41	.89	1.22	49.2

aim their strikes at a sympathetic government whose intervention might tip the scales toward the workers. But surely too much should not be made of this, because the exact same years witnessed a rebellion in the ranks of labour against both their own union leaders and the leadership of the parliamentary Labour Party, and it is unlikely in such circumstances that they would have turned to a Liberal Government for aid in achieving their industrial aims. So it seems that the Liberal 'dummy' is playing as much a descriptive as an explanatory role in the equation.

The variable whose presence and the size and direction of whose coefficient make most sense in Equation 5.1.1 is the rate of trade union growth. It will become evident that trade union membership or growth are the variables which figure most prominently in almost all of our equations. Can this be interpreted as proving that unionisation is the crucial missing link between economic forces and strikes? The importance of trade union variables does suggest that the impact of economic change on workers' attitudes may be manifest directly and in the first instance in organisational growth, and through this in strikes. But one cannot be confident about the direction of causation. If unionisation were causally prior to strikes, it would seem reasonable in this case to expect it to be temporally prior also. But the correlations between strike activity and union membership and growth are closer in the same year than when the latter are lagged by a year. So strikes may themselves affect unionisation, or both may reflect deeper shifts in worker consciousness. Still, the connection is not a trivial finding; if nothing else, it shows that workers did not strike without also joining unions in the prewar period.

Equations 5.1.2 and 5.1.3 again feature trade union membership as an important predictor of a three year moving average of strikes and confirm the probable mediating role of organisation between economic change, consciousness and strikes. Besides union membership, the most important variables are all political: the Conservative Government 'dummy', the Liberal 'dummy', and the number of Conservative MPs. Here too it is impossible to know how much their inclusion signifies about the real impact of politics on strikes and how much it is simply describing the years of unrest in political terms.[36] Something substantive does seem to be implied by the fact that in addition to the Liberal Government 'dummy', the number of Conservative MPs is also included with a high positive coefficient. This is a clear reference to the relationship of political forces in 1910-14. It is tempting to see this particular political constellation as peculiarly susceptible to outside pressure, and the several studies which view these years as 'critical', in almost a clinical sense, point in the same direction.[37] Still, even if these variables are accepted as having some analytical significance, do they really reveal causal relations at a level other than that of mere timing? Finally, note should be taken also of the surprising negative coefficient on strikers in mining lagged one year in Equation 5.1.2 concerning the number of workers directly involved in strikes. How is this to be reconciled with its positive relation to the number of strikes in Equation 5.1.1? The answer is that apparently the effect of large mining strikes (and possibly of large strikes generally) is to stimulate the workers in small, unorganised industries to take action in the following year. A classic case is 1913 and the first six months of 1914. This 18-month period saw a pause in large-scale strike movements, but a flowering of small strikes following the big battles of 1912.

Table 5.2 excludes the effects of mining strikes and in so doing generally accentuates the relationships reported in the previous table. Economic factors are again poorly represented — included if at all with negative coefficients. The importance of trade unions is reinforced. So are the major political variables, to which has been added the 'dummy' representing the influence of legal repression, in this case the Taff Vale decision. The lagged indicators of strikes take coefficients similar to, but greater than, those in Table 5.1, suggesting that the direction of influence is from the miners to other sectors of the working class, rather than *vice versa*.

Attempts to explain striking in mining and quarrying are somewhat less successful, as shown in Table 5.3. Strangely, the number of strikes is less susceptible to prediction than the number of strikers. Thus, no realistic combination of the 19 variables can account for more than 50 per cent of the variance in strikes, while all three of the equations for strikers account for better than 85 per cent. The equation for strikes (5.3.1) is highly enigmatic. The effects of legal repression and unemployment are straightforward enough, but the price and wage change variables take unexpected negative coefficients. This unusual pattern requires special consideration.

An answer can possibly be found by viewing Equations 5.3.1-5.3.4 together. In Equation 5.3.1, predicting strikes, the most important contribution to R^2 is made by the variable representing the number of strikers in mining the previous year — it takes a positive coefficient. On the other hand, the equations for strikers includes the same variable but with the opposite sign. There is thus an alternating rhythm to mining strikes. The occurrence of large-scale strikes in one year prevents their happening the next; instead there will be a proliferation of small strikes. Hence the low correlation (.44) between strikes and strikers in mining, and the frequent divergence in the movements of the two indices over time. (See Figure 5.1.) Widespread but small-scale mining strikes seem to represent a distinctly secondary form of struggle for miners. They increase when large-scale confrontation is not possible, due either to exhaustion from previous battles, or to political repression (thus the peak of strikes during 1901). So the curious economic correlates of the number of mining strikes are probably due more to the internal logic of mining unionism than to any causal economic relationship.

Equations 5.3.2 to 5.3.4, in which a moving average of mining strikers is the dependent variable, pose fewer interpretative problems. Unquestionably the most important variable is the level of trade union membership, while GDP seems to be acting as a 'suppressor' on the former. The negative effects of the previous year's total of mining strikers have already been discussed, while the similar effect of the lagged number of non-mining strikes confirms what was noted earlier: that the emulative effects between mining and other industries are not mutual; mining strikes have a pattern of their own.

More confusing is the positive influence of the rate of productivity increase. One obvious problem — and this applies to some extent to all the variables when used with mining data — is that the measure of productivity refers to all industry not just to mining. So the relationship may be entirely accidental. On the other hand, the pace of productivity growth is quite difficult to measure. It has a complex relationship with other economic factors. Figure 5.2 graphs both the rate of productivity increase and the unemployment rate against time between 1888 and 1921. Movements in employment and production, it can be seen, have distorting effects on productivity. This is due to the operation of two fairly obvious factors:

(1) the effects of innovation and capital improvements make themselves felt more forcefully only in upswings, when they are fully utilised;

(2) conversely, productivity drops as production and employment drop because employers cannot divest themselves of labour (especially labour not directly involved in production). Hence the ratios of capital to labour and to output rise, and productivity falls.

These influences distort the figures for productivity increases by causing the effects of innovations to show up some time after their implementation. Concretely, Figure 5.2 shows a tendency for productivity to increase in prosperous years, so it is possible that it is included in the equation as a weak prosperity variable. This might

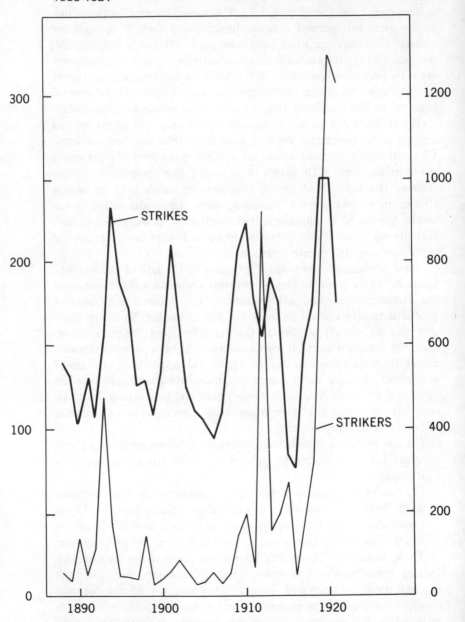

Figure 5.1: Strikes and Strikers (in thousands) in Mining and Quarrying, 1888-1921

account for the unexpected positive coefficient on unemployment in Equation 5.3.3 which may be acting as a 'suppressor' on productivity. There are, however, two other possible substantive interpretations of the productivity variable. First, it could simply be that increased productivity signifies a heightened intensity of work and leads to more workers going on strike. This, however, is unlikely. If anything, one should expect the opposite in these years, when miners complained that owners were intensifying work instead of increasing productivity. Second, and more likely, the positive association between strikes and productivity may mean that when workers cannot use the strike weapon they turn to on-the-job action to restrict output and boost wage rates. This is at least one possible explanation of the negative, or very low, rates of productivity increase during the tenure of the Taff Vale ruling, which also suppressed strikes.

It appears, therefore, that neither in mining nor in other industries were economic factors and fluctuations narrowly conceived responsible for variation in strikes. More broadly conceived, however, this is precisely what one should expect of a period of time when the economy was growing, but in such a way as to destabilise social class relations by mingling prosperity with intensified pressure at the point of production and by causing prices to rise just fast enough to make workers feel that their increased inputs were entirely unrewarded. Given this highly charged economic setting, explosions of strikes became almost inevitable, but their timing was left to the exact combination of political circumstances, some of whose connections with strikes may have been otherwise wholly fortuitous.[38]

With the coming of war, the normal patterns of strike activity were interrupted, and the industrial battles looming in late 1914 were postponed in favour of those of a bloodier type against a different foe. Conjuncturally, however, the war and immediate postwar years were still of a piece with the period 1896-1913, though between 1914 and 1920 the trends prevalent before 1913 were violently accentuated. Pressures at work intensified, as old customs and restrictions were discarded and as dilution was pushed forward. Probably the major additional stimulant to working class anger was inflation, but it is important also to understand how, during the war, economic problems became political. 'The War,' wrote one of the Commissioners on Unrest in 1917, 'has introduced a new element into questions affecting Labour, viz., the Government.' Specifically, 'The Munitions of War Acts . . . revolutionised industry,' while the prohibition of the right to strike had

Figure 5.2: Unemployment Rates and Rates of Productivity Increase, 1888-1921 (in percentages)

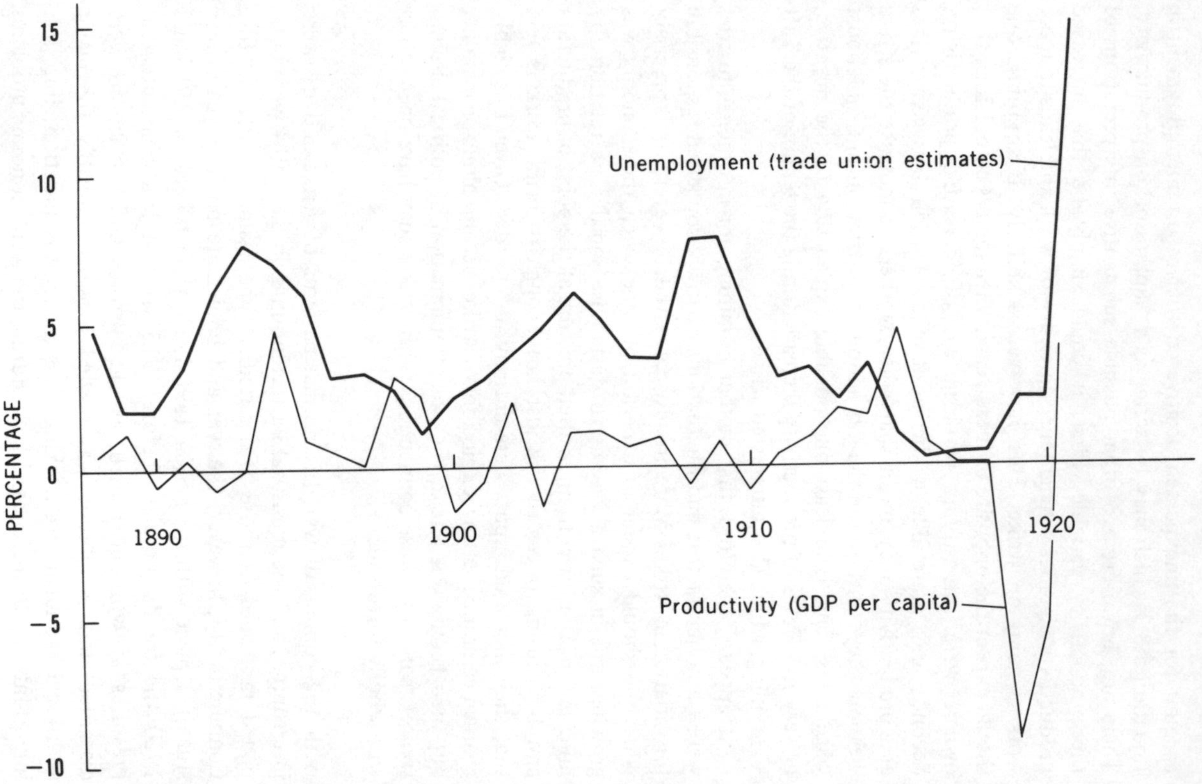

'undoubtedly taken authority out of the hands of the responsible officials and given it to Shop Stewards . . .' The 'trade union world,' was, as a consequence, 'in a state of flux and ferment.'[39] As a result of the concentration of control over much of the economy in official hands, economic grievances were politicised, and as a consequence of blocking redress of grievances through normal procedures, it was almost guaranteed that the politicisation would be of a rebellious or even revolutionary kind.

The reports of the 1917 Commission of Enquiry into Industrial Unrest, which are basically distillations of interviews with hundreds of workers and their spokesmen, contain numerous examples of this process. The proximate spur to unrest was high prices – by 1917 retail prices were approximately 170 per cent of their 1914 level – especially for food. Quickly, however, this complaint assumed a political form: 'Men begin to ask themselves whether the sacrifices they are making are really necessary.' Many came to believe 'that there has been inequality of sacrifice,' and 'the suspicion' rose 'that a portion of the community is exploiting the national crisis for profit.' 'Complaints of exploitation, profiteering, and bad distribution' echoed through the reports of each of the commissioners, and pointed comparisons were made between the continued availability of luxury foods for the rich and the plight of the poor, who were often reduced to eating sterilised tuberculous meat.[40] In his summary of all the reports, Minister of Labour Barnes claimed to have detected, behind the specific grievances, a generalised 'want of confidence' in the government and its local agents, and pleaded for more understanding of the 'difficulties which have beset all in authority . . .'[41]

The enhanced role of the government in social life was not, of course, entirely a product of the war. The nationalisation of politics and the growth of bureaucratic intervention in economic activity were two of the central structural developments occurring in all European countries in the first two decades of the century with extensive ramifications on social class relations.[42] In England, the imperial thrust of the late nineteenth century was transmuted into a programme for social reform and mobilisation for 'national efficiency' espoused by important sections of the Edwardian establishment. More concretely, the measures of the Liberal Government elected in 1906, especially its unemployment and pension schemes, marked decisive advances in the politicisation of economic problems, and the increasing involvement of the central authorities in labour disputes from 1907 onward was rightly seen as setting dangerous precedents which could impair the state's ability to remain detached from the escalating social confrontation.[43] Indeed, the bulk of the working class was literally pushed into political action by those very actions of government, beginning with Taff Vale, designed to ward off and, if necessary, suppress unrest. The war took the process several steps further, but in such a situation as to guarantee that the government would come to be viewed increasingly as an ally of the employers and an obstacle to social justice. Important structural changes, in other words, were developing in a tense and trying context that profoundly conditioned their evolution.

The upper-class bias that pervaded government intervention in society exacerbated social contrasts and the antipathy between rich and poor. Simultaneously, the conditions and problems confronting workers during the war tended to weld together the disparate elements of the class into a more unified social and political bloc. Mention has already been made of the growth of working-class communities which, with their dense social networks, facilitated collective organisation. Such informal ties were bound to increase in significance as the normal leaders of the unions and other institutions were sucked up into the inflated apparatus of government control. Divisions within the working class were further eroded by the drift of wages and earnings, which became much more equal. In many industries, the differential between skilled and unskilled narrowed by almost a third, and, despite some nasty immediate reactions, the long-term effect was to create a more homogeneous working class.[44]

There is no need to offer here yet another chronicle of the postwar unrest, although a good analytical history of 1917 to 1921 is sorely missed. What requires emphasis is, first, the radical and insurgent character of the unrest, and, second, its democratic form. Of late the tendency has been to downplay the former and ignore the latter, but this will not do. Even the most unflappable observers were struck by the militancy and truculence of the rank-and-file, and its refusal to abide by the instructions of its leaders. Beatrice Webb, for example, consistently emphasised the reasonable and moderate nature of labour and its demands, but she was forced to admit that 'it was not the leaders but the mass of the men who have gone "red" '.[45] Basil Thomson, Director of Intelligence at Scotland Yard, who usually minimised the depth of discontent and harped on the 'sane and sensible' character of the men, felt that in 1919 'The number of British-born persons who desire a violent revolution is apparently stationary, but the number who are determined to have a revolution by constitutional means is certainly increasing . . .' He later proclaimed that, as of January 1920,

'It is doubtful whether at this period the revolutionaries exceeded 10 per cent of the total number of trade unionists,' but also admitted that the trade union leaders had virtually no control over their members and would probably in the future 'again follow the line of least resistance' and consent to massive strike action.[46]

The Times wavered in its assessment. One day it would see a moderation in the intensity of social conflict, the next day it was back to attacking the 'gang of revolutionaries' determined to wreck the nation's recovery. In a relatively calm moment, a leader writer editorialised that:

> This unrest and restlessness of workers really means that our industrial population has made up its mind that for the future, no matter what the national need may be, it will not be disciplined, managed or controlled by an authority, [whether that authority be] a private employer or a State department, which it does not choose by its own unfettered will to recognize as fit and suitable and whose dictates it does not consider sound and reasonable.[47]

The new consciousness among workers took many forms and pervaded diverse aspects of social intercourse. Even language seems to have reflected an embittering of class divisions. In an extremely perceptive article, Bernard Waites has written of how the meaning and implications of the term 'class' shifted noticeably around this time. After entering into common usage between 1800 and 1850, the word degenerated in its specificity, and the prosperity and temporary social harmony of the second half (especially the third quarter) of the nineteenth century tended to replace the notion of class polarisation with a more elaborately graded spatial imagery. From 1910 to 1920, the awareness of class and class distinctions was again heightened. 'Class' also became tinged with overtones of conflict and battle, as metaphors generated in wartime were carried over into the analysis and description of domestic events.[48]

It also appears that this polarisation went hand in hand with an escalation of workers' expectations. As Runciman perceived, there was a 'sudden but short-lived explosion of aspirations' after the First World War. The escalation of expectations arose from several factors. Contemporaries like Basil Thomson and the *Economist* felt that workers were simply emulating the wealthier sections of society who were then indulging in an 'orgy of extravagance'. Resentment at such conspicuous consumption may also have merged with memories of war-induced shortages and inequities to produce an image — powerful if nonetheless not strictly authentic — of the rich as profiteers. Inflation probably also played a role, for rapidly rising prices seem to encourage a sharp calculating mentality and to invite those 'invidious comparisons' which generate anger and jealousy, particularly when established and customary differentials are upset. Whatever the origins of the sentiment, both the conduct and the content of working-class protest reveal a novel and expanded sense of what was due to workers and what they were morally justified in demanding.[49]

Testimony on this transformation abounds in contemporary literature. From our point of view, however, what is most interesting are the links between the social and economic roots of the militancy and its organisational and ideological manifestations. Primarily, the economic problem was inflation, but the enhanced economic role of the government, and the crippled role of union leaders, gave it a particular political character. It also led to deep doubts about the justice and viability of the existing economic system; around the issue of inflation crystallised a wide range of grievances, and ultimately a critique and an indictment of the whole society. The demands of the strike movement, as usual, varied enormously, but, also as usual, higher wages was the demand most often voiced. But the extent of these demands and the coupling of them with projects for nationalisation of the mines and railways, show at the very least that increasing numbers of workers saw drastic changes in the social system as a prerequisite for the granting even of limited wage demands.

In form, the movement was also advanced. There was a recognition of the need for a 'general staff' for the labour movement, to serve as a co-ordinator for the massive, synchronised strikes seen by many militants as the only winning strategy. This was reflected in the reforms of the structure of the TUC, particularly the strengthening of its General Council.[50] At a more local level, there was a rapid extension of shop stewards and workshop committees, or other organs of rank-and-file control. This occurred not simply in engineering, where they were actually recognised by management, but also on the railways, and in a mass rank-and-file movement among the miners based on the lodges.[51] In retrospect, these two thrusts appear in some ways contradictory, and they must have seemed so to many at the time, but both served to answer needs felt by large sections of the labour movement.

The form and content of the post-First World War militancy was therefore analogous to those of the prewar outburst — in both instances the comprehensiveness of the challenge from below corresponded to the complex and ubiquitous nature of the problems workers faced at this conjunctural moment. In neither case can the problems be reduced to the simply economic, though the litany of grievances in each can be traced back to the particular pattern of economic change that obtained between 1896 and 1920. It should not be surprising for that reason to find that when we specify predictive equations for the entire span of years from 1893 to 1921, the results are quite similar to those for 1893-1913 only. In Tables 5.4-5.6, therefore, most of the relationships picked out previously continue to hold; the determinants of strikes seem to remain relatively constant through 1921. The equations predicting the number of strikes in all industries from 1893 to 1921 (Equations 5.4.1-5.4.2), for example, are very similar to Equation 5.1.1. Once again trade unionism, as measured both by the level and the rate of growth of membership, is the critical variable. The main economic variable, the retail price index, again takes a negative value, apparently acting as a 'suppressor' on trade unionism. Likewise the number of strikers in mining the year preceding is included, indicating an emulation effect, as is the Liberal Government 'dummy'. Also included is time, the trend variable, which appears to be functioning as a 'suppressor'. The same is basically true of equations predicting strikers in all industries. The only major change in Equations 5.4.1 to 5.4.4, as compared with 5.1.1 to 5.1.3, is that the importance of trade unionism is strengthened. All four of the new equations include both union variables with positive coefficients.

So, too, do the four equations generated to explain strikes in nonmining industries (Table 5.5). In all four cases, the combined effects of the trade union variables account for well over half of the explained variance (R^2). Equations 5.5.1 and 5.5.2 are almost exactly the same as Equations 5.2.1 and 5.2.2, their counterparts for the years 1893 to 1913 only, except for the addition of one of the trade union variables and a trend term. The equations for strikers present a few minor changes. The effect of a Liberal Government is still in, but its importance is much less. Three other political variables, the Conservative 'dummy', the number of Conservative MPs and the repression 'dummy', are left out, and in their place is an election year 'dummy' with a positive, but rather marginal effect. Gross Domestic Product is brought in with a negative coefficient, apparently as a 'suppressor' on one of the trade union variables. Also included is the rate of change of real wages. There was thus a tendency for greater numbers of workers to strike as real wages rose; perhaps the habit of solidarity was becoming more firmly implanted. It seems more likely, though, that past successes

Table 5.4: Determinants of Strike Activity, All Industries, 1893-1921

Equation	Dependent Variable	Beta coefficients on:						R^2	D–W	SEE
		P_t	TUM	TUG	$SRSMQ_{t-1}$	LIBG	T			
5.4.1	STS	-1.19	2.61	.31	.41	.13	-1.28	.92	2.13	101.6
5.4.2	STS	-1.39	2.69	.31	.45		-1.22	.91	2.22	106.8

Equation	Dependent Variable	Beta coefficients on:						R^2	D–W	SEE
		GDP	TUM	TUG	$STSNOM_{t-1}$	LIBG	Cons			
5.4.3	SRS(3)	-.38	1.33	.08	-.16	.42	.34	.97	1.82	197.0
5.4.4	SRS(3)	-.36	1.20	.12		.35	.25	.96	1.64	118.9

Table 5.5: Determinants of Strike Activity, All Industries except Mining and Quarrying, 1893-1921

Equation	Dependent Variable	Beta coefficients on:						R^2	D–W	SEE
		P_t	TUM	TUG	$SRSMQ_{t-1}$	$STSNOM_{t-1}$	T			
5.5.1	STSNOM	-.88	1.77	.47	.42	.22	-.91	.92	2.71	94.1
5.5.2	STSNOM	-1.38	2.63	.33	.44		-1.18	.91	2.33	98.6

Equation	Dependent Variable	Beta coefficients on:						R^2	D–W	SEE
		GDP	$\dot{R}_t$	TUM	TUG	LIBG	EY			
5.5.3	SRS(3)NOM	-.22	.13	.93	.26	.09	.12	.91	1.86	86.4
5.5.4	SRS(3)NOM	-.35		1.07	.30	.10	.15	.90	1.95	86.9

Table 5.6: Determinants of Strike Activity, Mining and Quarrying, 1893-1921

Equation	Dependent Variable	Beta coefficients on:						Cons.	R^2	D–W	SEE
		P_t	$\dot{R}_t$	$\dot{R}_{t-1}$	$\dot{P}rod$	LIBG	CG				
5.6.1	STSMQ	.33	.11	.22	−.25	.78	−.20	.72	.60	1.62	35.0
5.6.2	STSMQ			.46	−.36	.47	−.40	.60	.53	1.74	36.4

Equation	Dependent Variable	Beta coefficients on:				Cons	R^2	D–W	SEE
		GDP	TUM	$SRSMQ_{t-1}$	LIBG				
5.6.3	SRS(3)MQ	−.42	1.14	.13	.33	.21	.96	1.75	60.5

caused rising expectations and widened 'orbits of comparison'.

The results for mining are again somewhat disappointing. The by now familiar political variables are in, and contribute significantly to explained variance. Still, the R^2s of Equations 5.6.1 and 5.6.2 are rather low, despite the inclusion of up to seven variables. The interpretation of these equations is also troublesome. They differ in several respects from their earlier analogue, Equation 5.3.1. The lagged number of strikers in mining is out, the signs of the price and wage variables are opposite to those in Equation 5.3.1. and, finally, productivity has been entered with a sign opposite to that taken in the equations predicting strikers in mining up to 1913.

The major factor causing this shift appears to be the fading away, between 1914 and 1921, of the tendency evident in prewar data for forms of mining struggle to alternate. In these later years, strikes and strikers in mining move up together vertically without pause. The peculiar economic correlates of strikes in mining therefore cease to hold, and a more normal positive relationship between strikes and prosperity is established. Hence the positive signs attached to the price and wage increase variables in Equations 5.6.1 and 5.6.2, the exclusion of the lagged number of mining strikers in these equations, and its inclusion with a positive coefficient in the next equation – the reverse of the situation when only 1893-1913 were involved. Still slightly confusing are the negative coefficients on productivity in Equations 5.6.1 and 5.6.2. These are probably due to their role as 'suppressors' on other economic variables, although they may also be a simple reflection of the coincidence of many strikes and plummeting productivity immediately after the First World War.

There are no such interpretative problems with the equation (5.6.3) developed to account for the fluctuations of miners on strike. Here again one finds the combination of political variables which describes so well the period of the 'Labour Unrest', together with the all-important level of union membership. Also included are Gross Domestic Product, as an apparent 'suppressor' on union membership, and the lagged number of strikers in mining, discussed above.

In general, then, the equations designed to predict strikes over the extended period 1893-1921 remain quite similar to those from which the post-1913 data were excluded in that political and organisational factors are crucial in both sets in accounting for fluctuations. This does not mean that the entire experience of increasing militancy and working-class mobilisation was not rooted in the economic movements of the period. It is rather that the latter were extremely complicated and contradictory as well as highly explosive, and their influence was appropriately mediated by politics and organisation.

Let us summarise the argument of this rather complex chapter once more. We began by discussing the impact of the Great Depression on the 'New Unionism'. Here the links between economic trends and workers' problems, shifting attitudes and consciousness, organisational innovation and strikes were relatively clear and unambiguous, although statistics were not available to permit a direct test of the relationships. It did prove possible, however to combine quantitative tests with a more conventional discursive treatment of the mediated impact of the phase of growth 1896-1920 upon strike activity. It was argued that the peculiar nature of this particular trend period — especially when its destablising tendencies were accentuated by war — did not so much confront workers with one discrete economic problem like unemployment as it served to present an inventory of injustices which deepened dissatisfaction with the entire system. This generalised discontent produced a fundamental social polarisation, and strike demands often escalated beyond specific grievances to broad statements of class interest and class politics. Similarly, new strategies and tactics were developed, like the sympathetic and general strike, which were thought capable of winning major political confrontations and initiating systematic change. And, finally, our statistical analyses revealed, again as expected, that what permitted or stimulated strikes in the short run was not the course of one or another economic indicator, but the balance of organisational and political resources.

None of this, to be sure, is definitive proof of an historical model of strikes based on the transformation of attitudes and collective organisation by succeeding and qualitatively distinct phases of growth, but it does constitute very suggestive evidence to that effect. And perhaps the most important point of all is that the blocks of years exhibiting certain common economic developments and designated as trend periods also seem to form the proper units for analysing strikes. Thus far, we have discussed industrial conflict in two such economic units; the next chapter will treat it in the years since 1919.

Notes

1. A.L. Levine, *Industrial Retardation in Britain* (London, 1967).
2. See S.B. Saul, *The Myth of the Great Depression, 1893-1896* (London,

1969), pp. 30-4.

3. Wood's index of the 'standard of comfort' is presented in Wages and Standard of Living, Table 1B in B. Mitchell and P. Deane, *Abstract of British Historical Statistics* (Cambridge, 1971).

4. In engineering, for example. See J.B. Jefferys, *The Story of the Engineers 1800-1845* (London, 1946), pp. 94-8.

5. Royal Commission on the Depression of Trade and Industry. Appendix. Part II 'Appendix D', 'Answers received from Associations representing the interests of the Working Classes to the Questions addressed to them', *Parliamentary Papers* (1886), vol. XXII, pp. 3-98, esp. pp. 71, 75.

6. Quoted in S. and B. Webb, *The History of Trade Unionism* (London, 1920), p. 378.

7. See R. Page Arnot, *The Miners. A History of the Miners' Federation of Great Britain, 1889-1910* (London, 1949), pp. 56-90.

8. H.A. Turner, *Trade Union Growth, Structure and Policy. A Comparative Study of the Cotton Unions* (London, 1962), pp. 122-8, 144-6; G.C. Miller, *Blackburn, Evolution of a Town* (Blackburn, 1951), pp. 144-9.

9. S. and B. Webb, *The History of Trade Unionism*, p. 375. See also D.W. Crowley, 'The Origins of the Revolt of the British Labour Movement from Liberalism, 1875-1906' (unpublished Ph.D. dissertation, University of London, 1952); and K. Laybourn, 'The Attitude of Yorkshire Trade Unions to the Economic and Social Problems of the Great Depression, 1873-1896' (unpublished Ph.D. dissertation, University of Lancaster, 1972). This process of re-education can also be studied and seen working in the lives of particular individuals in the labour movement. For an excellent example, see F. Reid, 'Keir Hardie's Conversion to Socialism', in A. Briggs and J. Saville (eds.), *Essays in Labour History 1886-1923* (London, 1971), pp. 17-46.

10. For a detailed, if somewhat uninspired account of these developments, see A.E.P. Duffy, 'The Eight Hours Day Movement in Britain, 1886-1893', *Manchester School of Economic and Social Studies*, XXXVI (1968), pp. 203-23 and 354-63. See also B. McCormick and J.E. Williams, 'The Miners and the Eight-Hour Day, 1863-1910', *Economic History Review*, XII (1959), pp. 222-38. For a more comprehensive view, consult the documentary collection by E.J. Hobsbawm, *Labour's Turning Point* (London, 1948).

11. H.W. Richardson, 'Retardation in Britain's Industrial Growth, 1870-1913', in D.H. Aldcroft and H.W. Richardson, *The British Economy, 1870-1939* (London, 1969), p. 117.

12. E.H. Phelps Brown, with M.H. Browne, *A Century of Pay* (London, 1968), pp. 190-1.

13. Ibid, p. 193.

14. Calculations based on data in table E9 in B.R. Mitchell, *European Historical Statistics, 1750-1970* (New York, 1975).

15. According to D.H. Aldcroft, 'The Problems of Productivity in British Industry, 1870-1914', in Aldcroft and Richardson, *The British Economy*, p. 131, 'The quantity of fixed industrial steam power in use in the U.K. rose from 500,000 horse power in 1850 to 2 million in 1880 and then increased to over 9 million in 1907.'

16. Ibid., p. 131.

17. See the literature cited in Ch. 3, n. 28, and D. Landes, *The Unbound Prometheus* (Cambridge, 1969), pp. 336-9.

18. M. Barratt Brown, *The Economics of Imperialism* (London, 1974), pp. 104-5, 190-1.

19. See Phelps Brown, *A Century of Pay*, pp. 174 for example. See J.B. 'Retardation in Britain's Industrial Growth', pp. 101-25, for what are probably the

most sensible overall discussions; and Hobsbawm, *Industry and Empire*, pp. 134-53, on the importance of international trade and investment in the British economy before 1914. See also W.P. Kennedy, 'Institutional Response to Economic Growth: Capital Markets in Britain to 1914', in L. Hannah (ed.) *Management Strategy and Business Development* (London, 1976), pp. 151-83.

20. On this, see R.C.K. Ensor, *England, 1870-1914* (Oxford, 1936), esp. pp. 501-2.

21. Jefferys, *The Story of the Engineers*, p. 118.

22. Crowley, 'The Origins of Revolt', p. 140.

23. Peter Stearns, *Lives of Labor* (New York, 1975), p. 197.

24. E.J. Hobsbawm, 'Custom, Wages and Work-Load', in *Labouring Men*, p. 406.

25. Landes, *The Unbound Prometheus*, pp. 297-323, gives a good description of the working out of 'the pursuit of speed' in these years.

26. Joseph White, *The Limits of Trade Union Militancy* (Westport, Conn., 1978), contains an excellent discussion of the pressures upon textile workers in this period.

27. On the mid-Victorian balance, see R. Samuel, 'The Workshop of the World: Steam Power and Hand Technology in mid-Victorian Britain', *History Workshop*, no. 3 (Spring, 1977), pp. 6-72. On the events and processes of 1890-1914, see P. Stearns, 'The Unskilled and Industrialization: A Transformation of Consciousness', *Archiv für Sozialgeschichte XVI*, (1976) pp. 249-82.

28. As Eric Hobsbawm argues, 'between 1870 and 1900 the pattern of British working-class life which the writers, dramatists and TV producers of the 1950s thought of as "traditional" came into being. . . . it was probably the first kind of life since the Industrial Revolution which provided a firm lodging for the British working class within industrial society.' See Hobsbawm, *Industry and Empire* (Harmondsworth, 1969), p. 164. Recent writers have been distinctly less favourable to the emergence of these traditional communities. See, among others, Robert Roberts, *The Classic Slum* (Manchester, 1971); and S. Meacham, *A Life Apart. The English Working Class, 1890-1914* (London, 1977). On urbanization and housing, see R. Dickinson, *The West European City* (London, 1961), pp. 463-4; J.P. McKay, *Tramways and Trolleys. The Rise of Mass Transport in Europe* (Princeton, 1976), pp. 205-25; and S.D. Chapman (ed.), *The History of Working-Class Housing* (Newton Abbot, 1971), *passim*.

29. Jefferys, *The Story of the Engineers*, p. 122; and Phelps Brown, *A Century of Pay*, p. 180-1.

30. See Stearns, *Lives of Labor*, Chs.4 and 6.

31. G. Dangerfield, *The Strange Death of Liberal England* (New York, 1961), p. 235. Dangerfield's book was written in 1935. More recent accounts, not unsympathetic to Dangerfield's view, can be found in R.V. Sires, 'Labor Unrest in England, 1910-1914', *Journal of Economic History*, XV (1955), pp. 246-66; S. Meacham, ' "The Sense of an Impending Clash": English Working-Class Unrest before the First World War', *American Historical Review*, LXXVII (1972), pp. 1343-65; and, of course, in E.H. Phelps Brown, *The Growth of British Industrial Relations* (London, 1965). Perhaps the most interesting local study for the period is H.R. Hikins, 'The Liverpool General Transport Strike, 1911', *Transactions of the Historic Society of Lancashire and Cheshire*, CXIII (1961), pp. 169-95.

32. Memo on 'Labour Unrest' to the Cabinet by G.R. Askwith, 14 April 1912, in Lloyd George Papers, C/21/1/11. Askwith's *Industrial Problems and Disputes* (London, 1920), esp. Chs XV to XXVI, is still an indispensable source for an understanding of the events of 1910-14.

33. On the Triple Alliance, see G.A. Phillips, 'The Triple Industrial Alliance in 1914', *Economic History Review*, XXIV (1971), pp. 55-67; and P.S. Bagwell,

'The Triple Industrial Alliance, 1913-1922', in Briggs and Saville, *Essays in Labour History*, pp. 98-128, whose discussion of the postwar events is extremely useful.

34. A particular source of discontent was what the workers felt to be the unfair working of various conciliation schemes. This sentiment was widespread in textiles, engineering and among railwaymen. See E. Wigham, *The Power to Manage* (London, 1973), pp. 63-70 on engineering; G. Alderman, 'The Railway Companies and the Growth of Trade Unionism in the Late Nineteenth and Early Twentieth Centuries', *Historical Journal*, XIV (1971), pp. 129-52, esp. p. 146ff.; J.H. Porter, 'Industrial Peace in the Cotton Trade, 1875-1913', *Yorkshire Bulletin of Economic and Social Research*, XIX (1967); and more generally, Porter's 'Wage Bargaining under Conciliation Agreements, 1860-1914', *Economic History Review*, XXIII (1970), pp. 460-75. Sidney Pollard also discusses the failure of unions to alter the distribution of income in labour's favour in 'Trade Unions and the Labour Market, 1870-1914', *Yorkshire Bulletin of Social and Economic Research*, XVII (1965), pp. 98-112.

35. Askwith, *Industrial Problems and Disputes, passim*. Askwith, one of the most perceptive figures in the history of British industrial relations, was one of the first to note both the wave-like character of strikes and the association of strike waves with breakthroughs and innovations in organisation. In June 1911, he informed the government that

'it looks as if we were [sic] in the presence of one of those periodic upheavals in the labour world such as occurred in 1833-34, and from time to time since that date, each succeeding occurrence showing a marked advance in organization on the part of the workers and the necessity for a corresponding change in tactics on the part of the employers.' – Askwith, 'The Present Unrest in the Labour World', 25 June 1911, cited in J.M. Winter, *Socialism and the Challenge of War* (London, 1974), p. 22.

36. It might be useful to define some of our terms here. All of the relationships captured by our equations are significant in the statistical sense described in Ch. 4. Significance in this sense is easy to determine; much more difficult is the problem of whether a statistical relationship actually implies any substantive relationship. This involves two problems: first, whether the statistical measures of association involve any sort of causal relation; and second, the direction of causality or influence.

Because our data are non-experimental, all of our statistics are technically speaking 'descriptive' as opposed to inferential statistics, which involve controlled experiments and random samples. In the text, however, we use the term 'descriptive' in a different, more normal sense. It is possible for statistically significant relations to possess only a descriptive meaning, without any causal implications. In equations like ours, involving so many possible variations in so many possible combinations with relatively few cases (years), it is likely that sometime variables may be included whose relationship to the dependent variable is largely fortuitous. The Liberal Government 'dummy' may be an example. Clearly there was an upsurge of strikes during the Liberals' tenure of office, so most equations for 1893-1913 show a positive coefficient on the Liberal Government 'dummy'. But this may simply be a descriptive relationship.

Even when relationships between variables are substantive, however, the direction of causation is not always obvious. This can only be determined by examining the nature of the variables involved. The classic example is the relationship between traffic accidents and snowfall. The nature of the variables clearly precludes one type of causal explanation. In practice, the problem is seldom so easy. The nature of our variables is much more complex; the possibilities for

subtle interactions almost unlimited. See R.B. Darlington, 'Multiple Regression in Pyschological Research and Practice', *Psychological Bulletin*, LXIX (1968), pp. 161-83 for a discussion of several of these points.
    37. George Dangerfield, *The Strange Death of Liberal England* (reprinted, NY, 1961) is the best articulation of this view. A more recent treatment is Standish Meacham, ' "The Sense of an Impending Clash": English Working Class Unrest before the First World War', *American Historical Review*, LXXVII (1972), pp. 1343-64.
    38. The argument advanced here may leave some readers a bit mystified: how can we say that the absence of economic variables from the equations actually confirms the thesis about the impact of the trend period 1896-1913 upon industrial conflict? The answer is simply that the process of building an explanatory model is not equivalent to estimating an equation. The components of a model may not all be translatable into quantifiable variables, but their effect will nonetheless be reflected in certain predictable behaviour of other variables or of the entire equation. A helpful example of this distinction between models and equations is provided by David Snyder's work. Snyder's model gives prominence to trade union strength and the institutional structures of industrial relations systems in explaining strike activity. There are, however, times and places where organisation and procedures are established, so that the balance of resources shifts very little from year to year. In these situations, Snyder claims that strikes may and do correlate with economic movements because organisational considerations are in the background. Specifically, he finds that for much of the history of France and Italy, unionisation and political forces were key to explaining conflict, and that much the same relationship obtained in the US before the Second World War. Since then, the structural contours of the US industrial relations system have stabilised, and changes in organisation have receded to a less prominent place in the causation of annual variation. Snyder's work shows, therefore, that factors need not figure explicitly in predicting equations in order to be considered important in one's model. It also demonstrates how the temporal span of an equation itself can be of great significance. See Snyder, 'Institutional Setting and Industrial Conflict', *American Sociological Review*, XL (1975), pp. 259-78.
    39. Commission of Enquiry into Industrial Unrest. 'Report of the Commissioners for the North-Eastern Area' (Cmd. 8662) in *Parliamentary Papers* (1917-18), vol. XV, II; 'Report . . . for the West Midlands Area', (Cmd. 8665), ibid., p. 5.
    40. 'Report . . . for the North-Western Area' (Cmd. 8663), ibid., p. 11; 'Summary of the Reports of the Commission' (Cmd. 8696), ibid., p. 7; 'Report . . . for Wales, including Monmouthshire' (Cmd. 8668), ibid., p. 24; and 'Report . . . for the South-Western Area' (Cmd. 8667), ibid., p. 3; *Manchester Guardian*, 4/8/17.
    41. 'Summary . . .' (Cmd. 8696), ibid., p. 7.
    42. On this general development, see C., L., and R. Tilly, *The Rebellious Century* (Cambridge, Mass., 1975), and also Shorter and Tilly, *Strikes in France*, for a specific application. The intertwining of political and economic power on the national level is likewise the theme of the provocative essays in H. Winkler (ed.), *Organisierter Kapitalismus* (Göttingen, 1974).
    43. The most recent and informed discussion of these trends in England is R. Scally, *The Origins of the Lloyd George Coalition: The Politics of Social Imperialism, 1900-1918* (Princeton, 1975).
    44. Consider the following ratios of the wage rates of unskilled to skilled workers:

	Building	Shipbuilding	Engineering	Railways
1914	.67	.55	.59	.54
1920	.81	.77	.79	.81

The figures are based upon K. Knowles and D.J. Robertson, 'Differences between the wages of Skilled and Unskilled Workers, 1880-1950', *Bulletin of the Oxford University Institute of Statistics*, XIII (1951), p. 111.

45. Beatrice Webb, *Beatrice Webb's Diaries. 1912-1924*, M.I. Cole (ed.) (London, 1952), entry for 21 October 1920, p. 197.

46. Directorate of Intelligence (Home Office), 'A Survey of Revolutionary Feeling during the Year 1919', PRO, Cabinet Papers, CAB 24/96, CP 462, 4; and Directorate of Intelligence (Home Office), 'A Survey of Revolutionary Movements in Great Britain in the Year 1920', PRO, CAB 24/118, CP 2455, 4,2.

47. *The Times*, 29 April 1919, p. 6.

48. B. Waites, 'The Language and Imagery of "Class" in Early Twentieth-Century England (circa 1900-1925)', *Literature and History*, no. 4 (Autumn, 1976), pp. 30-55.

49. See W.G. Runciman, *Relative Deprivation and Social Justice* (London, 1967).

50. V.L. Allen, 'The Re-organisation of the Trades Union Congress, 1918-1927', *British Journal of Sociology*, XI (1960), pp. 24-43.

51. See J. Hinton, *The First Shop Stewards' Movement* (London, 1973); S. Pollard, *A History of Labour in Sheffield* (Liverpool, 1959), pp. 271-9; more generally, B. Pribicevic, 'The Demand for Workers' Control in the Railway, Mining and Engineering Industries, 1910-1922' (unpublished Ph.D. dissertation, Oxford University, 1957); and the long-neglected study by Carter Goodrich, *The Frontier of Control* (London, 1974).

6 DEFEAT, REORIENTATION AND RENEWAL, 1919-74

The central fact of the interwar years was the long slump with which it has become almost synonymous in the public memory, and no amount of talk about the new industries and the housing boom and no romantic visions of shared hardship can negate or soften that identification.[1] Explicating the connection between conjuncture and strikes for this period will therefore involve primarily a dissection of the developing consequences of the depression of labour's consciousness and organisational capacity. Three distinct and successive effects can be discerned. In its early stages, the slump acted to derail the momentum of expectation, demands and strikes coming out of the war. As the depression wore on, however, it refashioned workers' attitudes in the direction of an intense commitment to securing employment stability. And, finally, these harsh decades ushered in the reorientation of the British economy so painfully and urgently needed, and in this created new challenges and difficulties for a demoralised and bureaucratised union movement. Let us begin with the initial taming of the rebellious mood of 1919-20.

When assessing the impact of aspects of economic history upon consciousness, strategy, and organisation, we must always remember that economic movements must work upon the ideas workers have already developed in response to previous phases of economic evolution. The learning process involves first unlearning, and then learning again. In the 1870s and 1880s, workers first had to unlearn many of the tenets of 'new model' unionism; they had to be dissuaded from, among other things, sliding scales and the concomitant principle that wages should rise and fall with prices. A similar process of re-education was necessary to counteract the militant consciousness and bright hopes which gripped so many workers just after the First World War.

Such was the task of the first years of the depression. As Runciman argues, 'The story of the period between the two wars ... is of a decline or, at least, a considerable appeasement of [the consciousness of] relative deprivation among the less fortunately placed.'[2] Actually, the job was done between 1920 and 1926, when a profoundly conservative process of stabilisation occurred.[3] This process operated on many levels simultaneously. There was a growth and strengthening of employers' organisations, economic concentration, and a reorganisation

126

in government, the main effect of which was to consolidate Treasury and Civil Service control. This, many hoped, would prevent any drastic and 'fiscally irresponsible' programmes. The restoration of the gold standard must also be understood against this background: it was 'knaveproof', and would provide an economic check to the demagogic programmes and promises of politicians. On the labour front, the strategy of the general or sympathetic strike was defeated and discredited, the authority of union leaders was to some extent restored, and successive wage cuts helped to lower workers' expectations.

Perhaps the best evidence of the depth of class antagonism in 1919-20 is how long it took to abate. The economic downturn came fairly early in 1920, and began to show up in unemployment rates by the summer. Nevertheless, workers continued to strike on a massive scale throughout the year. Still more impressive, coalminers and cotton operatives fought serious battles against wage decreases in 1921, when things were much worse, and all of the engineering unions entered a test of strength with the Engineering Employers' Federation in 1922. Each of these strikes was lost, but it took another four years and the defeat of the General Strike finally to stabilise the industrial situation.

The build-up to the General Strike of May 1926 is a story which has been told many times over, and the recent fiftieth anniversary celebration of the event has only added to the myriad of chronicles and reminiscences already available.[4] By now the story is well known, so one may with no essential loss skip the narrative and focus more clearly on two related problems: the effects of 1926 on the workers as a whole and on the trade unions in particular; and the role of the depression in bringing about whatever changes occurred. Some years ago Professor Hugh Clegg wrote a long article deprecating the alleged effects of the General Strike. He argued instead that the roots of the industrial peace which lasted from 1927 to the 1950s could be traced back beyond May 1926 to at least 1921, and possibly even further back to the beginnings of industrial conciliation in the 1890s.[5] A similar perspective informs the otherwise admirable account by G.A. Phillips.[6] Both men see the General Strike as having little significance in and of itself: however great its impact on the mining industry, its broader effects were negligible. The argument is not entirely without basis, but it ignores the sharp and fundamental contrast between the state of the labour movement in 1919-20 and in 1927-8. At best, this approach serves to place the General Strike at the end of a prolonged process of stabilisation, but makes it no less an important aspect of that process.

The contrast between 1919-20 and 1927-8 can be glimpsed to some degree by focusing on leadership. In 1919-20, what worried politicans most was the nearly total loss of control by union bureaucrats over their members. *The Times*, for instance, complained of a 'lack of discipline' within the ranks, and, as early as 28 January 1919 recognised that the strikes then in progress were 'in every case unauthorized by the governing bodies of the trade unions whose members are involved. In some cases they are emphatically repudiated by the trade union executives; in none are they countenanced, at any rate openly.' Further, '. . . the instigators of these revolts have almost as bitter a distrust and hatred of those trade union officials as they have of the "bosses" or the Government.'[7] On 8 February 1919, Tom Jones echoed a similar concern in a memo to Lloyd George: 'Much of the present difficulty springs from the mutiny of the rank and file against the old established leaders and there seems to be no machinery for bringing about a quick change of leaders.' The Coalition Government tried by various means to bolster the authority of trade union leaders, but it was a difficult task. As Jones pointed out: 'The Government's decision to stand by the accredited leaders is the only possible policy, but it does not get over the fact that the leaders no longer represent the more active and agitating minds in the labour movement.'[8] The aspirations of the rank-and-file had obviously outrun the tactics, strategy and outlook of the leaders and produced a crisis of confidence.

After the General Strike the situation was completely different. The authority of the leaders was more or less restored, the militants were checked or isolated, and the rank-and-file reduced once more to passivity and cynicism. Two examples of this new situation must suffice. In January 1927, a special conference of the TUC almost unanimously endorsed the General Council's handling of the events of the previous May. At that meeting, moreover, the moderate leaders of the General Council were not at all cowed or defensive. Ben Turner, soon to become president of the General Council, proclaimed 'great satisfaction with the general strike of 1926. I think it was a great movement and a great effort . . .' No apologies were offered. On the contrary, Walter Citrine, presenting the official view, actually went on the offensive against the miners and denounced their leaders. When the vote finally occurred, the official report was approved by an overwhelming majority.[9] A second example is the series of meetings known as the Mond-Turner talks which took place mainly in 1927 and 1928. Mond, the founder of ICI, represented a group of employers and Turner represented the TUC in discussions on how labour could help 'promote and guide the scientific reorganization of industry'.[10] Ultimately these conciliatory moves came to naught, but the fact that they were made, and with so little opposition from within the TUC, aptly symbolises the new spirit or lack thereof in the trade union world.[11]

This transformation, or demobilisation, was brought about by the economic crisis of the 1920s, but was aided by developments in union structure and other factors. Most important, the employers' bargaining position was enormously strengthened by the state of trade, and as a result they won most of the major strikes. On the other hand, the fall in prices may have cushioned, for those in work, the effects of somewhat lesser decreases in wages. Third, the astronomical levels of unemployment in some of the most militant and strike-prone industries must have served to lower the expectations of workers and to erode the bases of workshop organisation. This latter point is crucial. The upsurge of 1919-20 was directed from below and its primary organisational innovation was the shop stewards' or workshop committee. None of this could be sustained when unemployment decimated the ranks of the militants who were often blacklisted and driven out of industries entirely.[12] To all this must be added the way the re-organisation of the TUC strengthened the deadening influence of the bureaucrats.

Still, none of this would have sufficed to stabilise the situation without the General Strike itself. Thus Beatrice Webb noted that even the failure of Black Friday had not produced a resolution of the conflict between moderates and 'direct antagonists'. Direct action had not been tried, so it had not failed; and as a result 'all those who believe the strike would have succeeded will go on working for it . . .'[13] And, of course, Black Friday did little to restore rank-and-file confidence in the union leaders. So when confronted again by the threat of a General Strike in 1926, the union leaders remembered April 1921 and this time acted differently. As Bevin pointed out, 'I with others went through the 1921 dispute, and the one thing that was laid down at the General Council was that we must not have another 1921.'[14] The result of the General Strike was partly to erase the memory of 1921 by temporarily casting the TUC leadership in a militant role, and to that extent it served to reduce tension and opposition within the trade union movement.

But the General Strike did more than to redeem a few miserable leaders like J.H. Thomas. It also revealed the bankruptcy of a purely industrial strategy at a time of mass unemployment, and by so doing caused a constriction in the minds of the workers of the 'limits of the possible'. Dame Margaret Cole has put the point with extreme cogency: '. . . what really perished in 1926 was the romantic idea, dating from before the first world war, of the power of syndicalism, "direct action", and the rest of it.'[15] Realising that when faced with a determined and antagonistic government, a general strike would fail even if it was 100 per cent solid — as that of May 1926 virtually was — the organised British working class seems to have simply resigned itself to an inability to counter the economic catastrophes of the interwar years. The defeat of the General Strike meant more than a temporary retreat; it also served to complete the process of stabilisation begun in 1920-1.[16]

One must not, of course, exaggerate the magnitude of the 1920s' defeats. The earlier movement of 1919-20 advanced trade unionism to many positions from which it never was pushed back. For example, tortured struggles for union recognition (or acceptance) in transport, on both the docks and the railways, were finally won. So also was the 47-hour week — the major positive economic gain of these years. Real wages also advanced, due to the relative firmness of money rates and the decline in prices, and all of these gains persisted throughout even the worst years of the depression.

This then was the first effect of the interwar slump: to lower the collective temperature of the workers and to make Britain safe for capital. As happens so often, though, the prolonged crisis ultimately provoked yet a further shift in working-class attitudes. Blocked in their hopes for a more prosperous and more egalitarian society, labour militants and many of the rank-and-file became more resolute in the pursuit of more modest aims. Indeed, a new consciousness of unemployment and of the necessity of preventing its recurrence took hold among large sections of the working population during the 1930s, and it seems likely that this would have turned itself into a wave of strikes and unionisation parallel to those which occurred during 1935-7 in France and the USA, were it not for two additional complications. First, the organised trade union movement was still reeling from the defeat of 1926, while the parliamentary Labour Party was itself virtually destroyed by MacDonald's and Snowden's collapse and desertion in the fiscal crisis of 1931. Labour was generally on the defensive, its leadership cautious and tentative at best in taking initiative. The second factor preventing an outburst was structural, and related once again to the direction of economic development. The recovery of the mid-to late 1930s did not involve the revival of old industries, but rather a dramatic expansion of new ones producing new products with more advanced technologies and located in different geographical regions from the old. This situation created a host of novel organisational problems which the entrenched labour leaders were in no position and no mood to solve, and which thus delayed the industrial expression of discontent for the duration of the decade.

The content of the attitudes fostered by the depression were touched upon briefly in Chapter 3. Essentially they amounted to a resolve to prevent unemployment in the future, even if that entailed drastic social and political change. As Eric Hobsbawm has argued, '. . . the main result of the hard-faced inter-war decades was to alienate a solid core of millions of citizens permanently . . . from any party which does not promise socialism.'[17] Most of the industrial population, which was concentrated in the centres of the old industries at the beginning of this period, felt the pain and frustration of unemployment directly. Even among the more traditional groups of workers, like those in textiles, this had a profound effect. The change can be traced even in the pages of the *Cotton Factory Times*, an organ of moderation through all the turbulence of 1910-26. By December of 1932, the leading article on 'The Promise of the New Year' declared: 'The "common interest" may ultimately demand a different industrial and economic regime from the one we are under at present. We are not fastidious as to the name of the new social and industrial order, assuming that it will come.'[18] Similar developments occurred in widely disparate industries all over England.[19]

A parallel process of re-education occurred at the top of the trade union movement during the crisis of 1929-32. The lessons learned at that exalted level concerned the role of deficit financing, public works, and planning in bringing the economy up to full employment. Politically and economically, the unions also came to see the policies and influence of the City rather than industry as their main enemy and to postulate that future Labour governments must strive to break Civil Service and Treasury control over policy.[20] Both at the peak and at the base of the labour movement, then, a new set of attitudes and resolutions seems to have been established.

The depression also stimulated transformation in the economy. The decline of the old staple industries is a familiar theme in British economic history, but we have lately been informed of the contemporaneous growth of new ones.[21] The new industries — vehicles, chemicals, rubber, rayon, radios, etc. — differed in several ways from the old, and each of these differences posed problems for trade union organisation. They were located in different areas, mainly the South and the Midlands, where union organisation was always weaker than it had been in Scotland, Wales or the industrial North. They tended also to be mass production industries employing mainly semi-skilled or unskilled workers, who 'have for the most part no such lifelong attachment to a particular trade as the skilled craftsman'. The situation in the new industries simply did 'not make for stable or continuous organization', except among the relatively small number of skilled maintenance workers in the new plants who often formed the nucleus around which crystallised some minimal organisation. And finally, workers in the new industries lived in different, less solid communities than workers in older industrial areas. This problem was accentuated by the growth of working-class suburbs, facilitated by cheap mass transport, and by the simple fact that many of the industries' workers were recent migrants from areas of high unemployment and for that reason happy just to have a job.[22]

The timidity and bureaucratic rigidity of the TUC leadership compounded the problem. G.D.H. and Margaret Cole noted in 1937 that it was 'remarkable with how many of the strikes of the past few years official Trade Unionism has had nothing to do, or at any rate nothing but to deplore the impulsiveness of the workers' action.' Rank-and-file attempts at unionisation evoked little response among trade union leaders, perhaps because of the involvement of the Communists, but mainly because their efforts contradicted the cautious conservatism of the leaders. What little progress was made resulted from 'sporadic and unofficial strikes', initiated at the shop floor level. To the Coles, it was clear that new methods were needed, which would combine 'an inclusive appeal' with 'a sort of shop steward and works committee organisation'.[23] Unfortunately, the spread of these new methods had to wait upon the return of full employment during and after the Second World War. The industrial peace of 1927-55 was thus in one sense the result of the slowness with which the organisational problems of the new industries were solved. There were no mechanisms to translate the consciousness developed out of the depression into strike action.

Or so it appears judging from the non-quantitative evidence alone. The statistical results generally confirm this analysis, while adding a few additional wrinkles to the argument. The difficulty, of course, is in disentangling the impact of various influences on strikes when several factors were all working to discourage militancy at the same time. It seems clear, for example, that economic depression undercut union organisation, lowered expectations and decreased the chances of successful strikes. From this it follows that either some economic variable or one of the two measures of union strength should turn up as a strong predictor of strike activity, although it could be pointing to any one or all of the concurrent processes. On the other hand, we have also argued that the history of industrial relations between the wars involved a qualitative transformation from the militancy of the early 1920s to the more subdued mood of the thirties. One should therefore also expect the equations to register somehow a major discontinuity in strike patterns. Both of these expectations are happily fulfilled in the equations presented in the following tables.

These tables summarise the best sets of predictors for strikes and strikers in all industries, in all industries except mining, and in mining and quarrying respectively. Two distinct patterns can be discerned, one generally applicable to predicting the number of strikes, the other the number of strikers. Apparently the discontinuity in strike experience before and after 1926 is picked up statistically in the divergent determinants of the two indices of conflict. In determining strikes (e.g., Equations 6.1.1, 6.1.2, 6.2.1, 6.2.2, and 6.3.1) the role of trade union membership or growth is critical, and the most important economic variables enter as 'suppressors' with negative coefficients. For strikers (e.g. Equations 6.1.3, 6.2.3, 6.2.4, 6.2.5, 6.3.2, 6.3.3), trade union variables are left out and replaced in large measure by political variables. In the latter equations, therefore, economic variables enter with the expected effects. Let us look more closely, and explore the implications.

Equations 6.1.1 and 6.1.2 illustrate the first pattern. Trade union membership dominates both equations, and the price level and unemployment rate are opposite to what would normally be expected. Apparently the effect of the slump on strikes is mediated via its effect on workers' ability to organise. Once this incapacitating effect is taken into account, the depression actually seems to have increased the desire to strike. In these equations, the role of the rate of inflation and productivity increase are again somewhat confusing. They are probably acting as somewhat subtle indicators of the positive relation between prosperity and strikes, and more capable of capturing year-to-year movements within the generally depressed economy than the other economic variables. The election year 'dummy', whose coefficient is not too large, may have a substantive interpretation — that certain election years (1918, 1924, 1929) stimulated hopes and led to strikes — or its inclusion may be entirely fortuitous.

Equation 6.1.3, with the total number of workers involved in strikes as the dependent variable, is quite different. Each of the economic variables takes a coefficient suggesting a positive connection between strikers and prosperity. This poses no particular problems for interpretation, but the most important predictor is the legal repression 'dummy'.

Table 6.1: Determinants of Strike Activity, All Industries, 1919-38

Equation	Dependent Variable	Beta coefficients on:						R^2	D–W	SEE
		P_t	U_t	$\dot{P}_t$	$\dot{Prod}$	TUM	EY			
6.1.1	STS	−.56	.17	.26	.15	1.51	.12	.96	2.06	84.7
6.1.2	STS	−.60	.19	.19	.12	1.44	.09	.95	1.54	91.9

Equation	Dependent Variable	Beta coefficients on:					R^2	D–W	SEE
		P_t	$\dot{R}_{t-1}$	U_t	RL	EY			
6.1.3	SRS(3)	.35	.29	−.16	−.35	−.16	.91	2.34	192.3

Table 6.2: Determinants of Strike Activity, All Industries except Mining and Quarrying, 1919-38

Equation	Dependent Variable	Beta coefficients on:						R^2	D–W	SEE
		P_t	U_t	$\dot{P}rod$	$STSNOM_{t-1}$	TUM	TUG			
6.2.1	STSNOM	.42	.55	.19	−.61	1.50	.39	.98	2.21	52.1
6.2.2	STSNOM		.41	.12	−.56	1.75	.17	.97	1.85	60.9

Equation	Dependent Variable	Beta coefficients on:						R^2	D–W	SEE
		P_t	$\dot{P}rod$	$SRSMO_{t-1}$	$STSNOM_{t-1}$	RL	EY			
6.2.3	SRS(3)NOM	.57	−.29	.24	−.59	−.60	−.30	.85	2.70	129.7

Equation	Dependent Variable	Beta coefficients on:						R^2	D–W	SEE
		GDP	P_t	$\dot{R}_{t-1}$	U_t	RL	EY			
6.2.4	SRS(3)NOM	−.41	−.25	.25	−.55	−.36	−.27	.85	2.21	130.1

Equation	Dependent Variable	Beta coefficients on:					R^2	D–W	SEE
		GDP	$\dot{P}_t$	RL	EY	T			
6.2.5	SRS(3)NOM	.30	.16	−.24	−.25	−.92	.84	2.10	125.6

Table 6.3: Determinants of Strike Activity, Mining and Quarrying, 1919-38

Equation	Dependent Variable	Beta coefficients on:					R^2	D–W	SEE
		GDP	P_t	$\dot{P}\text{rod}$	TUM	EY			
6.3.1	STSMQ	.50	−.86	.35	1.57	.19	.87	2.00	41.0

Equation	Dependent Variable	Beta coefficients on:				R^2	D–W	SEE
		P_t	$\dot{R}_t$	$\dot{R}_{t-1}$	CG			
6.3.2	SRS(3)MQ	.69	.09	.28	.16	.95	1.94	77.2
6.3.3	SRS(3)MQ	.73		.30	.14	.94	1.87	78.7

Unfortunately, it is impossible to separate out the effects of repressive legislation, in force from 1927, from the long-term effects of the defeat of the General Strike, one of which was the 1927 legislation itself. In any case, from 1927 on there seems to have been a consistent depressant on large-scale strikes, a depressant strong enough, it seems, to prevent the revival of union membership of the mid- to late 1930s from resulting in any large-scale strike action (and thus to drive trade union variables out of all equations predicting the number of strikers). In addition, this equation includes the election year 'dummy'. Again, there is the choice of regarding it as fortuitous or expressive of some real relationship. The importance of this same variable in Equations 6.2.3 to 6.2.5. suggests that its effect is real: apparently union leaders, whose role has always been more important in determining the level of strikers rather than of strikes, exerted pressure against large-scale strikes during election years.

For the most part, the exclusion of mining strikes from the dependent variables merely accentuates the relationships in the first table. Equations 6.2.1 and 6.2.2 differ from 6.1.1 and 6.1.2 in only two ways: the importance of unionisation is increased by including the rate of union growth as well as the level of membership; and the lagged number of strikes in non-mining industries is included with a high, negative coefficient. This latter variable is probably acting as a suppressor on the very high coefficient of the union variable, but it also may suggest a pattern of strikes which reverses itself from year to year. This is consistent with what we already know to be the outstanding feature of interwar strike history — workers' inability to develop any sustained offensive.

Equations 6.2.3 to 6.2.5 generally affirm the model implicit in the first estimation. The trend variable and the impact of repressive legislation together reinforce the point made earlier about the decisive turning away from large strikes in this period. Economic depression, political repression, and the memory of 1926 all seem to have worked to prevent a resurgence of big strikes. It seems, however, that this represented primarily a shift in tactics. Workers shied away from major confrontations in favour of small-scale guerrilla warfare in the pits and shops — a grudging recognition of the power of capital concretised in successive governments, and a determination to win as much as possible through small struggles.

This same turn from mass confrontation to small, localised forms of struggle is equally evident in the equations for strikes and strikers in mining, reported in Table 6.3. Strikes rise and fall primarily with trade union membership; they are able to bounce back after the worst years of the depression. The number of strikers, however, the best indication of the number of large scale confrontations, follows the price level most closely, and that did not rebound in anything like the fashion of union membership until after the Second World War. In all industries between the wars, the scale of strikes and the frequency of major battles declined under the combined effects of defeat and depression. On the other hand, workers continued to use frequent, small strikes, which were much easier to mount and win, whenever and wherever they could, depending primarily on the state of union organisation. Thus, the behaviour of strikes in the interwar years seems to have contained intimations of what was to emerge during the late 1950s as the classic British pattern of small, unofficial strikes. So, both in terms of the tactical style of strikes and of the outlook of much of the labour movement, the depression was a crucial formative influence.

The dialectic between patterns of strike activity and the economic problems and social transformations attendant upon different phases of growth persisted after the depression, but as usual the correspondence was imprecise. During the early postwar period of full employment, workers seem to have continued to operate within a depression mentality; only since the 1960s have their attitudes and demands become in some sense appropriate to the prolonged upward movement of the economy. Of the two postwar strike waves, therefore, that of 1957-62 belongs ideologically and in terms of union strategy to the interwar experience, while that of 1968-72 reflects more contemporary conditions.

The preceding analysis of the interwar labour movement suggests that the industrial calm prevailing after 1926 was extremely precarious. Expectations in terms of wages or general social progress were no doubt lower in the 1930s than just after the war, but in the main they were different. Workers' attention was focused primarily on achieving full employment and economic security, and it seems obvious that workers were waiting only upon a catching-up by trade union organisation before turning these new desires and expectations into demands and attempting to enforce them by industrial action if necessary. The peculiarities and unevenness of Britain's recovery coupled with weaknesses in union strategy and leadership postponed the eruption of the massive strike wave that would have been expected in the late thirties. It is less clear what prevented an outbreak of strikes in the 1940s and early 1950s, when prosperity stimulated a huge increase in trade union membership.

Several factors do seem relevant, however. Most obviously, the victory of Labour in 1945 ushered in a period of social reform on an unprecedented scale. In response, most workers seem to have been genuinely willing to heed the government's plea not to strike and thereby jeopardise the economic growth upon which further reforms allegedly depended. In addition, the postwar period was marked by an increasing prosperity. From a peak of 3.1 per cent in 1947, unemployment declined steadily; throughout the 1950s it was minimal. During the Labour Government's tenure of office, there may have been some trade-off between wages and social services, so that the former stagnated while the latter expanded. But after 1951, real wages began to increase. Coupled with the continued high levels of employment, these trends gave workers less reason to organise and strike than they previously had.[24]

A third factor, though, was an underlying weakness of union organisation. The quantitative gains in members from 1940 to 1945 do not seem to have been matched by a comparable qualitative advance in organisation of equal magnitude. Membership had increased under hothouse conditions, and the factory level organisation urged by the Coles does not appear to have materialised, at least not to any great degree. The building up of a network of shop stewards and workshop committees took place later on, during the 1950s, first in the vehicles industry and then throughout the rest of industry.[25] As was pointed out to the Royal Commission on Trade Unions and Employers' Organisations of 1965-8 (the Donovan Commission), the modern shop stewards' movement was a relatively recent growth, with extremely tenuous links to the movement of the same name generated during the First World War.[26] It appears, in fact, that the real elaboration of a network of shop stewards happened quite late, either in the decade just prior to or during the strike wave of 1957-62. And because the sort of small-scale unofficial strike characteristic of this little outburst required intense participation at the local level, the growth of workshop organisation may be seen as an essential precondition for its occurrence.

If the rise in strikes from the mid-fifties was possible only with an adaptation of organisation, however, both were fuelled after 1955 by the catalytic effect of postwar economic problems upon the ideas and attitudes of the workers. Probably the strongest evidence of the moderate and security-oriented expectations of workers during the 1950s was the coexistence of unemployment levels of 1 to 2 per cent with modest wage demands and low rates of inflation. Numerous attitude surveys taken from 1950 to the mid-1960s tell us that workers wanted steady employment and a slightly increasing standard of living, rather than intrinsically rewarding work or very high wages.[27] But the mid- and late 1950s were anything but reassuring. From about 1950 to 1965, the two primary characteristics of Britain's economic performance were its erratic, 'stop-go' pattern and a rapid structural transformation.[28] Recurring balance of payments crises caused governments alternately to fan and then cool the flames of prosperity and inflation. Consequently, earnings for many workers fluctuated sharply and, as Turner *et al.* pointed out for the motor industry, the resulting insecurity led to demands against redundancy and for wage increases, in hopes of balancing fluctuating employment by high wages.[29] The other feature of economic development in the 1950s was the transfer of labour from coal, textiles and shipbuilding to the newer industries and into the service sector. This, too, increased workers' sense of insecurity and stimulated concern over the problem of redundancy.

Most of the labour and social history of the postwar period remains to be written, but even now it is possible to see these factors coming to a head in the late 1950s and to detect a deterioration in the climate of industrial relations around 1955-7. The turn coincided with the first severe check to industrial growth since 1947, during which both workers and employers were forced to recognise the country's underlying economic difficulties. The result was a new firmness on both sides of the bargaining table, and also a shift in 'public opinion'. *The Times* began to rail against unofficial strikes and the 'lack of discipline' (a recurring phrase) in certain industries. The strikers and their unofficial leaders at Briggs Motors came in for bitter criticism, for example, during their 1957 strike.[30] Encouraged by Macmillan at the Treasury (and later as Prime Minister) and MacLeod at the Ministry of Labour, the Engineering Employers' Federation decided to confront the unions in a showdown in 1957. The Federation was also supported by the Federation of British Industries and several other businessmen's organisations. Simultaneously, the government prepared to resist a claim from the National Union of Railwaymen. Apparently, the government's loss of support after the Suez affair brought with it a loss of will, and the unions won wage increases all round. Nevertheless, the incident seems to have set the tone for the next several years in industrial relations. The strike wave of 1957-62 was therefore the result of the interaction between a set of working-class ideas and attitudes, largely about economic security, and fortified by the spread of organisation at the workshop level, with the insecure and contradictory character of economic growth in the 1950s.

Still, it bears repeating once more that the aims and expectations of working people were stable and restrained at least into the early 1960s. Runciman's work on relative deprivation is particularly apposite in this context. His attitude survey was conducted in 1962, at the very end of the first postwar strike wave, when any significant inflation of expectations occurring until then should have been manifest. What he found, however, was that 'comparative reference groups among manual workers and their wives [are] so far restricted as to result in a marked discrepancy between relative deprivation and actual inequality . . .'[31] Workers compared their incomes not with those of doctors, lawyers and businessmen, but with those of people in the same shop who were single or had fewer children and thus lived a little better, or with those who had more opportunity to capture overtime earnings or, possibly, with those in comparable jobs in different companies or industries. Down to 1962, in other words, frames of reference remained limited in scope, and there is little evidence, in Runciman's or other studies, of any so-called revolution of rising expectations. The revival of conflict at that time must therefore be seen as a response to the economy of the 1950s dictated largely by the mentality of the 1930s and 1940s.

Once tried and perfected, however, the tactics of plant bargaining and unofficial strikes spread widely throughout industry, and once joined, the battle over wages continued.[32] From 1957 onward, the problems of prices, exports and unofficial strikes became inextricably (though, it can be argued, incorrectly) linked in the minds of businessmen, government ministers, newspaper editors and even some union leaders. But, again, the moderation of workers' demands is attested to by their apparent willingness to endure more or less stagnating real wage levels from 1964 to 1968. It required the surge in prices following the devaluation of 1967 to upset expectations sufficiently to produce the strike wave of 1968-72.[33] To some degree, of course, the strikes and 'pay explosion' of 1968-72 can be seen as the logical progression of militancy since 1957, as the product of a continuous development, but, as noted earlier, the most recent strike wave differed from the previous one both in terms of its personnel and its characteristic demands. It was also accompanied by a rapid increase in union membership among both manual and white-collar workers that was absent during 1957-62. Considered together, these facts point to a sharp discontinuity in strike experience and in the contours of Britain's industrial relations system.

The escalation of conflict in the late 1960s has produced a flurry of speculation on its origins and on the general viability of the institutional mechanisms that had served to mute and channel discontent

throughout most of the postwar era. With the latter we are quite uncon-
cerned here, though they afford many useful insights into the politics
of industrial sociology. The debate on the sources of militancy is more
interesting, and two basic arguments can be discerned. One group of
writers seeks the answer in the stagnation of real incomes. Jackson,
Turner and Wilkinson maintain that the increased incidence of taxation
upon lower incomes undermined money wage increases during the mid-
1960s and thus stimulated the inflation of wage claims and the incidence of strikes. In their view, workers were forced into disputes simply
to keep up their real after-tax earnings. A second approach has emphasised the alienating effects of several consecutive years of government
badgering to hold down wages and to eschew stoppages – the Labour
Government's statutory incomes policy, *In Place of Strife*, the Conservative Industrial Relations Act of 1971, and so on – upon the rank-
and-file of the unions. Labour was driven by a sustained attack upon
free collective bargaining and workshop autonomy into an unaccustomed, insurgent position.[34]

It is quite possible to combine these interpretations, as Douglas
Hibbs has done in a recent article.[35] He argues that the outburst of
industrial conflict was produced by the lag of real wage increases
behind gains in industrial productivity, coupled with the impact of the
legislative attempt to reform industrial relations. Since the connection
between the economic difficulties of workers in the 1960s and the
political disadvantages they faced was in practice quite close, it seems
eminently reasonable to stress their joint effects. Still, what is lacking
in all of these formulations is any sense of the workers themselves as
actors in the drama, who may very well have moved from a primarily
defensive to an offensive stance during its unfolding. Several aspects
of the most recent strike wave suggest that this did, in fact, happen,
and that elements of a new set of attitudes towards society and towards
social inequality lay behind the new militancy of 1968-72.

What defines this new consciousness, and what produced it?
Obviously, at this stage of research it is difficult to obtain a clear and
objective description of workers' changing attitudes. In-depth surveys
covering the period 1968-72 have yet to be published, and the implications of the new ideas probably still have to be worked out in many
cases. We are left with the statements made by workers to the press,
strike demands, and other circumstantial and impressionistic pieces of
evidence. Words uttered in the middle of a struggle are inevitably
infused with a certain amount of rhetoric, and the problem of inter-
preting strike demands is a familiar and thorny one. Despite such

problems, the available evidence presents us with an outline of the novel ideological impetus behind the 1968-72 strike wave.

Increased wages was the demand of most participants in the strike wave of 1968-72 and the percentage of strikers out over wages sky-rocketed in these years. The wage claims, moreover, were much higher than any raised previously and suggest a whole new standard of what is and what is not a justified demand. The very scope of pay claims has led several writers to infer that the wages explosion of 1968-72 was due basically to an explosion of expectations. While many workers still argue their claims by reference to rates for comparable jobs in other plants or even within plants, it seems that they are probably also casting an eye towards the incomes of quite different groups and beginning to compare their conditions with those of quite distant social location. It is possible of course to read too much into increased wage militancy, but even on *a priori* grounds it appears likely that no such dramatic escalation in money demands could occur without some major re-orientation in workers' perceptions of their social roles. One worker has argued, for example, that when asking for more cash, workers are actually 'seeking those things that make them human – a certain dignity, a measure of equality, and above all their self-respect. In our culture', he adds, 'a man's pay is a status symbol as well as a means of existence, so "not getting the rate for the job" is a blow to a man's pride as well as his pocket.' By the same logic, the normal way for an enhanced sense of personal worth and social value among workers to express itself 'in our culture' is through an escalation of wage demands.[36]

That something new is indeed involved in the current inflation of demands and expectations it also indicated by the odd variety of issues with which pay claims have come often to be coupled and by the bolder and more expansive rhetoric with which the struggles have been conducted. All of these phenomena attest to a growing and persistent demand for workers' rights and for equality. Frequently, workers on strike have expressed a lack of concern with the actual monetary gains and losses. 'Money don't count when you're fighting for principle,' proclaimed a striking seamstress from Dagenham in 1968. 'In the ultimate no strike is worthwhile [economically],' argued another striker, 'but there are principles.' These sentiments were echoed by many other workers, especially by opponents of the Government's White Paper, *In Place of Strife*, who felt, 'This is our last right – to strike.' In contrast to the rhetoric of poverty surrounding strikes in the past, workers are not ashamed now to complain of the effects of layoffs on 'my social life . . . as far as going out for a drink . . . I've just got to give that up.' Nor are they reluctant to complain about the quality of work. 'The monotony has to be seen to be believed,' said a member of the AEF in 1969, explaining further that the fundamental source of discontent was the 'monotony and tempo of work as much as the economic matters connected with the work'. Workers, it seems, feel less need, or are less willing, to plead for support on grounds of pity and poverty.[37]

Much has been written recently of the problem of wage differentials, of how many strikes are basically an effort to maintain or restore inequality within the working class. There is some truth in this, although often the concern for equality has emanated from sources whose own egalitarian commitments are somewhat suspect – the *Financial Times*, for instance.[38] But fundamentally this analysis is incorrect. Most often, demands concerning differentials have been demands for equality. In the lists of 'Prominent Stoppages' in the annual articles on strikes in the *Department of Employment Gazette* in 1972 and 1973, for example, 37 stoppages were mentioned as having been in some way related to questions of wage differentials. Of these only 4, or 11 per cent, were concerned with maintaining, restoring, or widening differentials. The rest were apparently motivated by the desire to maintain or establish parity. Typical were the demands of chemical workers at Paisley, 'For an increase of 10p an hour and parity for Grade "B" process operators with maintenance workers'; and of vehicle workers at Peterborough for 'parity with similar workers in the West Midlands'.[39]

The enhanced sense of workers' rights and dignity and the growing demand for equality have taken various forms. One is the willingness to defend shop stewards and convenors in their hassles with management. Another is the sustained and surprisingly popular fight for equal pay for women, which both women and men have supported.[40] Still another is the solidarity shown in the face of redundancies – as in the strike of mechanical engineering workers at Wigan of July 1972, which was 'in sympathy with workers at another plant of the same company who had stopped work in protest against threatened lay off'. And there have even been strikes in support of workers' physical attacks on foremen and supervisors. At West Kilbride 270 construction workers, for example, went out 'against the dismissal of a worker for alleged threatened violence to a foreman and the resultant issue of 160 dismissal notices to other workers who stopped work in sympathy'. Similar strikes involved motor-car workers at Ellesmere Port and Dagenham in defence of fellow workers charged with assaults on foremen in 1973.[41] All in all, workers appear to have manifested a new set of ideas and attitudes in the late 1960s and early 1970s.[42]

Again, the roots of these changes in consciousness seem to lie in the cumulative impact of economic trends. Two influences must be distinguished. Over the long term, that is, from about 1945-68, the prevailing high levels of employment and continually advancing real wages have in all probability gradually raised workers' expectations. As we have seen, Phelps Brown feels that this heightening of expectations primarily affected younger people, with no direct experience of the depression. He also argues that by 1968 the number of such people reached a critical mass within the labour movement and this led to the outburst of 1968-72.[43] Yet there is little or no evidence in recent studies of significant generational differences among workers in attitudes or expectations. Twenty or more years of prosperity would probably raise the expectations of anyone – young or old.

On the other hand, it seems to have been the jump in prices of the late 1960s that provided the short-term stimulus for escalating expectations, coming as it did at a time when trade union rights and workers' living standards were both being tested by the incomes policy and the struggle over unofficial strikes. Inflation is in this sense social dynamite because it lifts workers' eyes from their immediate friends and family and focuses them on the whole society. John Foster has recently argued that the dominant form of social control in industrial society is social fragmentation. The growth of an industrial society based on factory labour leads inevitably, he asserts, to alienation and inequality, so that 'in order to recreate the conditions for a meaningful "social" existence – to establish *apparent control* over what society produces – people tend to limit their social contacts to those possessing roughly the same purchasing power as themselves'.[44] If this is true, inflation can be a major threat to social stability, because it overcomes social and ideological fragmentation and makes the entire hierarchy of rewards and opportunities problematical. The operations of successive incomes policies in England may have had a similar destabilising effect. Both inflation and wage controls involve by their very nature an 'explicit rejection of custom and convention as a sufficient justification of any given level and relationship of pay'.[45] Thus it might well be that government attempts throughout the 1960s and early 1970s to limit inflation by controlling incomes had effects precisely opposite to those intended.

What emerges from the foregoing discussion of Britain's recent strike history is the sense that since 1945 there has been yet another qualitative shift in labour outlook and patterns of industrial conflict. The set of relatively cautious expectations which prevailed from sometime in the 1940s to about the mid-1960s has given way to a novel constellation of working-class objectives, imparting a distinct and different logic to strike behaviour since 1968. It is not surprising that the two econometricians, Shorey and Pencavel, found it possible to develop economic models of strike determination with stable parameters for the years 1950-67. But, as one might also guess, no such simple formula as they provide suffices when the time frame is broadened to include all the years from 1947 to 1974. Indeed, recent increases in the levels of strikes and strikers have been on a scale and of a magnitude which no serious student of strikes considered possible before 1965. Kenneth Knowles, for example, writing in the early 1950s, picked out the decline of major confrontations since 1926, but missed the resilience of small-scale, local action. Nor did he suspect any resurgence of either index of strike activity.[46] Back in 1963, H.A. Turner picked out the beginning of the now historic rise of the late 1950s in his inaugural lecture on *The Trend of Strikes*, but he did not anticipate a strike movement like the one of 1968-72.[47] We should therefore be wary of any overly simple model of strike determination for the post-1945 period.

This sceptical attitude is amply justified by the equations governing these years, which are presented in Tables 6.4 to 6.6. First of all, the R^2s and Durbin-Watson statistics, while still high, are not as good as for previous periods. More important, in six of the nine equations time, the trend variable, figures very prominently. Its inclusion boosts the amount of 'explained' variance, but does not really explain it at all. Theoretically, time is included in a time series model to pick up '. . . the regular effect of variables which are not explicitly part of the model . . .'[48] As John Shorey explains, 'A simple trend term has no unique meaning. Its significance in statistical results indicates the importance of an omitted variable.'[49] Thus while Snyder, following Shorter and Tilly, generally ascribes the importance of trend variables to the unmeasured 'consequences of the processes of industrialization and urbanization', this is merely an assumption.[50] Time may be a stand-in for any factor whose impact is synchronised with time.

So whenever time dominates an equation, it is a sign that none of the other variables — 18 in this instance — accounts very well for the movement of the dependent variable. In this particular case, the logical deduction seems to be that time is substituting for a major transformation in worker attitudes, an erosion of deference and a rising demand

Table 6.4: Determinants of Strike Activity, All Industries, 1946-74

Equation	Dependent Variable	Beta coefficients on:						R^2	D–W	SEE
		GDP	$\dot{R}_{t-1}$	U_t	TUG	$SRSMO_{t-1}$	T			
6.4.1	STS	−3.13	.20	−.29	.66	.22	4.05	.83	1.24	260.1
6.4.2	STS	−2.71		−.22	.68	.29	3.67	.83	1.41	273.7

Equation	Dependent Variable	Beta coefficients on:					R^2	D–W	SEE
		$STSNOM_{t-1}$	Cons	RL	EY	T			
6.4.3	SRS(3)	.51	.40	−.39	−.47	.35	.70	1.61	290.3

Table 6.5: Determinants of Strike Activity, All Industries except Mining and Quarrying, 1946-74

Equation	Dependent Variable	Beta coefficients on:						R^2	D–W	SEE
		GDP	$\dot{R}_t$	TUG	$STSNOM_{t-1}$	RL	CG			
6.5.1	STSNOM	.75	−.20	.37	.26			.93	1.62	250.6
6.5.2	STSNOM	.69		.21	.33	−.12	−.08	.93	1.51	261.0

Equation	Dependent Variable	Beta coefficients on:					R^2	D–W	SEE
		$STSNOM_{t-1}$	Cons	RL	EY	T			
6.5.3	SRS(3)NOM	.50	.32	−.42	−.44	.43	.71	1.54	295.9

Table 6.6: Determinants of Strike Activity, Mining and Quarrying, 1946-74

Equation	Dependent Variable	Beta coefficients on:					R^2	D–W	SEE
		$\dot{R}_{t-1}$	$SRSMQ_{t-1}$	$STSNOM_{t-1}$	CG	RL			
6.6.1	STSMQ	.18	.23	−.47	.43	−.36	.88	1.48	234.3

Equation	Dependent Variable	Beta coefficients on:					R^2	D–W	SEE
		$\dot{R}_{t-1}$	$SRSMQ_{t-1}$	CG	LG	T			
6.6.2	SRS(3)MQ	.32	.35	.35	−.21	−.45	.92	1.39	18.9

Equation	Dependent Variable	Beta coefficients on:							R^2	D–W	SEE
		P_t	$\dot{R}_t$	$\dot{R}_{t-1}$	U_t	CG	Cons	T			
6.6.3	SRS(3)MQ	.49	.18	.34	−.23	.45	.24	−1.01	.91	1.44	21.3

for a greater share of society's goods and services. Of course, the equations do not in themselves imply this. It is simply the inability of other variables to account for postwar strikes that allows one to propose such an explanation. Still, no other explanation readily presents itself.

Equations 6.4.1 and 6.4.2 are relatively simple. Two economic variables — unemployment and the rate of wage change — are included with the expected positive coefficients, conforming to the well-known link between prosperity and strikes. The lagged number of mining strikers indicates that other workers are still somewhat influenced by what the miners do. As one might expect, the rate of trade union growth also affected strikes positively. But the most important variable is clearly time, which takes a coefficient larger than any reported thus far in this study, and which apparently causes the third economic variable, Gross Domestic Product, to be entered with a high negative coefficient, as a 'suppressor'. Clearly there are some unspecified factors at work here.

Equation 6.4.3, still dealing with all industries, is also fairly straightforward. Election years and repressive legislation tend to hold down big strikes, while large numbers of Conservative MPs apparently evoke a fighting mood among workers. There is also an unambiguous 'strike wave effect', indicated by the role of the lagged number of non-mining strikes. And time again contributes significantly to the equation's explanatory power.

The equations developed to deal with all industries except mining differ slightly from those used to predict strikes in all industries. Equations 6.5.1 and 6.5.2 give pride of place to three factors: prosperity, the rate of trade union growth, and the 'strike wave effect'. This is not unexpected. Also included in successive equations are the rate of wage change and the impact of political factors like repressive legislation and the strength of Conservatives in Parliament. The latter, it appears, at the same time prevents the proliferation of small strikes and promotes large strikes. Repressive legislation is more successful in deterring most workers from launching either small or large strikes, except for the miners who, according to Table 6.6, respond to repressive legislation and Conservative Governments by concentrating their efforts into a few big battles. Equation 6.5.3, which attempts to account for the number of non-mining strikers, is almost an exact replica of Equation 6.4.3, which has already been analysed.

Strikes and strikers in mining are predicted best by three curious equations. In Equation 6.6.1, the lagged number of non-mining strikes explains the main proportion of the variance, an obvious statistical reference to the fact that mining strikes began to fall just when strikes in other industries began to rise. The lagged measure of strike activity in mining itself is simply an indication of the consistency of the trends in mining strikes throughout the period. The other three included variables, the lagged rate of wage change, and the particular combination of political variables, carry modest coefficients whose influence in each case is in the expected direction. This suggests that, once the general downward movement is taken into account, mining strikes respond in the short run to familiar and normal influences.

Equations 6.6.2 and 6.6.3, predicting the number of strikers in mining, need little comment. A negative trend factor is the most important term in both. After this, economic variables enter in expected ways, as do the lagged number of mining strikers, the Conservative Government 'dummy', and the number of Conservative MPs. The only new addition is the Labour Government 'dummy', which acts as a depressant on the number of strikers. Miners seem, more than any other group, to time their strikes to embarrass their political enemies and to support their allies.

Overall, then, the equations for 1946-74 reveal two general characteristics of the period. First, most of the influences important in earlier periods still matter. Prosperity, the political situation, and especially trade unionism, all operate as they tended to in the past. Secondly, however, added to this set of determinants are two crucial trend factors, which signify major transformations in strike patterns. The first is the tendency for strike activity to decline in mining as the industry is run down and its pay structure rationalised. The second is the blossoming of strikes in almost all other industries, barely discernible in the late 1950s, but crystal clear in the late sixties and seventies.

The aim of this and the previous chapter was to demonstrate in detail the interrelationship between economic and technical change and strikes, and its mediation through consciousness and organisation. To recapitulate thoroughly would be tiresome, but a few summary points are in order. Most significant about these chapters is the way the ordinary descriptive analysis of conjuncture and development and their impact upon conflict was reinforced by the use of multivariate statistical analysis. The two modes of explanation neatly dovetailed, such that expectations, generated by the examination of economic change, about shifts in the structure of the working class, its attitudes and organisational strength were consistently confirmed by the statistical results.

The significance of this needs to be stressed, because it greatly strengthens the general argument of this book. In earlier chapters (2-4) our interpretation of various statistical models was marked by a persistently pessimistic note, since the main concern was to demonstrate how competing theories fail to explain British strike history. Now the position has been reversed. We have elaborated a model of our own which says that strikes respond to different situations at different times because the economic context changes and with it workers' ideology and tactical resources. A first corollary is that strikes do follow relatively consistent patterns during blocks of years constructed with attention to economic periodisation, and that these patterns can be described and analysed statistically. A second is that the movement from economic development to shifts in consciousness to alterations in union strategy and form is not automatic, and that union strength concretised in one or another measure should play an important part in equations developed to predict strikes in particular periods. The hypothesis and its corollaries are strongly supported by the results of multivariate analysis. Strikes turn out to be quite predictable when the right combinations of years are chosen, so that even though the impact of long waves of economic history is not explicitly represented in any equation, they are clearly operative in the background, imparting a consistency and coherence to strike behaviour during successive periods. On the other hand, some trade union variable was included in no less than 28 of the 42 equations in these two chapters, and in many it was the most powerful predictor. Together these findings add up to a striking confirmation of the basic argument.

Notes

1. John Saville has put the case well: 'For the mass of the people of Britain, unemployment and insecurity of jobs were the biggest social facts of their lives. Economic historians have rightly emphasized the improvement in real incomes during the thirties, but what mattered for most working people was the regularity of the job. Historical hindsight commends the labour mobility which helped to encourage the growth of the new industries in the Midlands and the London area, but at the same time, even with a job, life was not altogether sweet for the Welshman, separated from his family and living an alienated existence in Oxford or Slough.' See his 'May Day 1937', in A. Briggs and J. Saville (eds.), *Essays in Labour History, 1918-1939* (London, 1977), p. 261.
2. W.G. Runciman, *Relative Deprivation and Social Justice* (London, 1967).
3. No detailed and explicit study has been made of this process in England as yet, certainly nothing on the scale or of the quality of Charles S. Maier's *Recasting Bourgeois Europe: Stabilization in France, Germany, and Italy in the*

decade after World War 1 (Princeton, 1975). The story can largely be pieced together from a careful reading of the following works: M. Cowling, *The Impact of Labour, 1920-1924* (Cambridge, 1971); D.E. Moggridge, *The Return to Gold, 1925* (Cambridge, 1969), and *British Monetary Policy, 1924-1931, the Norman Conquest of $4.86* (Cambridge, 1972); Susan Armitage, *The Politics of Decontrol of Industry: Britain and the United States* (London, 1969); P.B. Johnson, *Land Fit for Heroes* (Chicago, 1968); Nona Newman, 'The Role of the Treasury in the Formation of British Economic Policy, 1918-1925' (unpublished Ph.D. dissertation, University of Durham, 1972); and the introductory sections of S. Blank, *Industry and Government in Britain: the Federation of British Industries in Politics, 1945-1965* (Lexington, Mass., 1973).

For a theoretical perspective on this period and process, see the provocative essays in H.A. Winkler (ed.), *Organisierter Kapitalismus* (Göttingen, 1974).

4. See the literature cited in Ch. 3, notes 12-14, for general histories of the General Strike and for further references. Perhaps the best recent studies of the events of 1926 have been those with a local focus. See, in particular, Anthony Mason, *The General Strike in the North East* (Hull, 1970); D.E. Baines and R. Bean, 'The General Strike on Merseyside, 1926', in J.R. Harris (ed.), *Liverpool and Merseyside: Essays in the economic and social history of the port and its hinterland* (London, 1969), pp. 239-75; R.P. Hastings, 'Aspects of the General Strike in Birmingham', *Midland History*, II (1974), pp. 250-73; and part 2 of J. Skelley (ed.), *The General Strike 1926* (London, 1976).

5. H.A. Clegg, 'Some Consequences of the General Strike', *Transactions of the Manchester Statistical Society* (1953-4).

6. G.A. Phillips, *The General Strike* (London, 1976).

7. *The Times*, 24 and 28 Jan. 1919.

8. Tom Jones, *Whitehall Diary, 1916-1925*, K. Middlemas (ed.), (London, 1969), p. 73.

9. Trades Union Congress, General Council, *The Mining Crisis and the National Strike, 1926. Official Reports* (London, 1927), p. 187A, 36-44, and *passim.*

10. Report of the General Council to the 1928 Trades Union Congress, quoted in S. Pollard, *The Development of the British Economy, 1914-1967* (New York, 1969), p. 178.

11. The failure of the talks was due largely to the active opposition of the Engineering Employers' Federation, according to Wigham, *The Power to Manage*, pp. 130-2. For an interpretation of the talks as 'an attempt by the main victims to combine forces against the Treasury and the City . . .', see S. Pollard, 'Trade Union Reactions to the Economic Crisis', *Journal of Contemporary History*, IV (1969), p. 106. See also G.W. MacDonald and H.F. Gospel, 'The Mond-Turner Talks, 1927-1933: A Study in Industrial Cooperation', *Historical Journal*, XVI (1973), pp. 807-29.

12. See J. Hinton and R. Hyman, *Trade Unions and Revolution* (London, 1975), who see this 'emasculation of the rank-and-file movement', due to unemployment, as the key to the stabilisation after 1920. They note, for example, that 'As union strength on the shop floor was eroded by unemployment and victimization, the focus of power and influence within the unions shifted upward to the full-time officials,' whose numbers actually increased during the prolonged decline of membership in the 1920s. See esp. pp. 11-22, 41.

13. Beatrice Webb, *Beatrice Webb's Diaries*, entry for 16 April 1921, p. 208.

14. As quoted in TUC, General Council, *The Mining Crisis*, p. 173A.

15. Letter from Dame Margaret Cole, *Society for the Study of Labour History Bulletin*, no. 34 (Spring, 1977), p. 14.

16. This conclusion is in general agreement with Hinton and Hyman, *Trade*

154   *Defeat, Reorientation and Renewal*

Unions and Revolution. M. Jacques, 'Consequences of the General Strike', in Skelley (ed.), *The General Strike 1926*, pp. 275-404, makes some of the same points, but puts too much stress on the rise of real wages in promoting stabilisation.
17. E.J. Hobsbawm, 'Trends in the British Labour Movement', in *Labouring Men*, p. 388.
18. *Cotton Factory Times*, 30 December 1932.
19. See Saville, 'May Day 1937', pp. 238-84.
20. Pollard, 'Trade Union Reactions', pp. 101-15.
21. See Aldcroft and Richardson, *The British Economy*, Chs 7 and 8.
22. This analysis owes a good deal to G.D.H. Cole and M.I. Cole, *The Condition of Britain* (London, 1937), pp. 397-404.
23. Ibid., pp. 407-10.
24. Perhaps the clearest evidence on the redistributive aspects of the Labour Government of 1945-51 is the shift in factor shares of GNP in these years. On this, see A.B. Atkinson, *The Economics of Inequality* (Oxford, 1975), pp. 161-8. A useful discussion of the social effects of the creation of the welfare state can be found in R.M. Titmuss, *Essays on 'the welfare state'* (London, 1958). The economic history of the early postwar period is treated in detail in G.D.N. Worswick and P.H. Ady, *The British Economy, 1945-1950* (Oxford, 1952); A.A. Rogow, *The Labour Government and British Industry, 1945-1951* (Oxford, 1955); and J.C.R. Dow, *The Management of the British Economy, 1945-1960* (Cambridge, 1964).
25. H.A. Turner, G. Clack, and G. Roberts, *Labour Relations in the Motor Industry* (London, 1967), pp. 61, 192-5, 234-5, 271-5. See also A.I. Marsh and E. Coker, 'Shop Steward Organisation in the Engineering Industry', *BJIR* I (1963), pp. 170-90.
26. W.E.J. McCarthy, *The Role of Shop Stewards in British Industrial Relations*, Research Papers 1, Royal Commission on Trade Unions and Employers' Organisations (London, 1967), pp. 4-5.
27. This, at least, is my interpretation of the consistent finding about the importance to workers of job security, a concern central to many workers, especially older, married ones. See S. Wyatt and R. Marriott, *A Study of Attitudes to Factory Work*, Medical Research Council, Special Report Series, no. 292 (London, 1956), *passim*; D. Wedderburn and R. Crompton, *Workers' Attitudes and Technology* (Cambridge, 1972), p. 39; H. Beynon and R.M. Blackburn, *Perceptions of Work* (Cambridge, 1972), p. 62; and the literature cited in these works.
28. See Pollard, *The Development of the British Economy* Cn. VIII; A.J. Youngson, *Britain's Economic Growth, 1920-66* (New York, 1967), Ch. VI; and G.D.N. Worswick and P.H. Ady (eds.), *The British Economy in the Nineteen-Fifties* (Oxford, 1962), esp. pp. 1-75.
29. As Turner, Clack, and Roberts, *Labour Relations in the Motor Industry*, p. 128, explained, 'The reappearance of the trade cycle in the 1950s, bringing with it sharp periods of unemployment and redundancy, seems to have led to heightened insecurity and the return of old fears on the part of car workers, especially from 1956 onwards. And it is precisely from the mid-1950s that the frequency of car workers' strikes began its steep upward slope.'
30. See the leader, 'A Sorry Story', in *The Times*, 1 Feb. 1957, p. 9. On unofficial strikes more broadly, see Robert A. Shea, 'A General Analysis and Case Study of Unofficial Strikes in the Manual-Worker Section of the British Engineering Industry' (unpublished MSc dissertation, London School of Economics, 1961). See also Wigham, *The Power to Manage*, pp. 178-88, 195.
31. Runciman, *Relative Deprivation*, p. 207.
32. Harold Wilson summarised the situation created by the enhancement of

rank-and-file control in a speech of 1970, where he argued that 'the growth of shop floor power, industrial militancy, part of it spontaneous and part of it capable of being created by unscrupulous unofficial leaders . . . is the central fact of the 1970s'. Quoted in L. Panitch, *Social Democracy and Industrial Militancy* (Cambridge, 1976), p. 230.

On the inroads and activities of the left, see P. Shipley, *Revolutionaries in Modern Britain* (London, 1976), pp. 50-7, 125-9, 135-43. On the general role of oppositional movements in unions, see J.D. Edelstein and M. Warner, *Comparative Union Democracy* (New York, 1976), pp. 150-87, 209-318.

33. On real net incomes, see D. Jackson, H.A. Turner and F. Wilkinson, *Do Trade Unions Cause Inflation?* 2nd ed. (Cambridge, 1975), pp. 78-89. They calculate that median earnings for manual workers after taxes increased by 1.45 per cent annually in 1960-4, by .88 per cent in 1964-8, and 1.49 per cent in 1968-70.

A. Glyn and R. Sutcliffe, *British Capitalism, Workers, and the Profits Squeeze* (Harmondsworth, 1972), have also pointed to the period around 1967 as a key turning point in economic history, suggesting that it marked a decisive break with Treasury orthodoxy, and a reorientation of policy toward the interests of industry rather than those of the City of London. For further discussion of the influence of the City on policy during postwar years, see Pollard, *The Development of the British Economy*, pp. 483-4.

34. Jackson, Turner and Wilkinson, *Do Trade Unions Cause Inflation?*, pp. 63-103; and also J. Johnson and M. Timbrell, 'Empirical Tests of a Bargaining Theory of Wage Rate Determination', *Manchester School of Economic and Social Studies*, XLI (1973), pp. 140-67, on the effects of taxes upon incomes.

For the political perspective, see Panitch, *Social Democracy*; and C. Crouch, *Class Conflict and the Industrial Relations Crisis* (London, 1977).

35. D. Hibbs, 'On the Political Economy of Long-Run Trends in Strike Activity', *British Journal of Political Science*, VIII (1978), pp. 153-75.

36. K. Hawkins, *British Industrial Relations, 1945-1975* (London, 1976), pp. 136-8; H. Behrend, 'The Impact of Inflation on Pay Increase Expectations and Ideas of Fair Pay', *Industrial Relations Journal*, V (Spring, 1974), pp. 5-10; E.H. Phelps Brown, 'New Wine in Old Bottles: Reflections on the Changed Working of Collective Bargaining in Britain', *British Journal of Industrial Relations*, XI (1973), pp. 329-37.

On wage demands, see E. Sutcliffe, 'Factory Money', in R. Fraser (ed.), *Work 2: Twenty Personal Accounts* (Harmondsworth, 1969), p. 295.

For a much more sceptical view of the extent of recent changes in the attitudes of workers, see C. Crouch, 'The Drive for Equality: Experience of Incomes Policies in Britain', in L. Lindberg, *et al.* (eds.), *Stress and Contradiction in Modern Capitalism* (Lexington, Mass., 1975), pp. 228, 230-5.

37. These statements are taken from various BBC interviews with strikers made available to me at the British Institute of Recorded Sound. The following records were used: LP30583, LP31816, and LP32418.

38. See, for example, the article on 'The Top Brass at Leyland', in the *Financial Times*, 3 April 1976.

39. 'Stoppages of Work due to Industrial Disputes in 1972', *Department of Employment Gazette* (June 1973), p. 557; 'Stoppages of Work due to Industrial Disputes in 1973', *Department of Employment Gazette* (June 1974), p. 512.

40. R. Hyman and I. Brough, *Social Values and Industrial Relations* (London, 1976), p. 244. See also J. Goldthorpe, 'Social Inequality and Social Integration in Modern Britain', in D. Wedderburn (ed.), *Inequality and Class Structure* (Cambridge, 1974), p. 228. On the issue of equal pay, see S. Lewenhak, *Women and Trade Unions* (New York, 1977), pp. 285-7.

41. 'Stoppages ... in 1972', pp. 558, 563; and 'Stoppages ... in 1973', pp. 511-12.

42. While we await systematic survey data on these issues, one small but suggestive study may be mentioned. A team of American sociologists conducted a series of interviews during 1974-5 designed to compare British and American attitudes toward social equality and, incidentally, societal alienation. The British sample proved to value equality substantially more, and to be much more alienated, than previous studies would have predicted. Though the sample was small (N=101), the results are quite consistent with the argument presented here. See R.V. Robinson and W. Bell, 'Equality, Success, and Social Justice in England and the United States', *American Sociological Review*, XLIII (1978), pp. 125-43, for a first report of the findings.

Also consistent with our argument are the results of recent surveys of British political attitudes, in terms of social class voting, political satisfaction and alienation. See R. Inglehart, *The Silent Revolution. Changing Values and Political Styles among Western Publics* (Princeton, 1977), pp. 149-76, 214-15.

43. H. Phelps Brown, 'A Non-Monetarist View of the Pay Explosion', *Three Banks Review*, 105 (March 1975), p. 19.

44. J. Foster, *Class Struggle and the Industrial Revolution* (London, 1974), p. 4.

45. Hyman and Brough, *Social Values*, pp. 230-46.

46. K.G.J.C. Knowles, *Strikes* (New York, 1952), *passim.*

47. H.A. Turner, *The Trend of Strikes* (Leeds, 1963).

48. D. Snyder, 'Determinants of Industrial Conflict' (unpublished Ph.D. dissertation, University of Michigan, 1974), p. 127.

49. John C. Shorey, 'A Quantitative Analysis of Strike Activity in the United Kingdom' (unpublished Ph.D. dissertation, London School of Economics), p. 123.

50. Snyder, 'Determinants of Industrial Conflict', p. 125.

7   INDUSTRIAL CONTRASTS

Strike rates vary not only over time, but also from one group of workers to another. To take one obvious case, between 1963 and 1968 the average docker struck more than once a year, six times more frequently than the average miner, ten times more often than the ordinary engineering worker, and about forty-five times more often than most construction workers. These ratios are extreme, but they do help to explain why so many students of strikes have been fascinated by inter-industry differences, often to the virtual exclusion of patterns over time.

Aside from the natural predisposition of an historian, three empirical considerations dictated that the core of this study would be the analysis of the chronological dimensions of strike variation. One was the dramatic nature of temporal fluctuations in strike activity; a second was the simultaneity and comparability of movements in most industries over the years; and a third was the instability of inter-industry patterns themselves. Still, it remains that industries have contrasted sharply in the past and continue to behave differently today. It is only logical to suggest that the argument developed to explain the variations over time in industrial conflict should also provide guidance concerning the differences between groups of workers. This chapter therefore will apply insights spawned in the previous chapters to the analysis of inter-industry differences in strikes.

Two competing paradigms dominate the extensive literature on industrial variation in strike propensity — the economic and the sociological.[1] The economic approach fixes upon elements in the market situation of particular groups of workers — susceptibility to fluctuations, adverse working conditions, piece-work, peculiarities of bargaining procedures, and so on — as predisposing some groups to conflict by multiplying the causes and occasions for disputes. The sociological paradigm is concerned above all with the relative social cohesion of different sorts of workers, in the belief that solidarity is the key to strike-proneness. The basic thrust of this book leads us to come down heavily in favour of the economic perspective. Let us preview the argument briefly.

Theoretically, there is little reason to dispute the sociologists' insistence upon social networks as the precondition for effective collective action. What is doubtful is how much workers differ in this respect. Aside from the extreme situations of miners and, possibly, dockers, the variation does not appear to have been great. This is probably due to the fact that the bulk of the working class in Britain has lived in those stable residential communities consolidated some time around the turn of the century.[2] While there has been some tendency for such neighbourhoods to decay and disintegrate since the Second World War, the process is by no means complete, and those who have moved out of the old neighbourhoods have been those in industries where shop-floor associations have been able to substitute as a basis for cohesion and collective action.[3] In short, the argument from community is unobjectionable in general terms, but fails to discriminate sufficiently between one group of workers and another.

Economic forces, by contrast, discriminate viciously between industries, as the entire economic history of twentieth-century Britain reveals. Most important for our point of view, those qualitatively different stages of economic growth, which seem to propel conflict forward, affect different industries at uneven rates and with varying degrees of severity. It should therefore be possible to extend the argument about the time pattern of strikes to the problem of inter-industry differences in the following fashion: strike propensity will vary with the extent to which particular 'phases of economic evolution' impinge upon the day-to-day working of different industries. How central an industry is to the economy and how thoroughly subject it is to market vagaries and imperatives should determine how prone it is to industrial conflict.

Several steps are involved in demonstrating this theory — the first is to examine the actual record of strike-proneness. The information on strike propensity is unfortunately limited by a lack of precision in the government's industrial classifications. Comparable data can be obtained back to 1888 only if all industries are divided into eight broad groups: building; textiles; clothing; metal; engineering, and shipbuilding; vehicles; mining and quarrying; transport and communications; and miscellaneous industries. Out of these eight, separate figures for vehicles were not available prior to 1949, and textiles and clothing have been combined since 1949. At any given date, therefore, all strikes are classified into one of only seven broad industrial groupings.

The seriousness of the measurement problem becomes evident when one realises the disparate workers lumped together in these groupings. In the miscellaneous category old established craftsmen, like printers and glass makers, sit uneasily alongside social workers, teachers, chemists and dustmen. Even in what appear as relatively homogeneous groupings like textiles, there are many different occupational levels. In transport and communication there are dockers and telephone workers, both of whom have been relatively strike-prone in recent years, plus railwaymen, who strike much less often. Obviously, such groupings often may conceal as much as they reveal.

Granting all these difficulties, the figures do reveal certain basic trends in strike-proneness. Figure 7.1 depicts visually calculations of strike-proneness for 8 four-year periods at approximately ten-year intervals since 1888. Two different measures of strike-proneness are used: the number of strikes per 1,000 workers and the number of strikers per 1,000 workers. As measured by the former, mining and quarrying usually heads the list, while miscellaneous industries brings up the rear. Mining is generally followed by vehicles, metal-working, textiles, and transport; but the order among these relatively strike-prone industries is by no means stable. Textiles, for example, was much more strike-prone before 1932 than since. Transport, on the other hand has experienced more conflict as the present century progressed. Metal, engineering and shipbuilding fluctuated from first down to sixth place between 1888-92 and 1899-1902, between second and fourth thereafter. Vehicles has been consistently high in strike-proneness, but here there are relatively few observations, and other evidence suggests that this is a relatively recent development.[4] The strike-propensity of building also fluctuates substantially.

When the probability of striking is measured by the number of strikers, these patterns become more pronounced. Mining is still the most, miscellaneous industries the least, strike-prone. Textiles appear even more strike-prone before 1932, even less after that. Building appears less strike-prone, owing apparently to the prevalence of small strikes in that industry. Transport and communication, on the other hand, come out as more strike-prone than as previously measured, due to the importance of large strikes in this group. Metal-working has consistently held third or fourth place in striker rates. Clothing, despite some militancy in 1899-1902 and again, for unexplained reasons, in the late 1940s, is generally one of the less strike-prone industries.

The consistency of the pattern of rank ordering according to strike-proneness, however, does less than justice to historical reality, for the general level moves up and down dramatically. Between 1889-92 and 1899-1902 the number of strikes per worker decreased by almost half, strikers by two-thirds. Between the latter date and 1910-13 the strike ratio increased slightly, but the rate for strikers increased by almost

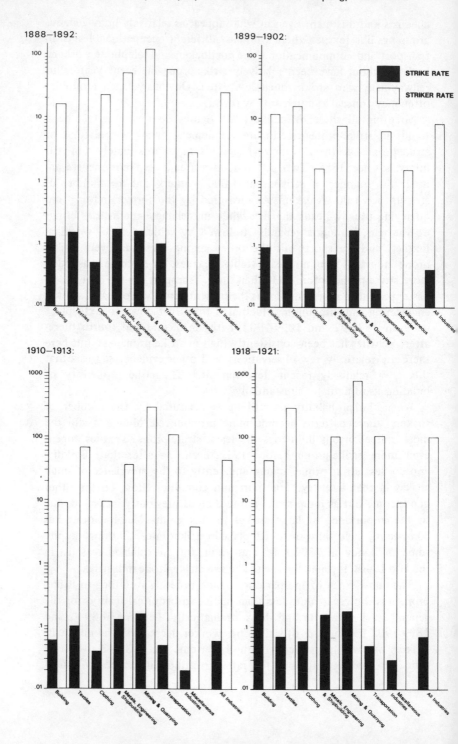

Figure 7.1: Strike Propensity by Broad Industrial Grouping, 1888-1972

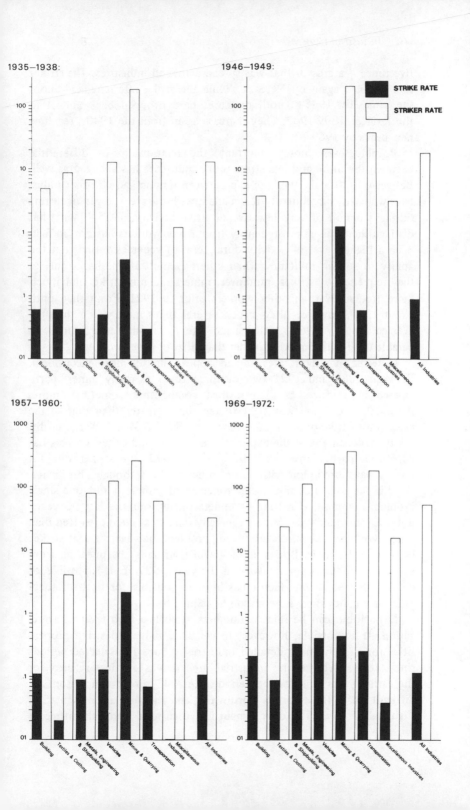

1935–1938:

1946–1949:

STRIKE RATE
STRIKER RATE

100

100

10

10

1

1

.1

.1

.01

.01

Building
Textiles
Clothing
Metals, Engineering & Shipbuilding
Mining & Quarrying
Transportation
Miscellaneous Industries
All Industries

1957–1960:

1969–1972:

1000

1000

100

100

10

10

1

1

.1

.1

.01

.01

Building
Textiles & Clothing
Metals, Engineering & Shipbuilding
Vehicles
Mining & Quarrying
Transportation
Miscellaneous Industries
All Industries

five times – a growth that was spread across all industries. The striker rate doubled again by 1918-21, while the strike rate remained about the same. By 1935-8, both measures have dropped back almost to the level of 1899-1902. They increase again from the 1940s, reaching new peaks by 1969-72.

Possibly even more important, the relationship or differential between the more and less strike-prone industries has changed as well. Between 1920 and 1949 the gap between mining and all other industries widened, subsequently it declined; with the greatest gap occurring during a period of very low overall strike activity, 1935-8. What has distinguished miners most sharply from other workers has not, in fact, been a higher level of activity during eras of general conflict, but the ability to sustain militancy when others cannot. If one looks only at the frequency of strikes, moreover, miners did not strike that much more frequently than other workers prior to 1921. From then until about 1960, however, they struck several times more often than the average, but by 1969-72 the strike rate for mining was again comparable to, if still somewhat higher than, that of other workers.

In terms of striker rates, miners appear slightly more exceptional. Between 1889 and 1921 two or three times as many miners participated in conflicts as their nearest competitors, sometimes more. After 1921, the rate was eight to ten times greater than that of the next most strike-prone group. Since the Second World War, the disparity between the strike experience of miners and other workers has narrowed, particularly after 1957. By 1969-72, the striker rate for miners was more in line with that of other workers, though a bit higher.

This suggests that the strike-proneness of miners is not one single problem common to mining or miners throughout the last 90 years, but two separate issues. Miners generally tend to strike more often than other workers. The more interesting problem, however, is that strikes became endemic in British mining while virtually disappearing from the rest of industry, particularly in the years 1927-56. It is possible, of course, that some one factor has been responsible for both of these phenomena, but there is no reason to assume so.

Little more can be said of numbers at such a high level of aggregation. It is possible, however, to calculate industrial strike propensities for slightly more detailed industrial groups for selected periods since 1888. Because the industrial breakdowns are less refined for the earlier years than for the period since 1945, direct comparisons are difficult. Still, the effort is worthwhile, and the data are presented in Figures 7.2 - 7.3. The data remain less than ideal, but will suffice to

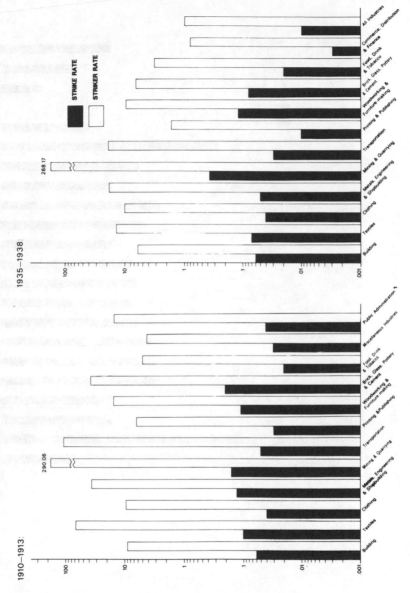

Figure 7.2: Strike Propensity by Industry, 1910-38

Figure 7.3: Strike Propensity by Industry, 1954-72

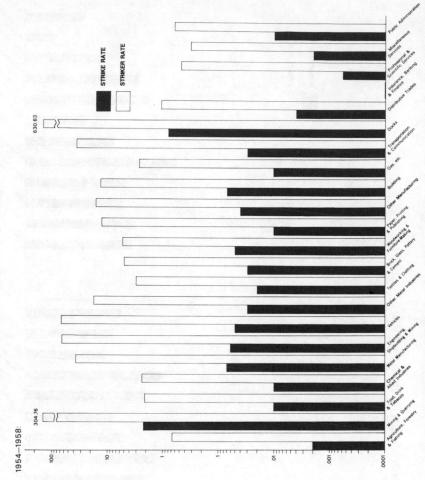

1954-1958:

STRIKE RATE

STRIKER RATE

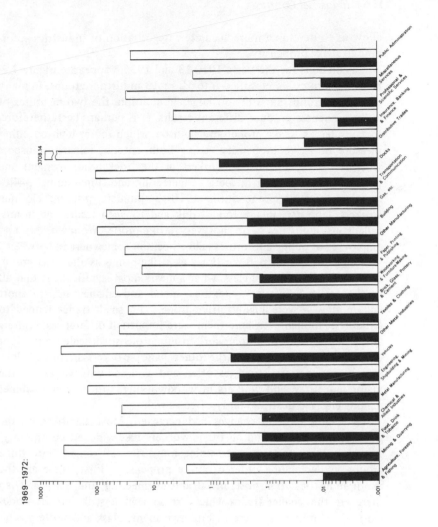

1969—1972:

Public Administration
Miscellaneous Services
Professional & Scientific Services
Insurance, Banking & Finance
Distributive Trades
Docks
Transportation & Communication
Gas, etc.
Building
Other Manufacturing
Paper, Printing & Publishing
Woodworking & Furniture Making
Brick, Glass, Pottery & Cement
Textiles & Clothing
Other Metal Industries
Vehicles
Engineering, Shipbuilding & Mining
Metal Manufacturing
Chemical & Allied Industries
Food, Drink & Tobacco
Mining & Quarrying
Agriculture, Forestry & Fishing

3708.14

1000
100
10
1
0.1
0.01
0.001

allow us to develop a more accurate categorisation of industries according to strike propensity.

Calculations for the years 1910-13 and 1935-8 appear in Figure 7.2, in which strikes are classified into 12 or 13 industrial groups. In many cases, the groups are still too large. In addition, the two measures of strike-proneness produce different results. It is perhaps best, therefore, to consider as 'strike-prone' any industry which scores high on either measure of strike propensity. Using both criteria, miners, transport workers, textile operatives, workers in the brick, glass, cement and pottery industries, and in metal, engineering and shipbuilding qualify as relatively strike-prone during 1910-13. Builders, printers, clothing workers, labourers in the food, drink and tobacco trades and in miscellaneous industries were not very strike-prone. Woodworkers and employees of public authorities held a position somewhere in between.

Miners were almost three times as strike-prone as the next group, the railwaymen. Nevertheless, what appears most significant is that all of the major industries — textiles, metal and engineering, transport and mining — were highly strike-prone. The small trades tended to strike less, though even here there were important differences. Printers and building, both of whom work in numerous small-scale units, went on strike infrequently. On the other hand, workers in brick, glass, cement and pottery struck as often and as broadly as workers in the major industries, and workers in woodworking, furniture and cabinet making engaged in strikes fairly often as well.

By 1935-8, several changes had occurred. Most significantly, the gap between miners and all other workers had widened enormously. Leaving mining aside, the remaining industries fall roughly into three groups in descending order of strike propensity. First, there are the major industries: transport, metal and engineering, and textiles. Then there are the smaller trades which are somewhat strike-prone: woodworking, clothing, workers in bricks, cement, glass and pottery, and builders. Lagging a good distance behind are those who for various reasons seldom strike: printers, employees in food, drink, tobacco, and clerical labour.

Jumping to Figure 7.3 and data from the mid-1950s, the amount of information improves considerably, and reveals a good deal more. Miners were still more likely to strike than other workers, except dockers, who had become most strike-prone of all. Information relating specifically to dockers is unfortunately lacking for earlier periods, so it is not clear when they emerged as the most militant group. It probably occurred in the late 1940s, but we cannot be sure. In any case, several other shifts are apparent from Figure 7.3. Textile operatives and clothing workers have become less strike-prone than any other group in manufacturing. Once can also detect a new leading role for workers in the manufacture of motor vehicles, who have by this time become the most strike-prone of all manufacturing employees. Building workers have also turned more strike-prone, while those in transport and communications more or less maintain their previous role. Paper manufacture and printing have become marginally more strike-prone, although this seems due almost entirely to one or two large strikes of printers. Workers in bricks, glass, etc. and woodworking and associated industries still strike with some frequency, but less than in earlier periods. White-collar employees, workers in chemicals and allied industries, and in food, drink and tobacco engage in disputes quite infrequently.

By 1968-72, however, a new and distinct pattern had emerged which requires close analysis.[5] Almost every sort of labourer has become more strike-prone. In old industries like textiles and clothing, striker rates increased by about ten times between 1954-8 and 1968-72, while those for public administration increased approximately 40 times over the same period. Dockers have clearly replaced miners as the most strike-prone workers, their striker rate being almost ten times that of the miners. Three more phenomena stand out. With the exception of gas workers and those in woodworking, all sections of manual labour have striker rates above 20 per thousand, a figure surpassed by only four manufacturing industries in 1954-8. Second, the most strike-prone industry within manufacturing is vehicles, with a strike rate almost equal to mining and a striker rate still higher. Nevertheless, militancy is general throughout the metal-working industry. Shipbuilding and marine engineering, metal manufacture, and mechanical, electrical and industrial engineering, all have participation rates above 100 per thousand.

Perhaps most interesting, many white-collar workers have become as highly strike-prone as workers in manufacturing industries. Some of these are included under transport and communications, others under professional and scientific services and public administration. White-collar unionism and white-collar strikes apparently began to climb around 1967-8. Between 1964 and 1970, white-collar union membership increased by one-third; from 1964 to 1974, the density of white-collar unionisation jumped from 29 per cent to 39 per cent. One white-collar union, the Association of Scientific, Technical and Managerial Staff (ASTMS) saw its membership rise from a mere

80,000 to over 200,000 between 1968 and 1970.[6] Similarly, from 1963-8 to 1968-72, the striker rates for professional and scientific services workers and for those in public administration jumped fully twenty times.

All in all, the figures present a complex picture of differences between industries, but it is possible to discern certain patterns and regularities. It appears, in fact, that the historical variability of strike-proneness is not quite absolute, and that industries can be classified into three categories whose propensities for conflict normally fluctuate in tandem.[7] Most of the major industries have relatively high strike propensities and make up the first, most strike-prone group. This would include metal, engineering and shipbuilding, textiles, mining, and transport for most of the years since 1888. Within this group, three major deviations occur: the miners from 1927 to 1956 and the dockers since 1945 have exceeded the norm, while textile workers have by the same standard 'underachieved' since 1932. Granted these significant exceptions, the industries in this group behave in very similar ways and have strike propensities of a roughly comparable order of magnitude.

The second category encompasses mostly small-scale industries: it is composed of builders, brick, cement, glass and pottery workers, woodworkers, and furniture and cabinet makers. While one of these groups, like builders or brick-makers, may temporarily attain a strike rate equal to that of a major industry, its striker rate approaches such levels rarely. The least strike-prone group includes printing and paper workers, labourers in the food, drink and tobacco industries, public service employees and white-collar workers. Here, too there are exceptions, mainly those white-collar workers whose strike propensities have increased since the mid-1960s and, for one or two very brief periods, printing and paper workers.

By locating three distinct patterns and groupings, the task of explaining industrial variation in strike activity is reduced to more manageable proportions and divided into two discrete and analytically separate problems. The first is to understand the general breakdown by discovering what unites industries in each group and divides them from those in other categories. This exercise will necessarily constitute the main aspect of our discussion of inter-industry differences. Second, one must also explain the extreme cases, the exceptions and the major transformations. Here the focus will quite naturally be upon the dockers and miners, and to a lesser extent the textile workers and white-collar employees.

Ideally, it should be possible to apply the same techniques of multi-variate analysis used earlier to this cross-sectional data on industrial conflict in order to test competing theories of strike-proneness. But because the statistical information necessary for such an exercise is not available for much of the period under consideration, we must make do with a less elegant survey.[8] In what follows, we shall begin by isolating those characteristics that set off the most highly strike-prone industries from those less prone to conflict. We then assess the other two groups on the same criteria, and seek to differentiate between the moderately and minimally strike-prone industries.

What do the highly strike-prone industries — mining, textiles, transport, and metal-working — have in common that predisposes their workers to take so readily to the picket lines? No one critical factor stands out, but one can easily discern a cluster of features that distinguishes them from other industries. Workers most prone to strike are likely to be found in industries which are highly unionised, unusually susceptible to economic fluctuations, with a marked proclivity toward the use of piece-work as a stimulus to production, and, most important, with a central role in the economic life of the nation. Obviously, these features are related, and can be seen collectively to describe large-scale, modern industries highly integrated into the market or strategic to its smooth operation.[9] Let us look in more detail.

Unionisation

The structure of British unions is famous for its irrationality: craft, industrial and general unions compete for members and overlap in their coverage. This makes it difficult to calculate precisely the density of organisation in different industries. Nevertheless, official government statistics dating from 1893 and TUC data going back still further suggest clearly that the most strike-prone industries have all been highly unionised. The miners, metal-workers and engineers, and the textile operatives set the pace for unionisation between 1870 and 1914, and transport workers began to organise massively after 1889. By 1913, over 900,000 miners were unionised, over half a million were in unions in both metal-working and textiles, and almost three-quarters of a million in various branches of transport. The only other trades with large numbers of unionised workers prior to the First World War were clothing, construction, and printing, and only in the latter was density as high as in the strike-prone group.[10] A more systematic attempt to measure densities came in the 1930s — not the best years for unions — and it shows the same situation. As of 1936, about 70 per cent of coal miners and transport workers were in TUC-affiliated unions. Ship-builders could boast a comparable level of organisation; while workers in other branches of engineering, in cotton textiles and in printing and publishing had rates of membership of between 36 per cent and 47 per cent. All these except printing and publishing were in the most strike-prone group, and only one other industry — boot and shoe-making, with 52 per cent — came close to these in level of unionisation.[11]

Since the 1930s, union densities have increased across the board from 30.5 per cent in 1938, to 45.2 per cent a decade later, to just over 50 per cent by 1974. Most of the growth came in two bursts, 1938-48 and 1968-74, typical of the discontinuous and uneven patterns we have come to expect in strikes and labour organisation.[12] Calculations of relative union density are presented in Table 7.1. While the increase in membership has been widely dispersed, the most strike-prone industries remain among the best organised, with transport workers and coalminers achieving almost 100 per cent unionisation. Note, too, the substantial jump in density within the metal and engineering industry; the enhanced postwar strike propensity of engineering workers is matched by their organising efforts.

The postwar data also reveals a few anomalies, however. Industries like pottery, glass, and public service have joined footwear and printing as highly unionised industries that are but minimally or infrequently strike-prone. Two points deserve to be made about this. First, it is worth recalling that most industries have increased their strike propensity and union density since about 1960, so that the most strike-prone group is inevitably losing its monopoly over solidarity in collective organisation. Still, it is also necessary to recognise that union organisation has never been both a necessary and sufficient cause of striking; it has always been a critical prerequisite, but never the whole story. On the other hand, it is difficult to minimise the importance of organisation in distinguishing the most strike-prone group of industries over the long run.[13]

Economic Fluctuations

It is difficult to compare precisely the severity with which business cycles have affected different industries. Output indices are available, but are influenced by trend factors which make measurement of the magnitude of cyclical downturns problematical. Somewhat better are unemployment figures, but they must be used with caution. It is well known that in such industries as textiles the response to recessions

Table 7.1: Union Density in Selected Industries, 1948 and 1974

| | Percentages of labour force in unions: | |
Industry	1948	1974
Coalmining	84.1	96.2
Food and drink	38.1	51.2
Tobacco	53.1	
Chemicals		
Metals and engineering	50.0	69.4
Cotton and man-made fibres	70.0	
Other textiles	33.8	40.9
Leather	31.2	46.6
Clothing	33.9	60.0
Footwear	66.6	79.0
Bricks and building materials	40.8	40.4
Pottery	41.5	93.8
Glass	41.3	78.5
Wood and furniture	43.6	35.2
Paper, printing and publishing	58.0	71.6
Construction	45.3	27.2
Railways	88.1	96.9
Sea transport	89.3	99.6
Port and inland water transport	79.1	94.7
Post office and telecommunications	80.2	87.9
Insurance, banking, and finance	32.2	44.8
Health	38.9	60.9
Hotels and catering		5.2
Other professional services		3.7
Education and local government	61.9	85.6
National government	66.4	90.5

Source: R. Price and G.S. Bain, 'Union Growth Revisited: 1948-1974 in Perspective', *British Journal of Industrial Relations*, XIV (1976), pp. 342-3.

has been short-time working rather than unemployment. Since 1945, the response in engineering and a broad range of industries has been to cut back on overtime, a policy not captured by any available statistics, certainly not on an industry-to-industry basis. Nevertheless, unemployment statistics give some indication of the situation in different industries before 1940. Tables 7.2–7.3 summarise the existing data on relative rates of unemployment for these years. Two statistics are presented for each industry, and each has a particular significance. The average (mean) rate indicates the general level of unemployment, and reflects the level of hardship suffered by an industry's workforce. The standard deviation is a statistical measure of the annual dispersion about the average; the higher it was, the more unstable, the less certain, were unemployment prospects within an industry.

The data for 1888-1913 are obviously incomplete, because neither textiles nor mining are included. Still, the results show that the most strike-prone industry on the list — metal, engineering and shipbuilding — had the highest level and greatest fluctuation of unemployment. The building workers came next in susceptibility to fluctuations, and had the next highest strike propensity as well. Conversely, printing and bookbinding, known to have been relatively strike-free, had the least year-to-year fluctuation, despite a rather high average level of unemployment. If data were available on coalmining and textiles during this period, the correlation between susceptibility to fluctuations and strike-proneness would be still clearer. Both were notorious for their cycles of boom and bust, and they were extremely prone to industrial conflict.[14]

The data for the interwar period are more comprehensive. Worst hit by the depression were the older, staple industries: mining, shipbuilding, textiles, metal manufacture and, somewhat surprisingly, pottery and

Table 7.2: Economic Fluctuations as Indicated by the Course of Unemployment for Members of Different Unions, 1888-1913

Industry (Unions)	Average %	Standard Deviation
Engineering, Metal and Shipbuilding Unions	5.9	3.2
Amalgamated Society of Carpenters and Joiners	4.6	3.0
Woodworking and Furnishing Unions	3.9	1.7
Printing and Bookbinding Unions	4.3	.9
Other Industries	2.3	.9
All unions	4.3	1.8

Source: Based on Mitchell and Dean, *Abstract of British Historical Statistics*, Labour Force Table 3.

Industrial Contrasts

Table 7.3: Economic Fluctuations as Indicated by the Course of
Unemployment in Different Industries, 1923-39

Industry	Average (%)	Standard Deviation (%)
Coalmining	19.6	9.3
Brick, Tile, Pipe, etc. Manufacture	12.1	4.5
Pottery, Earthenware, etc.	23.0	7.9
Chemicals	10.2	3.6
Pig Iron	22.8	11.6
Steel Melting & Iron Puddling, & Iron & Steel Rolling & Forging	26.3	10.9
General Engineering: Engineers' Iron & Steel Founding	15.1	7.3
Electrical Engineering	7.6	4.2
Construction & Repair of Motors, Cycles & Aircraft	10.1	5.0
Shipbuilding & Repairing	36.8	13.5
Electrical Cable, Apparatus, Lamp, etc. Manufacture	9.0	3.4
Cotton Textiles	20.7	8.8
Wool Textiles	16.0	6.6
Hosiery Manufacture	10.5	3.6
Tailoring	13.0	3.4
Dressmaking & Millinery	8.3	1.8
Boot, Shoes, etc. Manufacture	14.5	4.0
Bread, Biscuits, Cakes, etc. Manufacture	14.5	4.0
Drink Industry	8.8	2.7
Sawmilling & Machined Woodcutting	13.1	4.0
Furniture Manufacture & Bookbinding	7.1	2.1
Building	17.3	5.9
Gas, Water & Electricity Supply	8.0	1.9
Railway Service	9.1	3.5
Tramway and Omnibus Service	4.0	1.1
Other Road Transport	15.7	3.7
Docks, Harbours, Canals, etc. Service	29.6	4.0
Distributive Trades	8.7	2.5
National Government Service	10.3	2.7
Total	14.3	4.1

earthenware manufacture. Not only did these industries have high average rates of unemployment, but large fluctuations as well. Dockers, on the other hand, experienced extremely high levels but little fluctuation. Engineering and vehicles by no means escaped the impact of the slump, but they were spared its worst effects. The industries with relatively full employment (if one can use that term to describe rates of 10 per cent unemployed) usually also experienced less fluctuation, and these were generally the least likely to experience strikes.

Employment fluctuations have been much less severe since 1948. Indeed, between 1948 and 1968 the average unemployment rate was a mere 1.5 per cent; even lower in manufacturing.[15] Unemployment has remained an annoyance to construction workers, and has affected some more marginal trades as well, but overall it has not been fluctuations in employment that have bothered workers since 1945. Much more serious have been the fluctuations in earnings associated with short-time working or the loss of overtime. For example, the industry most infamous for its strike propensity in recent years has been motor vehicles, which is extremely dependent upon export demand, highly vulnerable to market vicissitudes, and subject to marked instabilities in earnings.[16]

While the form which insecurity has taken has altered over the years, there is nonetheless a constant association between the lack of stability so obviously a feature of capitalist economies and the propensity of workers to strike. It may be a slight exaggeration to say, as one writer has, that 'In the final analysis it has been the insecurity of employment that has been the major focus of the workman's discontent in the market economy ..., rather than changes in his absolute or relative material condition,' but it is surely a factor of some importance.[17]

Piece-work

A high proportion of workers on some form of payment-by-results system also seems general among the most strike-prone industries. Between 1938 and 1961, the proportion of all workers paid by results increased from a quarter to a third. Table 7.4 gives breakdowns by industry for 1938 and 1961 which reveal the correspondence between the tendency toward piece-work and the propensity to strike. In 1938, textiles and engineering had the highest percentage of piece-workers, while many of the least strike-prone industries, like paper, printing and publishing, and food, drink and tobacco, had very few workers on such systems. In 1961, the metal, engineering and shipbuilding group — especially metal manufacture, shipbuilding and marine engineering and vehicles — had the highest proportions working on piece-rates, and were among the most strike-prone. The correlation between strike-proneness and payment-by-result systems has been quite close at all levels. In 1938, for example, leather and clothing, bricks, pottery, glass and cement, and miscellaneous manufacturing industries had modest proportions of workers on piece-work and comparably modest strike rates. By 1961, almost all manufacturing industries saw increases in the percentage of workers paid by the piece, and their strike propensities had increased correspondingly.

Systematic data on piece-work are not readily available for other industries, like coalmining and dockwork, about which we should very much like to know. There is, however, some recent data that can be projected backwards without great distortion. The Devlin Committee reported in 1966 that 70 per cent of dockwork was 'paid by the piece'. A similar situation prevailed in mining, where 'before the coal industry's national powerloading agreement of 1966 almost all faceworkers were on some form of payment by results'.[18] Since 1966, both industries have rationalised their pay structures and eliminated most piece-work, but the situation in 1966 was probably little different from that which

Table 7.4: Percentage of Workers on Payment-by-Result Systems — Selected Industries, 1938-61

Industry	% in 1938	% in 1961
Food, Drink and Tobacco	14	20
Brick, Pottery, Glass & Cement	35	40
Chemical & Allied Industries	9	21
Metal, Engineering & Shipbuilding:	41	
Metal manufacturing		59
Engineering & electrical goods		47
Shipbuilding & marine engineering		65
Vehicles		52
Other metal goods		41
Textiles	45	51
Clothing	35	47
Leather	27	33
Woodworking	15	26
Paper, printing & publishing	12	19
Other manufacturing industries	31	47
Construction	1	7
Public Administration & Utilities	1	2

Source: R.B. Ainsworth, 'Earnings and Working Hours of Manual Wage-Earners in the United Kingdom in October 1938', *Journal of the Royal Statistical Society,* Series A, CXII, Part (1949), p. 44; and *British Labour Statistics. Historical Abstract, 1886-1968* (London, 1971), Table 80.

prevailed at the turn of the century. In coalmining, piece-rates became issues of contention when geological conditions made work difficult after the turn of the century; hence the broad-based demands for minimum wages or for allowances for 'abnormal places'.[19] On the docks, it was common practice for a long time to negotiate a new rate for every task.

So, a high proportion of workers on piece-work of some sort seems to characterise the major strike-prone industries. There seem to be only two exceptions to this rule — one pertains to workers in transport (excluding dockers), whose relatively high strike rates have not been matched by a large percentage of workers paid by results; the other to labour in the textile industry. Many workers in textiles have been paid by the piece since the nineteenth century, and continue to be today, but they have not maintained the capacity or propensity to strike. Still, these exceptions are minor, and do not weaken the general link between piece-work and strikes.

Economic Importance

The most basic trait common to the more conflict-prone industries — and the one from which the other similarities may indeed arise — is the central role that each has played within the entire market economy. If we can bypass for present purposes the complicated and not very fruitful debates surrounding the definition of 'leading sectors', and use instead a rather common-sense notion of importance, it is clear that each of the most strike-prone industries has occupied a pivotal place in Britain's economic history. Before 1914, British coal, textiles and engineering produced for an enormous world market and each employed over a million workers and supported countless more indirectly. In the same years, the transport industry grew enormously, its labour force increasing by approximately 43 per cent between 1891 and 1911.[20] Between the wars, these industries remained the largest employers despite the slump. Since the Second World War, the situation has changed somewhat. New engineering industries have replaced the old, textiles has suffered a slow death, and since the mid-1950s coal has declined precipitously. Concomitant with the decline of these older industries has been the growth, somewhat later than the rise of the new engineering industries, of the service sector. Education, health services, and various clerical occupations have expanded at an enormous rate, fast enough to absorb much of the labour made redundant by the run-down of textiles and coal.[21]

Also noteworthy since the Second World War has been the enhanced role of the dockers in the economy. Of course, the importance of imports and exports has always made water transport workers crucial to Britain's economy, but this dependence has been highlighted by the prominence which almost all government programmes and proposals for economic growth have given to exports. Export-led growth has been a chimera chased equally and with a comparable lack of success by Labour and Conservative governments. The problem of exports and the particular difficulties in meeting orders on time have focused attention on the docks. This concentration has been increased further by the (verbal) commitment of governments to abolish the evils of casualism.

The rise and fall of the leading sectors of growth since 1890 bears an almost uncanny resemblance to the historical patterns of strike-proneness. The only exception is a partial one — the rise of the service sector has not produced uniformly higher strike rates for its component industries. Still, the recent upsurge in white-collar unions and strikes suggests that the workers most likely to strike are consistently found in large, strategically important or growing sections of the economy, where the problems of successive stages of capitalist development set in motion the processes that ultimately produce strike waves. The mechanism seems to be related to the peculiar structure and orientation of the British economy. The dependence on foreign trade has made Britain's major industries extremely susceptible to cyclical fluctuations and to pressures stemming from foreign price competition. Insecurity of earnings and jobs in strike-prone industries and the prevalence of payments-by-results are both probably reflections of this boom-bust pattern. Piece-work is adopted to encourage workers to respond to rapid expansions of demand; and fluctuating earnings are the result of the succession of these expansions by equally severe contractions.[22]

To put it simply, economic growth based on foreign trade is precarious. It tends to make employers very sensitive to problems of cost, and quick to attempt to reduce wages or speed up production through whatever means are at hand. It seems, therefore, that the character of a particular period of economic development becomes apparent to employers in major industries sooner than to other employers, and their responses to it are experienced that much more quickly by the industry's workers. In particular, to remain competitive export industries must adopt the latest available technology or extract the most from the present level. Such an imperative produces technological innovation, disruptive changes in work routines, and other pressures for production. This exposed position guarantees that those 'qualitatively different phases of economic evolution' which lie behind the changes in consciousness associated with strike waves, are felt more keenly, decisively, and earlier in the major industries facing international competition than in smaller industries producing primarily for home consumption.

Overall, it seems that the structural characteristics most important in discriminating between the workers with the greatest strike propensity and all the rest — unionisation, susceptibility to fluctuations, the extent of payment-by-results systems, etc. — are really functions of their role within the economy. Thus, we can restate the analysis in terms of the general argument of this book: the most strike-prone industries are those where, because of their strategic location in the nation's economic life, the problems and patterns of change accompanying the succession of one trend period by another impact themselves most quickly and most sharply. Strike propensity tends therefore to be associated with the dynamism of particular industries and their openness to change. By this logic our hypothesis concerning the essentially economic roots of strike waves can be extended so as to explain the general experience of Britain's major industries. The patterns prevailing in other sectors, on the other hand, may well diverge by virtue of the fact that they are less integrated into the capitalist market and so escape many of its vicissitudes; and likewise, the strike rates of such industries should come to approximate the standard among heavy industry as they are gradually subjected to the exigencies of the market.

The set of characteristics common to the most strike-prone of industries may be taken as a norm against which to measure other industries and, assuming we have settled upon the right constellation of features, to assess their potential for striking. Indeed, it is possible to consider the typical strike-prone worker as resting near one pole on the continuum that runs from those in major industries fully integrated into the market, feeling its every pulsation and reacting with a high propensity to strike, to those in jobs quite immune to the logic of capitalism and its market mechanism.

When workers from various industries are located at the appropriate spots along this continuum using the data presented earlier, they in fact cluster in much the same way as when they were grouped according to strike-proneness. The moderately strike-prone industries — building, clothing, brick and pottery making, woodworking and the like — clump together near the middle. They are production industries and hence prey to market forces, but small in scale, oriented ordinarily to the home market and relatively old-fashioned in their technologies and styles of management. By contrast, the least strike-prone group, made up of printers, workers in the food, drink and tobacco industries, public service and other white-collar employees, tend to be in the service sector, the luxury trades or industries where demand is inelastic, and hence protected from the vagaries of the market. They collect quite near the opposite pole, in terms of integration into the market, from the most strike-prone industries.

In sum, the strike experience of British workers falls into one of three categories. The most strike-prone are those in major industries whose complete domination by the market has made them specially sensitive to the new situations caused by the qualitative transformations of the economy. The industries with moderate propensities to strike have also been heavily involved in the market but, because they are less massive and depend more upon domestic demand, not so easily or rapidly affected by change. The least strike-prone industries are those whose workers do not feel the bite of insecurity and the pressure for productivity that has been the basic fate of the working class under industrial capitalism.

As a final exercise, we shall use this argument to explain the four cases whose strike experiences have (temporarily but noticeably) diverged from the three basic patterns outlined here — the miners, the dockers, the textile operatives and white-collar workers. This should allow us to illustrate once more the general utility of our basic analysis linking historical variation in strikes to the (differential) impact of phases of economic development. It should, at the same time, suggest some of the ways that sociological factors, like community structure, may interact with these economic forces.

Three of the exceptional cases occur within the most strike-prone class of industries: the abnormally high incidence of disputes among dockers since about 1945 and of miners from the 1920s to the mid-1950s, and the 'withering away' of strikes in textiles after 1932. Let us begin with the two industries that have deviated in the direction of excessive militancy.

Industrial sociologists have spilled much ink over the strike-proneness of dockers and coalminers. Most often, recourse has been had to some version of the Kerr-Siegel hypothesis about the isolated and inbred nature of dockers' and miners' communities. To many investigators, the communities of dockers and miners fit Kerr and Siegel's description of strike-prone workers very neatly:[23]

> The miners, [and] the longshoremen . . . form isolated masses,

almost a 'race apart'. They live in their own separate communities
. . . . These communities have their own codes, myths, heroes, and
social standards. There are few neutrals to mediate the conflicts
and dilute the mass. All people have their grievances, but what is
important is that all of the members of these groups have the same
grievances.

Testimony abounds concerning the distinctiveness of miners' and
dockers' communities and their peculiar characteristics. G.D.H. Cole,
writing in 1923, located the roots of 'the miners' intense solidarity and
loyalty to their Unions' in their physical and social 'isolation'.[24] He
was echoed in 1928 by T.S. Ashton, who felt that 'coal miners have
always been a class apart, with mentality and aspiration unlike those of
the rest of the working class'. Dockers have been viewed similarly. As
late as 1965 the Devlin Committee attacked their 'exaggerated sense
of solidarity'. According to a recent study, 'The conjunction of a
hostile society, the system of employment and strong kinship bonds
have had the effect of creating a sub-culture in the docks, a world of
clannishness and resentment of authority . . . '[25]

Despite such eloquent testimony, there are several reasons to question
these stereotypes. Most commentators have written of these communities in a timeless, abstract way, as if miners and dockers always
and everywhere live in isolated, tight-knit, and collective communities.[26]
This is highly unlikely on *a priori* grounds, and it conflicts with the
obvious fact that the extreme strike-proneness such communities
allegedly produce has been specific to particular historical periods.
Moreover, what little direct evidence does exist suggests that tightly
knit occupational communities are themselves peculiar to certain times
and places.

Miners, for example, seem to have had considerable difficulty
forming stable communities before 1914, when the industry was growing
rapidly and attracting large members of migrants from all over England.[27]
The whole religious and linguistic character of South Wales changed
between 1850 and 1914 due to the massive influx of English miners
and agricultural labourers.[28] And even before this, the Glamorganshire coalfield had absorbed significant numbers of Irish immigrants.[29]
In other areas, growth was slightly less rapid, but South Yorkshire
received a large number of migrants over the years. In fact, one stereo-
type of miners, as friendly, warm and open to strangers, seems to have
grown up as a specific response to the early fluidity of miners' communities.

The same holds true for the dockers. Between 1890 and 1920, employment in transport increased rapidly, and several factors combined to swell enormously the number of dockers. Most important was the casual nature of the industry and the ease of entry into it. Workers were hired by the day, and the daily demand could fluctuate wildly, not only with the regular industrial rhythm of prosperity and depression, but also with the winds and the weather. No employer knew how many workers he would need on a given day, and because it 'cost the employers nothing to keep a large pool' of workers available, many more men were encouraged to attend the daily calls than were ever employed. In January 1912, for instance, an average of 27,200 showed up each day, although the maximum hired on any given day was 19,861, and the average was approximately 15,000.[30] In addition to this chronic underemployment, there was the regular and predictable influx of non-dockers into dockwork during slack seasons for other trades. And this influx became still larger during periods of mass unemployment, when out-of-work builders, engineers, and every other sort of worker enlarged the available work-force on the docks.

The result was a fierce and selfish scramble for work. Ben Tillett, the dockers' melodramatic spokesman, remembered how hiring was done in the 1890s:

> In a building that would hold very few in comfort, men were packed tightly into suffocation, like the black hole of Calcutta, and those struggling men fought desperately and tigerishly, elbowing each other, punching each other, using their last remnants of strength to get work for an hour or half hour for a few pence . . . Coats, flesh, even ears were torn off. Men were crushed to death in the struggle. The strong literally threw themselves over the heads of their fellows and battled with the milling crowds to get near the rails of the cage, which held them like rats − human rats who saw food in the ticket.[31]

Tillett undoubtedly exaggerated. Nevertheless, it is hard to imagine how such a mobile and individualistically-organised workforce could become known as a tight, solid occupational group. As one Manchester docker explained in 1951, 'People would not say that dockers are solid if they saw us in the pen squabbling like a lot of monkeys to do ourselves a bit of good.' Another put it equally bluntly: 'Dockers are not really solid − it's each man for himself and the devil take the hindmost.' The authors of this study were so struck by the ferocious fighting over work as to argue that solidarity served a 'compensatory' function for dockers' psyches, 'help[ing] them to get rid of feelings of guilt aroused by the often selfish struggle in the call-stand'.[32]

Nevertheless, the picture of the dockers and miners as solid, closely-knit living and working groups is too specific and has been painted in with too many strokes of too many brushes to be dismissed altogether. Rather, it should be seen as applicable to a particular moment in history, dating since the 1940s for the dockers, and existing between approximately 1920 and 1960 among the miners. No doubt some elements of the picture apply earlier and some later, but the classic dockers' and miners' communities, producing large numbers of strikes, have probably been limited to these years in England.

Two historical factors seem to have caused miners and dockers to congeal in tight communities with militant attitudes — one economic, the other social. The oppressive conditions and wages on the docks and in the mines produced numerous bitter conflicts between 1890 and 1926. These struggles served to create traditions of militancy, antagonism and solidarity within each industry. At the same time, or shortly after, both industries' workforces began to stabilise. Migration to coal-mining areas ceased between the two world wars, and mining communities became more inbred and immobile. The common experience of unemployment, which struck whole communities all at once, served further to unite miners in a collective struggle to survive.

The hard-fought dock strikes of 1889 and 1911-12 are part of the lore of the labour movement. Less well-known is the slow, but steady, progress made by Bevin and other dockers' leaders in restricting the size of the dock labour-force after 1918. 'Decasualisation' was not ultimately achieved until September 1967, but relatively full employment had prevailed since 1940, and the National Dock Labour Scheme of 1947 marked a major victory in securing stable employment for dockers. It was no accident that the flare-up in the dockers' strike-propensity occurred just as the Scheme was introduced in the late 1940s.

The postwar dock strikes represented a critical turning point. Though the stoppages shocked and angered public opinion, more rational analysts knew that the 'causes of the recent strikes derive from the impact of the past on the present'. With justice, a union leader from Hull described a strike there as 'the final bursting of the canker present in every great port during the past fifty years'.[33] The role of a tradition of militancy is obvious, but what actually enabled this tradition to be maintained, and expressed in strikes, was the gradual tightening of the dockers' community. By the late forties, the dockers were much older than most workers.[34] In 1951, over 50 per cent of the dock labour force was aged 45 or above.[35] They had lived through many past battles. In an important sense, then, the strike-proneness of the post-war period stemmed from the success with which union organisers fought to instill patterns of solidarity in the men and to combat the problems of underemployment and casualism.

As with dockers, the history of mining is largely the story of the 'emergence of a feeling of community out of a common experience of hardship'.[36] But in mining the tight communities emerged earlier, possibly by 1914, certainly by the 1920s. Even during the worst periods of unemployment, miners maintained the collective strength and solidarity with which to wage frequent and successful strikes. When unemployment began to recede after 1938, aided no doubt by growing outmigration of sons and daughters to the centres of the new industries, a veritable explosion of strikes occurred. In mining and on the docks, therefore, the extremely high propensity to strike was due to the interaction between traditions of militancy and the gradual development of a social structure peculiarly adapted to preserving and extending those traditions. Theoretically, the history of strikes in these two industries shows how sociological, specifically demographic, abnormalities can exaggerate and intensify a propensity to strike generated in the first instance by exposure to the market and the difficulties that entails.

The drop in strike propensity among textile workers reveals precisely the opposite tendency, with social structures undermining a tradition of conflict. Textiles, too, had its share of sharp struggles in the prewar and interwar years, and unemployment in Lancashire was a deeply embittering experience. But these did not become embodied in a shared culture of militancy. During the 1930s, for example, observers noticed how the individualistic and conservative culture of Lancashire made unemployment there a personally isolating experience. The Pilgrim Trust's survey of the unemployed in Blackburn found that many 'keep themselves apart from any social institution rather because the tradition of independence which they have inherited causes them to do so — from feelings of "respectability" or whatever we choose to call it.'[37] The precise reasons for this tradition are unclear, but it seems to have deep roots. Anderson found that as far back as the mid-nineteenth century cotton operatives were not very sociable, and that neighbourhood and community played relatively minor roles in their lives. Even when 'critical life situations' did force individuals to turn to family and kin for help, the resulting 'relationships tended to have strong short-run instrumental overtones of a calculative kind'.[38]

Personal independence was probably encouraged in the Victorian era by the employment structure of textiles. There was a large demand for female and child employment, and 'once they had found a job, men and women could be more or less independent of kin at an early age'.[39] Child labour was effectively restricted from about 1850, but the percentage of female labour in textiles increased steadily until 1880, and took yet another leap during the First World War.[40] Some writers have argued that a high percentage of women in an industry in and of itself acts to deter strikes, but there is no statistical evidence that increases in the proportion of women in textiles brought decreases in strike propensity. Nor has there been any correlation between the percentage of women in various industries and those industries' strike propensities.[41] On the other hand, the employment of a large percentage of the female population of a particular community may well have encouraged a culture of independence and individualism that hindered the preservation of a culture of militancy.

The predominance of women in textiles also produced an unusual age structure among the workforce that probably was inimical to the creation of militant traditions. Such traditions are not easily built; bonds of trust and solidarity must knit together gradually, over a relatively extended period of time. But the age structure of female textile operatives suggests that they are an unusually structured force, with a huge gap among women of childbearing age. Figure 7.4 depicts the age distribution of female textile workers graphically. The enormous bulge at the younger end, the decline between ages 20 and 34, and the final peak at ages 35-44 suggests that young women have flocked into the mills at a tender age, left to marry and bear children, and returned some time after their mid-thirties. To sustain social ties and habits of mutual support in such a situation is obviously a difficult task.

It seems likely that the bitterness which the interwar years undoubtedly produced among textile workers simply could not be translated into increased strike rates due to the social structure of the industry. If we add to this historic weakness the gradual decline of the industry after 1955 and the consequent resignation and lowered expectations of its workers, their inability to mount a sustained offensive like that of the dockers or the miners becomes painfully comprehensible. The comparison with miners is particularly instructive. Both groups lived in predominantly one-industry towns, suffered acutely in the depression, and fought intense strikes in the same years. But while the miners remained a factor to be reckoned with throughout the reorganisation and run-down of the postwar years, textile workers have watched their industry die passively.

Figure 7.4: Age Structure of Female Textile Operatives, England and Wales, 1951

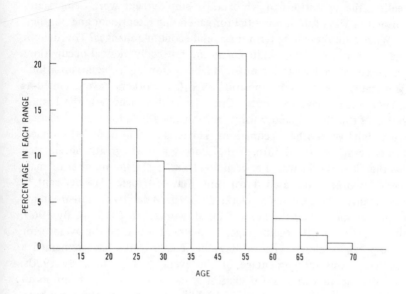

One final exception remains to be discussed — the jump in strike-proneness among white collar workers since the mid-1960s. Before then, most white-collar workers would fit into the least strike-prone category. Between 1968 and 1972, however, employees in professional and scientific services, public administration and defence achieved striker rates over ten times those of 1963-8. A comparable jump in union membership occurred simultaneously; again, unionisation and strikes interact. The suddenness and size of these twin explosions suggests that the specific economic conjuncture merely provided the spark to ignite what was already an extremely flammable situation. It would seem, then, that any explanation of the phenomena should relate long-term changes in the conditions of white-collar employment to the specific circumstances of 1968-74.

In fact, a substantial literature on the 'blackcoated worker' existed prior to 1968, an obvious recognition of his growing importance in the occupational structure of modern British society. Unfortunately, most investigators seem to have been misled by the slowness with which white-collar workers took to unionism into underestimating the significance of long-run, secular changes in pushing them in that direction, and concluding that rather special and unique circumstances had to conjoin to produce white-collar unionisation and militancy.[42] In reality, the conditions of white-collar employment were being transformed in ways full of potential for generating resentment and conflict.

What were these long-term social and economic changes? Throughout the twentieth century, white-collar and especially clerical occupations have experienced what some would label a growing 'proletarianisation'. The status and economic position of office workers have declined as their numbers have expanded. Critical to this process was the feminisation of the clerical labour force, accompanied by a lowering of clerical wages relative to other occupations. The replacement of male by female clerks began about the turn of the century and was greatly accelerated by the First World War. Between 1911 and 1921 the number of male clerical workers increased 4 per cent, that of females 215 per cent.[43] Predictably, the earnings of clerks declined. Male clerks earned almost a quarter more than the average for all workers in 1913-14. By 1960, they were even with the average, 18 per cent less than the average for male workers alone. The earnings of female clerks have remained a relatively constant percentage of the average since the early 1920s. The decline in earnings for clerical workers as a whole, from about 100 per cent of the average in 1913-14 to 75 per cent in 1960, has been therefore primarily a reflection of the increasing percentage of female clerical labour.[44]

This gradual erosion of the clerical workers' position formed the background to the outburst of white-collar unionism and strikes, but the immediate precipitant appears to have been the inflation and 'pay explosion' of the late 1960s. The exact mixture of influences in these years is difficult to disentangle, and assigning primacy to one factor almost impossible. Inflation was probably the major stimulus, but on top of this was the confrontation between organised labour and the Labour Government over the latter's incomes policy and its attempts to suppress unofficial strikes. This confrontation was clearly lost by the government and the incidents apparently convinced many hitherto unorganised groups to form or join unions.[45] These factors combined in some way to produce the great increase in strike propensity among clerical and other white-collar workers.

The fate of clerical labour is not surprising; and its evolution offers yet another confirmation of our basic argument. Beginning as a part of the labour force more or less removed from the impact of market forces, they have become more central to the workings of the economic system and more subject to its destabilising and disconcerting conjunctural rhythms. The distinct phases of economic development that drove workers in the hard-core production industries to develop a separate social consciousness and to elaborate various strategies of resistance by the problems they inflicted, are now affecting the conditions of white-collar work, with obvious and predictable consequences.

Let us recapitulate the argument on inter-industry differences. Most British industries can be classified into groups of high, medium, and low strike propensity, with a few exceptions for certain periods of time. Overall, the most strike-prone are the large, strategically important industries most thoroughly entangled in the ups and downs, the pressures and tensions, of the market. They feel most quickly and intensely the economic and technological changes that accompany each distinct phase of economic evolution and react accordingly, with innovative organising efforts and waves of strikes. The moderately strike-prone industries are also jostled about by the market, but not so violently, and they tend to be smaller and more artisanal in their technique and general modes of operation. The industries that strike least are above all else stable, sheltered from uncertainties of employment and from pressure at the point of production. At the core of this explanation is the market, and its effects upon the daily life of the various groups of workers.

The four exceptions we investigated confirmed the broad outlines of this analysis, while adding a few qualifications. The extreme strike propensities of miners and dockers were traced to the way unu—ally tight communities or work groups nurtured and inflamed traditions of militancy stemming in the first instance from the economic forces impinging upon the industry. Textile workers, on the other hand, lived and worked in communities that allowed grievances to die and made resistance harder and thus more rare. And, finally, we found the recent burst of activity among white-collar workers to be a product of the long-term growth of the service sector and the transformation of the clerical labour force, plus the impact of inflation — a sign that these workers can no longer avoid or escape the dictates and forces of the market.

It would be foolish to claim that this brief review of the problem of inter-industry differences has provided all the answers, or that the modest hypothesis proposed here has been proven definitively. Much more evidence remains to be gathered and evaluated, some of which may well serve to heighten our sensitivity to the subtle differences between the industries whose similarities we have been stressing. The danger, however, is that in fixing upon differences, one can easily miss the great social and economic movements that have transformed so much of industry and homogenised so much of daily life for the working population in modern society. So, is we have slightly overemphasised those things that have cut across the varieties of industrial experience, in order to demonstrate the impact of the evolution of the market economy upon strikes, it is because the normal focus on the distinctiveness of miners or dockers or pottery workers has so often led to a neglect of the broader changes that have made and remade the landscape of British society.

Notes

1. For the economic approach, see H.A. Clegg, *The System of Industrial Relations in Great Britain* (Oxford, 1970); for the sociological paradigm, see C. Kerr and A. Siegel, 'The Inter-Industry Propensity to Strike', in A. Kornhauser, R. Dubin and A. Ross (eds.), *Industrial Conflict* (New York, 1954), pp. 189-212; and the authors cited in Ch. 2, above.

2. S. Meacham, *A Life Apart. The English Working Class, 1890-1914* (London, 1977), pp. 30-59.

3. J.H. Goldthorpe, D. Lockwood, F. Bechhofer, and J. Platt, *The Affluent Worker*, 3 vols. (Cambridge, 1968-9); E. Bott, *Family and Social Network* (London, 1971); C. Lambert and D. Weir (eds.), *Cities in Modern Britain* (London, 1975), pp. 224-99; and M. Young and P. Willmott, *The Symmetrical Family* (London, 1973).

4. H.A. Turner, G. Clack and G. Roberts, *Labour Relations in the Motor Industry* (London, 1967).

5. The distinctiveness of the pattern that emerged by the late 1960s calls seriously into question J.C. Shorey's pioneering multivariate analysis of strike propensity. In focusing on the early and mid-1960s, he enshrined a particularly transitional phase of inter-industry differentials as a basic structural aspect of industrial relations. See Shorey, 'A Quantitative Analysis of Strike Activity in the United Kingdom' (Ph.D. dissertation, LSE, 1974); and 'An Inter-Industry Analysis of Strike Propensity', *Economica*, XLIII (1976).

6. G.S. Bain and R. Price, 'Union Growth and Employment Trends in the United Kingdom, 1964-70', *British Journal of Industrial Relations*, X (1972), p.371; Price and Bain, 'Union Growth Revisited: 1948-74 in Perspective', *BJIR*, XIV (1976), pp. 340-55; and K. Hawkins, *British Industrial Relations, 1945-75* (London, 1976), p. 138.

7. In February 1976 the *Department of Employment Gazette* carried an article on 'The Incidence of Industrial Stoppage in the United Kingdom', which gave strike propensities for industries broken down into very small groups for the years 1966-73. Their calculations are based on data not available in published form, so it is not possible to compare precisely their calculations with ours. However, they generally confirm what we have found and presented in this chapter.

8. Unfortunately, the data with which Shorey performed his elaborate analysis are not available for periods before the Second World War, so we shall follow a procedure more akin to that of Clegg, *System of Industrial Relations*.

9. Cf. M. Fiaz, 'Inter-Industry Propensity to Strike in France, 1891-1930', (Ph.D. dissertation, University of Toronto, 1973), for a similar argument with regard to the French experience.

regard to the French experience.

10. For union membership as of 1893, see the *Second Abstract of Labour Statistics* (London, 1895), pp. 10-11; for 1913, see the *Seventeenth Abstract of Labour Statistics* (London, 1915), p. 201.

11. See G.D.H. and M.I. Cole, *The Condition of Britain* (London, 1937), pp. 392-3. It must be remembered that these statistics relate only to those in TUC-affiliated unions. Total union density was thus somewhat higher in certain industries.

12. Price and Bain, 'Union Growth Revisited', pp. 340-3.

13. For a more sceptical view, however, see K. Armstrong, D. Bowers, and B. Burkitt, 'The Measurement of Trade Union Bargaining Power', *British Journal of Industrial Relations*, XV (1977), pp. 91-100.

14. See J. Cronin, 'Strikes in Britain, 1888-1974' (Ph.D. dissertation, Brandeis University, 1977), Figure 7.1, for data on the output of coal and on raw cotton consumption, which reveal the tremendous fluctuations to which coal and textiles were subject prior to 1914. More generally, see W.H. Beveridge, *Unemployment: A Problem of Industry* (London, 1909).

15. Cronin, 'Strikes in Britain', Table 7.8.

16. Turner, Clack, and Roberts, *Labour Relations*, p. 128. On the fear of insecurity more generally and its effects on attitudes and consciousness, see, among others, D. Wedderburn and R. Crompton, *Workers' Attitudes and Technology* (Cambridge, 1972); S. Wyatt and R. Marriot, *A Study of Attitudes to Factory Work* (London, 1956); H. Beynon and R.M. Blackburn, *Perceptions of Work* (Cambridge, 1972); and R. Martin and R.H. Fryer, *Redundancy and Paternalistic Capitalism* (London, 1973).

17. M.A. Bienefield, *Working Hours in British Industry* (London, 1972), p. 226. Cf. also J. Foster, *Class Struggle and the Industrial Revolution* (London, 1974), for an argument which places the cyclical nature of the early Victorian cotton industry at the core of an explanation of emerging class consciousness.

18. D.F. Wilson, *Dockers: The Impact of Industrial Change* (London, 1972), p. 34; Clegg, 'Some Consequences of the General Strike', p. 320; and J.W.F. Rowe, *Wages in the Coal Industry* (London, 1923).

19. See D.I. Gidwell, 'Philosophy and Geology in Conflict. The Evolution of the Wages Structure in the South Wales Coalfield, 1926-1974', *Llafur*, I (Summer, 1975), pp. 44-57; and R. Page Arnot, *The Miners: Years of Struggle* (London, 1953), pp. 57-86.

20. *British Labour Statistics. Historical Abstract 1886-1968* (London, 1971), Table 102, 'Analyses of the Occupied Population, 1841-1921'.

21. The role of the service sector has of course been an important aspect of economic growth throughout this century, but it has accelerated significantly since the Second World War, and especially since the mid-1960s. On the relatively slow growth of the output of the service sector, see J.A. Dowie, 'Growth in the Inter-War Period: Some More Arithmetic', *Economic History Review*, XXI (1968), Table 1. On the growth of unemployment in the industries which make up the service sector, see Bain and Price, 'Union Growth and Employment Trends', Table 9, 'Changing Industrial Distribution of Employment in the United Kingdom, 1948-1970', p. 377.

22. There is also a tendency for the major, strike-prone industries to be organised in more concentrated fashion with larger production units. For a review of the data on plant size by industry, see Cronin, 'Strikes in Britain', Table 7.9. Impressive documentation for the connection of plant size and strike propensity is provided in a recent study by the Department of Employment. See 'The Incidence of Industrial Stoppages in the United Kingdom', *Department of Employment Gazette* (Feb. 1976), p. 116. According to the Department's calculations, plants employing 11-24 persons average 8 strikes per 100,000 employees, those

with 25-99 average 19.2 per 100,000, while plants employing between 500 and a thousand workers experience almost 30 stoppages per 100,000. Cf. also G.K. Ingham, *Size of Industrial Organisation and Worker Behaviour* (Cambridge, 1970). Still, the link is not as clear and unambiguous as might be expected, due primarily to the fact that some of the industries with large plant sizes, like chemicals, or with high concentrations of workers per unit, like certain public utilities, have for various reasons not exhibited excessive strike-proneness.

23. Kerr and Siegel, 'The Inter-Industry Propensity to Strike', pp. 191-2. It should be pointed out, however, that an interesting and reasonable argument can be made about the negative effects which such isolation can have upon strike propensity by limiting expectations and horizons. Cf. Ian Rutledge, 'Changes in the Mode of Production and the Growth of "Mass Militancy" in the British Mining Industry, 1954-1974', *Science and Society*, XLI (1977-8), pp. 410-29. A more statistical approach to the topic is L. Lynch, 'Strike Frequency in British Coal Mining, 1950-74', *British Journal of Industrial Relations*, XVI (1978), pp. 95-8.

24. G.D.H. Cole, *Labour in the Coal-Mining Industry* (Oxford, 1923), p. 7.

25. T.S. Ashton, 'The Coal-Miners of the Eighteenth Century', *Economic History* (Jan. 1928), p. 307, cited in K.G.J.C. Knowles, *Strikes* (New York, 1952), p. 164. An interesting, if at times naive, discussion of miners and their communities can be found in the Report of the Commission of Enquiry into Industrial Unrest, Report of the Commissioners for Wales, including Monmouthshire, *Parliamentary Papers*, 1917-18, XV (Cmd. 8668) esp. pp. 11-17. On the dockers, see Wilson, *Dockers* (London, 1972), pp. 52-4.

26. An extreme example of this stereotyped docker, abstracted from both time and place, can be found in Raymond C. Miller, 'The Dockworker Subculture and Some Problems in Cross-Cultural and Cross-time Generalizations', *Comparative Studies in Society and History*, XI (1969), pp. 302-14 – a singularly mistitled article. Peter Stearns applies an equally stereotyped view of the difference between occupational groups in his article, 'National Character and European Labor History', *Journal of Social History*, IV (1970), pp. 95-124.

27. Using Table 102 in *British Labour Statistics. Historical Abstract*, it can be shown that in the thirty years from 1881 to 1911 the number of persons working in the mines and quarries of Great Britain increased from 612,000 to 1,210,000 or 98 per cent. On the ease with which labour entered the mines, and the difficulty this caused for organisation, see C. Storm-Clark, 'The Miners, 1870-1970: A Test Case for Oral History', *Victorian Studies*, XV (1971), pp. 63-6; and W.H. Chaloner, 'British Miners and the Coal Industry between the Wars', *History Today*, XIV (1964), p. 419.

28. K.O. Morgan, 'The New Liberalism and the Challenge of Labour: The Welsh Experience, 1885-1929', *Welsh History Review*, VI (1973), p. 290.

29. Brinley Thomas, 'The Migration of Labour into the Glamorganshire Coalfield, 1861-1911', *Economica*, X (1930), pp. 275-94.

30. Wilson, *Dockers*, p. 68.

31. B. Tillett, *Memories and Reflections* (London, 1931), p. 76.

32. Liverpool University, Dept. of Social Science, *The Dockworker: an Analysis of Conditions and Industrial Relations in the Port of Manchester, 1950-51* (Liverpool, 1956), pp. 66-7.

33. K. Knowles, 'The Post-War Dock Strikes', *Political Quarterly*, XXXII (1951), pp. 266-90.

34. Ibid., p. 270.

35. Cronin, 'Strikes in Britain', Table 7.14.

36. C. Storm-Clark, 'The Miners, 1870-1970', p. 60. Thus, the classic descriptions of tightly-knit mining communities all date from the period after the

impact of the interwar depression. See, for example, Eli Ginzburg, *Grass on the Slag Heaps* (New York, 1942); W.H. Scott, E. Mumford, I.C. McGivering, and J.M. Kirby, *Coal and Conflict* (Liverpool, 1963); and N. Dennis, F. Henriques, and C. Slaughter, *Coal Is Our Life*, 2nd ed. (London, 1969).

37. Pilgrim Trust, *Men Without Work* (Cambridge, 1938), p. 320. By contrast, the report noted the 'strong community spirit' (68) with which the depression was met in South Wales.

38. M. Anderson, *Family Structure in Nineteenth Century Lancashire* (Cambridge, 1971), p. 171.

39. Ibid., p. 171, also pp. 124-32.

40. In 1841, women made up 40.5 per cent of the labour force in textiles; by 1881, it had climbed to 57.4 per cent. It remained at about this level until the First World War caused another major increase. Thus, from 1911 to 1921, the proportion of women in textiles rose from 57.7 per cent to 66.9 per cent. See Cronin, 'Strikes in Britain', Table 7.15.

41. See Cronin, 'Strikes in Britain', Table 7.16. This contradicts John Shorey's argument about the depressing effects of a high percentage of women in the workforce upon strike propensity. See Shorey, 'A Quantitative Analysis of Strike Activity in the United Kingdom' (Ph.D. dissertation, LSE, 1974), p. 173ff.

42. G.S. Bain, *The Growth of White Collar Unionism* (Oxford, 1970), esp. p. 188.

43. G. Routh, *Occupation and Pay in Great Britain, 1906-1960* (Cambridge 1965), p. 25.

44. Calculated from Tables 103 and 105 in *British Labour Statistics. Historical Abstract*.

45. R. Price and G.S. Bain, 'Union Growth Revisited: 1948-1974 in Perspective', *British Journal of Industrial Relations*, XIV (1976), pp. 339-55.

8 CONCLUSION

From 1888 to 1975, there were more than 175,000 strikes in Britain, directly involving at least 52 million workers. Well over three-quarters of a million working days have been 'lost' to production or gained for rest and recreation, depending upon how one views it. These astronomical figures have dictated the adoption of a statistical approach, based on various sorts of aggregates, in order to discern the patterns which lie beneath this rich collection of facts. One cannot talk confidently at this level of cause and effect or of definitively demonstrating motivations and desires; one can only describe tendencies and probable relationships. The sense of certitude based on the case study is lost, replaced by statistical significance and reliability, in the hope that by moving beyond the specific and the individual, we can reach something deeper, something whose importance derives from its applicability to more than just a few people or a few instances. There is a risk and a benefit associated with such an approach. The risk is that the human details will be lost or forgotten in the focus on the interplay of social forces. Counterbalancing this, there is the great potential benefit of capturing and depicting patterns and connections in outline form that are simply not visible when the lenses are more narrowly focused. The hope implicit in this study is that by redrawing the contours of the problem from this broad and long-term vantage point, new questions and insights will emerge to inform further, more detailed, research. Our aim has been to write a prologue to the history of strikes, not the definitive narrative.

Because of the nature of the enterprise, the project has contained both methodological and substantive dimensions. Methodologically, we have tried to suggest and demonstrate that the dynamic concerns of the historian can be fruitfully allied with the statistical methods and rigorous modelling techniques of other social scientists. Neither approach is alone sufficient, and in combining history and social science we are transforming each in important ways. The methodological aspect of our argument has been discussed in some detail in earlier chapters and need not be recapitulated here; what does require more discussion are the substantive findings that have emerged from this interdisciplinary effort. After all, methods must in the end produce results.

Perhaps the simplest way to gauge the nature and import of our findings is to contrast them with the current received wisdom in the historiography of British labour.[1] Such a comparison is inevitably hampered by the overwhelming empiricism that dominates the writing of labour's history. Historians of the working class in the United Kingdom seem fascinated by the daily rounds and habits of the quaint craftsman or the lusty day labourer. We know much about the world of the pub and the music hall, but very little about the major turning points in the evolution of labour in society. Unfortunately, the better, more informed labour historians are often the most prone to sticking to local contexts, and thus leave the task of generalising to the less subtle interpreters. While this dilemma argues forcefully for the heuristic value of the current study, it also guarantees that it should be suggestive and tentative rather than definitive.

These caveats aside, a comparison between our findings and the prevalent conception of labour's development reveals striking contrasts. Labour historians have ordinarily stressed the gradual, evolutionary nature of the development of the labour movement and its increasing integration into broader society. The accent is strongly upon continuity and moderation; as one bold generaliser proclaimed, 'There is, in fact, a basic continuity in trade-union history, a gradual evolution, with few if any breaks or watersheds.'[2] This staid view of the labour past was once the characteristic outlook only of conservative chroniclers, while those historians with attitudes sympathetic to labour preferred to dwell upon the moments of conflict and struggle. Of late, however, a more radicalised version of the same position has emerged from more left-wing commentators.

Concretely, Marxist historians of more recent vintage have been concerned with uncovering the roots of reformism, Labourism and the long-term subordination of the working class in the social and political order. Surveying the broad sweep of England's past, they have found a record of half-hearted compromises and unrealised potentials, a general lack of clear and unambiguous class conflict. This historic aversion to confrontation, it has been argued, emerged first in the compromise and then symbiosis of aristocracy and bourgeoisie after 1660, and carried over into the relationship between labour and capital. Britain's 'supine bourgeoisie produced', as a result, 'a subordinate proletariat', which has been 'distinguished by an immovable corporate class consciousness and almost no hegemonic ideology'. Among the workers there has thus persisted 'an extreme disjunction between an intense consciousness of separate identity and a permanent failure to set and impose goals for society as a whole'.[3]

Such a pessimistic perspective has become quite influential in labour historiography, and has actually stimulated some important research into neglected areas of social history – into leisure and its uses, language and class, and class culture in general. In a seminal and creatively researched article, for example, Gareth Stedman Jones has argued that the 'distinct, hermetic culture' of the modern working class has been inimical to a more complete and sophisticated class consciousness, and that its development was a setback and an accommodation rather than an achievement. He claims that 'much of the cluster of "traditional" working-class attitudes described by sociologists and literary critics, dates . . . from the last third of the nineteenth century'. Between 1870 and 1900, the English working class was 'remade'; it evolved 'a dense and inward-looking culture, whose effect was both to emphasize the distance of the working class from the classes above it and to articulate its position within an apparently permanent social hierarchy.' The roots of this transformation can be found, according to Jones, in the decay of old industries and the radical artisan culture they supported, in rising standards of living, smaller family size and a growth of consumerism that led to the creation of a privatised life centred in the home. The result was a defensive, corporative posture affecting the whole working class, including its trade unions. Moreover, 'with the foundation of the Labour Party the now enclosed and defensive world of working class culture had in effect achieved its apotheosis.' Since then, by implication, little has happened to alter the situation, and reformism has maintained its hold over labour.[4]

There is some obvious validity to this argument: the British working class has not established its hegemony over the entire society (however loudly its opponents may decry the 'power of the trade unions'); no major social rupture has occurred since the mid-Victorian era; and, overall, labour has seemed inclined to compromise rather than to fight. Nonetheless, there is implicit in this critique of the incorporation of the workers an extremely high standard of alternative behaviour to which the British are being held up, and it derives not from the realities of British social development but from an abstract revolutionary norm lying entirely outside history.

The incorporation argument has another, more substantial flaw – it cannot explain or even minimally make sense out of the pattern of industrial conflict described in this book. Whether or not the precise explanations for British strike activity offered here are correct, one thing is certain: strikes have come in waves, in big, broad explosions of creative militancy. They occur fitfully and violently, and this uneven path of advance simply does not fit in with the notion of labour history which stresses the defensive, reactive, corporate mentality of labour and its gradual integration into society. We believe firmly that the sporadic and wave-like character of industrial conflict and union growth testifies unequivocally to the dramatic changes that have occurred in various aspects of working-class life and politics. Thus, those analyses that emphasise the elements of persistence, the tenacity of non-revolutionary 'labourist' beliefs, ideological passivity and social inertia, are missing or minimising changes of genuine social and political import. There is no need to further belabour this point. Virtually every piece of evidence presented in this book, from the very first graphs of the incidence of strikes to the statements of workers in the 1960s and 1970s, bears witness to a profoundly discontinuous path of working-class evolution. The whole thrust of this presentation can be summarised by saying that the 'making of the English working class' did not occur, once and for all and definitively, between 1790 and 1832, or even by 1848. Nor was it remade between 1870 and 1900, and cast in a mould which has persisted ever since. On the contrary, the working class is being made, unmade, and remade incessantly. Its social composition, its politics, values, institutions and actions experience frequent and manifold transformations, as new stages of economic and social development undermine the basis of old habits and beliefs. Naturally, some elements persist, but these are often superficial, formal and rhetorical. As historians, we must be particularly sensitive to the new meanings and significances which are constantly inserted into archaic forms and outdated slogans.

The basic point to emerge from this study is that social conflict is not the manifestation of some fixed and undifferentiated quantum of discontent that expresses itself in one form or another at different points in time. Rather, social and industrial conflict are the means used by ordinary working men and women to assert their changing needs and aspirations in the face of trends and problems that even their rulers and employers cannot control. The strike itself therefore changes its form and meaning as society and economy alter; and because the latter have developed so fast and in such diverse ways over the past hundred years, the nature of industrial conflict has been transformed dramatically as well. The only two constants in all this are the basic division of labour that gives rise to conflict, and the persistent function of the strike as the fundamental statement of the humanity and intelligence of the working class.

196 *Conclusion*

Notes

1. This is not intended as a review of the field of labour history and makes no pretensions to comprehensiveness. The most recent survey is W.H. Maehl, ' "Jerusalem Deferred": Recent Writing in the History of the British Labor Movement', *Journal of Modern History*, XLI (1969), pp. 335-67, but it is seriously outdated. More up-to-date lists of titles can be found in the *Bulletin of the Society for the Study of Labour History*.

Besides the approaches to labour history discussed here, three other traditions deserve brief mention. One is embodied in the work of the Webbs. a rich and critical source which bears the ideological marks of its authors. A second is the industrial relations approach, with its focus on institutions and rules and its neglect of the dynamic which led to their elaboration. Last, there is the vast heroic, almost hagiographic, literature produced by the labour movement itself, which requires no particular review.

2. A.E. Musson, *Trade Union and Social History* (London, 1974), pp. 8-9.

3. P. Anderson, 'Origins of the Present Crisis', in P. Anderson and R. Blackburn (eds.), *Towards Socialism* (London, 1965), *passim*. Cf. T. Nairn, 'The Nature of the Labour Party', in Anderson and Blackburn, *Towards Socialism*, pp. 159-217. For a critical perspective, see E.P. Thompson, 'The Peculiarities of the English', in R. Miliband and J. Saville (eds.), *Socialist Register 1965* (New York, 1965), pp. 311-62.

4. Gareth Stedman Jones, 'Working-Class Culture and Working-Class Politics in London, 1870-1900: Notes on the Remaking of a Working Class', *Journal of Social History*, VII (1974), pp. 460-508.

APPENDIX A: A NOTE ON STATISTICAL SOURCES AND METHODS

The basic material out of which this project has been fashioned has been statistics: of strikes and strikers, of prices, wages, employment and unemployment, production and productivity, trade union membership, and so on. For that reason, it might be useful to spend some time describing the nature of the sources from which the data were taken, and the primary techniques used in manipulating them.

The most important data were the totals of strikes and strikers. They were obtained from the Reports on Strikes and Lockouts, published by the Board of Trade and reprinted in the *Parliamentary Papers*, for the years 1888-1913. From then on, they were taken from the annual articles on industrial disputes in the *Labour Gazette*, whose name was changed successively to the *Ministry of Labour Gazette*, the *Ministry of Labour and National Service Gazette*, back to the *Ministry of Labour Gazette*, then to the *Employment and Productivity Gazette*, and, finally, to its present title, the *Department of Employment Gazette* (hereafter referred to as simply the *Gazette*). Also consulted on occasion were various *Abstracts of Labour Statistics*, particularly the Twenty-second, which summarised data for the years 1922-36.

The strengths and weaknesses of British strike statistics have been discussed by K.G.J.C. Knowles, *Strikes: A Study of Industrial Conflict* (New York, 1952), and, more recently, by Michael Silver, 'Recent British Strike Trends: A Factual Analysis', *British Journal of Industrial Relations*, XI (1973), pp. 66-104. However, several problems require comment here. First, in the early years, before 1900, there were still apparently some problems of classification to be worked out. Thus, it often occurred that the summary figures published in the *Abstract of Labour Statistics* differed slightly from the original figures. We have generally tried to utilise the latest revision available, but it proved impossible to do so in every case. Frequently, for example, revised figures would only deal with the totals for all industries or for all causes, in which cases we have had to stick with the original figures in order to obtain industrial or causal breakdowns. Still later revisions, again of aggregate data, for the years before 1914 have been published excluding Southern Ireland. These have not been used here. Our figures include all of Ireland up to 1913; from 1914, only Northern Ireland is included.

There are three main statistical series on strikes available on an annual basis: the number of strikes, of strikers ('workers directly involved'), and of man days lost due to strikes. The latter has not been extensively used in this study, because the issue it is meant to address, the economic losses of strikes, is not of concern here. [On this issue, however, see M. Fisher, *Measurement of Labour Disputes and Their Economic Effects* (Paris, 1793).] These three series are in any year broken down by industrial group and by cause, and for some years by region as well. Information is most complete for the years 1893 to 1913, when, for example, the number of strikes and strikers were given for each industrial group, by cause and result. From 1914 to the mid-1950s, only industrial breakdowns and aggregate classifications by cause are available, but since 1957 the range of data offered has increased again.

A few qualifications must be made regarding the methods of compiling the data. The official report for 1972 explained:

> The statistics compiled by the Department of Employment relate to stoppages of work known to the department which are the result of industrial disputes connected with terms and conditions of employment . . . There is no differentiation between 'strikes' and 'lockouts'. . . . Small stoppages involving fewer than 10 workers, and those lasting less than one day, are excluded from the statistics except where the aggregate number of days lost exceeded 100. (*Department of Employment Gazette* (June, 1973), p. 354.)

Three important points are raised here: the exclusion of political strikes, the confusion of strikes and lockouts, and the decision to ignore very small strikes. The lumping together of strikes and lockouts is not serious, and probably necessary. As Knowles has pointed out, 'the distinction is as difficult and subjective as that between "aggressive" or "defensive" war,' and the practical impossibility of making the distinction necessitates their joint treatment.

The exclusion of political strikes is a more difficult question, if only because it is not done consistently. Despite the Baldwin Government's contention that the General Strike of 1926 was a political act aimed at the constitution, it was counted in that year's figures. In 1974, however, the strike of 330,000 workers on 8 May against the sequestration of AUEW (the engineering union) funds by the National Industrial Relations Court was not counted, but a strike on 5 May of the same year of dockers at Liverpool, Hull, and Bromborough demanding that May Day be declared a public holiday was included in the list of 'Prominent stoppages in 1974'. Still, by all accounts, the number of explicitly political strikes is minimal, and this omission should not seriously bias the data.

It is impossible to say just how many strikes are excluded because they are too small. One study of the motor industry suggests the proportion may be quite large, and the fact that the typical strike since the Second World War has become smaller may mean that a slightly larger percentage is being excluded. But it would be a mistake to make too much of this weakness of the data. A line must be drawn somewhere, and if one wanted to include strikes smaller than what the official statistics report, there would still be the problem of distinguishing small strikes from a host of other industrial actions, such as 'go-slows,' 'downers,' overtime bans, lunch-time meetings purposely allowed to run over into working time, and so on. Any cut-off point will be arbitrary, and the question is not where it is fixed, but whether the standard is consistently applied. There is no evidence to the effect that it has not been. Thus, in terms of what is and is not included in the strike statistics, the British government's methods seem reasonable and unproblematical, and the information they provide is ideally suited to constructing a clear, telling picture of the dimensions of industrial struggle since the late 1880s.

The methods used for the classification of strikes by industry and by cause are somewhat more debatable. The industrial groupings are extremely broad and loose, and tell one nothing about the occupational status or skill level of the workers involved. All such information must be gathered independently of the strike statistics, and that creates serious difficulties when one attempts to determine the strike propensities of different sorts of workers within each broad industrial grouping. A further difficulty stems from the shifts that have occurred in the definition of industrial groups. Fortunately, however, changes in the classifications of strikes have parallel shifts in the census or occupational census classifications, the major shifts occurring with the introduction of new census categories in 1921, or with the adoption of new Standard Industrial Classifications in 1948, 1958 and 1968.

The categorisation of causes suffers from a comparable ambiguity that makes it very hazardous to infer anything about workers' desires or consciousness from the prominence of one or another issue. Demands for higher wages, for example, might suggest an essentially defensive mentality when raised in an inflationary situation, but an aggressive attitude at a different time. Strikes over trade union rights and employment issues might equally well betoken concern over unemployment, a desire to demonstrate social solidarity, or a petty and exclusivist outlook on the part of different groups of workers in different contexts. The slots into which all strike demands are fitted for the convenience of the bureaucrat/statistician are simply too imprecise to allow such data to be used as anything but crude indicators of workers' consciousness.

None of these problems is critical, however, in the framework of this study. The rationale offered here for the importance of analysing strikes stressed that the very act of striking — whatever the rhetoric and issues surrounding it — involved substantial risks and commitment which most of the articulated demands would seldom seem to merit. What needs to be explained in most cases, therefore, is why the decision to strike was taken, and what complex of factors moved people to such action. These considerations preclude an analysis that focuses mostly on inter-industry differences, or that stops at the level of explicit strike demands, and necessitate instead a careful and comprehensive search for links between strike movements and other social processes.

By 'other social processes' is generally meant economic and demographic variables. Data on various aspects of economic change — prices, wages, etc. — were obtained primarily from the main abstracts of historical statistics. Four were of particular importance: B. Mitchell, with P. Deane, *Abstract of British Historical Statistics* (Cambridge, 1962); B. Mitchell, with H.G. Jones, *Second Abstract of British Historical Statistics* (Cambridge, 1971); B. Mitchell, *European Historical Statistics, 1750-1970* (New York, 1975); and the Department of Employment and Productivity, *British Labour Statistics. Historical Abstract, 1886-1968* (London, 1971), which has been continued as the *British Labour Statistics Yearbook*, published annually since 1969. Of nearly equal importance was C.H. Feinstein, *National Income, Expenditure and Output of the United Kingdom, 1855-1965* (Cambridge, 1971), especially for data on production and productivity. Also used for productivity data was E.H. Phelps Brown, with M. Browne, *A Century of Pay* (London, 1968).

The main statistical series used in this book other than of strikes are presented in Appendix B, Tables B.7 to B.10. Before describing the make-up of these indices, we should mention briefly some difficulties involved in merging different indices covering limited periods of time into one composite index covering a much longer period. The technical problem is actually quite simple; all that is required is a base point where two series meet, when they are equivalent. A minor difficulty may arise from the magnitude of the numbers involved. If, for example, there is a marked long-term trend for an index to increase, then the numbers further along in time would be much larger than earlier ones. In absolute terms, therefore, this might make the pace or magnitude of change at earlier times look smaller, and less important than it appeared to contemporaries, which, after all, is what counts. A concrete instance of this can be seen in our retail price index. Rates of inflation since 1967 make the price rise of 1905-13 look puny by comparison, but we must not imagine it appeared so to workers in 1910.

A more serious problem relates to the comparability of index numbers over long spans of time. Retail prices again provide a very clear example. The index numbers for before 1914 were based on a weighted average of the basic necessities in the working class budget: food, clothing, coal and rent. As the years progressed, however, the normal ratio between food, clothing, fuel and rent changed. So, too, did the normal quality of each of these items. The cost of rent may have doubled between 1910 and 1960, but the quality of housing may also have increased by 100 per cent. Thus, in one sense the cost actually remained constant and, by implication, if workers were content now to live in the conditions of 1910, they would need only half the money. But, of course, housing of a comparable quality is probably not available, and it also seems clear that while being forced to live without hot and cold running water or an indoor toilet in 1910 was normal, having to do so today would constitute extreme deprivation. There are so many ways in which the quality of life has changed, so many differences in standards and expectations, that any attempt to quantify these changes with a single index number represents a considerable oversimplification and distortion. And, if this is true of indices of prices and living standards, it is no less true for indices of production and productivity.

Mindful of these inherent limitations in the production of index numbers, we can proceed to describe the main series used in the statistical analysis:

Index of Money Wages. Data were taken from Tables 11-13 of *British Labour Statistics. Historical Abstract*, for the years up to 1968, and for subsequent years, from various issues of the *Gazette*.

Index of Retail Prices (Cost of Living). This was calculated by splicing together data from Wages and Standard of Living Tables 1C of Mitchell and Deane, *British Historical Statistics*, for 1880 to 1892, with Tables 87 to 92 from *British Labour Statistics. Historical Abstract* for 1892 to 1968, and with data for subsequent years in various issues of the *Gazette*.

Index of Wholesale Prices. This was taken from Table I1 of Mitchell, *European Historical Statistics*, for the years up to 1970. For subsequent years figures were calculated, following Mitchell, by averaging the index numbers of wholesale prices for inputs and outputs published in the *Annual Abstract of Statistics*.

Index of Real Wages. These figures were calculated by dividing the index of money wages by the index of retail prices.

Index of Employment. This index was taken from Table T20 of Feinstein, *National Income*, for years up to 1965, and from various issues of the *Gazette* for later years.

Unemployment Rates. These were obtained from Labour Force Table 3 in Mitchell and Deane, *British Historical Statistics*, for the years before 1881, from Tables 159, 160, 161 and 165 in *British Labour Statistics*. *Historical Abstract* for 1881-1968, and from the *British Labour Statistics Yearbooks* and the *Annual Abstracts of Statistics* since 1968. Four different sorts of calculations are presented. Two are based on trade union returns, Method A being an estimate based on relief expenditure, Method B an actual count of unemployed members. The official returns relate to insured workers, and the estimated official returns are calculations based on the ratios of the trade union returns (Method B) to the official returns for 1912 to 1926, and of the trade union returns (Method A) to the estimated official rates for 1888 to 1892.

Gross Domestic Product. These numbers were taken from Feinstein, *National Income*, Table T20, for 1855 to 1965, and from various issues of the *Gazette* since then.

Total Productivity. This is simply Gross Domestic Product divided by Employment, and the figures were obtained from the same sources as Gross Domestic Product.

Industrial Production. This index was taken from Table T51 of Feinstein, *National Income*, for 1855 to 1965, and spliced together with output figures for the 'Index of Production Industries' found in various issues of the *Gazette* for later years.

Index of Industrial Productivity. These figures are somewhat problematical, primarily because of our inability to produce a continuous series, or to unite the three series with one base year. In addition, the figures lack comparability because for the interwar years they refer to productivity in manufacturing only, whereas other figures refer to industry generally. For the years up to 1960 they were obtained from Phelps Brown and Browne, *A Century of Pay*; for later years from *British Labour Statistics. Historical Abstract*, Table 204, and from relevant issues of the *Gazette*.

Trade Union Membership. The figures for TUC-affiliated membership were taken from S. Pollard, 'Trade Unions and the Labour Market, 1870-1914', *Yorkshire Bulletin of Economic and Social Research*, XVII (1965), p. 102. Those for total membership were obtained from Table 196 of *British Labour Statistics. Historical Abstract*, and from relevant issues of *Gazette*.

The sources of all other statistics have been given as they appeared in various chapters, and a general list of all statistical sources is provided at the end of this appendix.

Throughout this book, we have used standard statistical methods to calculate rates of growth, standard deviations, etc. A short and simple introduction is Roderick Floud, *Introduction to Quantitative Methods for Historians* (Princeton, 1973). For the more complicated statistical procedures involved in multiple regression analysis, and for the calculation of correlation coefficients, we used the various subprogrammes in SPSS, documented in H.H. Nie, C.H. Hull, J.G. Jenkins, K. Steinbrenner, and D.H. Bent, *Statistical Package for the Social Sciences*, 2nd edn (New York, 1975). Discussion of these procedures, and of the meaning of the results, can be found in the relevant sections of standard textbooks in economic and social statistics. Particularly useful are H.M. Blalock, *Social Statistics*, 2nd edn (New York, 1972), and J. Johnston, *Econometric Methods*, 2nd edn (New York, 1972). David Snyder's thesis, 'Determinants of Industrial Conflict' (unpublished PhD dissertation, University of Michigan, 1974) is also very helpful on the specific application of these methods to the study of strikes.

One final point should be registered as to methods. Numerous squabbles, largely pedantic, surround the use and interpretation of multiple regression in social research generally, and we have been forced to make choices among alternative techniques which will inevitably displease some. Specifically, we have not used logarithmic formulations of the dependent or independent variables because these have seldom proved useful in previous studies, such as Shorey's or Bean and Peel's. On the other hand, we have departed from these authors and chosen to follow Shorter and Tilly in the consistent use of standardised rather than non-standardised regression coefficients — i.e., we prefer Beta weights to simple Bs. This was done because, in contrast to the econometricians, our concern was with the relative causal importance of one factor versus another rather than with the overall predictive capacity of the equations alone. No doubt some will find fault with these decisions, and so see fit to question the results. We feel confident, however, that the interpretations proposed here are not dependent upon the particular methods adopted, but are supported by a wide range of evidence, and thus do reflect the underlying realities conditioning strikes in Britain.

Statistical Sources

British Government Publications:

Abstract of Labour Statistics, 1893-1936
Annual Abstract of Statistics, 1938-
British Labour Statistics. Historical Abstract, 1886-1968
British Labour Statistics Yearbook, 1969-
Census of England and Wales, 1951
Census of Production, 1907, 1924
Labour Gazette, 1893- (later *Ministry of Labour Gazette, Ministry of Labour and National Service Gazette, Employment and Productivity Gazette, Department of Employment Gazette*)
New Earnings Survey, 1968, 1974
Report on Strikes and Lockouts, 1888-1913

Other Publications:

Ainsworth, R.B., 'Earnings and Working Hours of Manual Wage-Earners in the United Kingdom in October 1938', *Journal of the Royal Statistical Society*, Series A, CXII (1949), pp. 35-65

Feinstein, C.H., *National Income, Output, and Expenditure of the United Kingdom, 1855-1965* (Cambridge, 1971)

Knowles, K.G.J.C., and Robertson, D.J., 'Differences between the Wages of Skilled and Unskilled Workers, 1880-1950', *Bulletin of the Oxford University Institute of Statistics*, XIII (1951), pp. 109-27

Mitchell, B.R., *European Historical Statistics, 1750-1970* (New York, 1975)

Mitchell, B.R., with Deane, P., *Abstract of British Historical Statistics* (Cambridge, 1962)

Mitchell, B.R., with Jones, H.G., *Second Abstract of British Historical Statistics* (Cambridge, 1971)

Phelps Brown, E.H., with Browne, M.H., *A Century of Pay* (London, 1968)

Pollard, Sidney, 'Trade Unions and the Labour Market, 1870-1914', *Yorkshire Bulletin of Social and Economic Research*, XVII (1965), pp. 98-112

Routh, Guy, *Occupation and Pay in Great Britain, 1906-1960* (Cambridge, 1965)

APPENDIX B: MAIN STATISTICAL SERIES

Table B.1: Annual Number of Strikes by Industrial Group*

	Total	M&Q	Tex	Cloth	ME&S	Veh.	Cons.	Tran.	Misc.
1888	517	139	186	7	138	n.a.	21	9	17
1889	1211	131	241	66	339	—	86	184	164
1890	1040	104	241	78	203	—	113	163	138
1891	906	132	220	63	164	—	125	61	141
1892	700	109	143	48	131	—	142	38	89
1893	782	156	105	82	136	—	198	43	62
1894	929	232	178	65	161	—	162	48	83
1895	745	187	124	39	160	—	146	27	62
1896	926	171	153	48	266	—	171	25	92
1897	864	127	108	56	229	—	193	48	103
1898	711	129	99	53	152	—	183	22	73
1899	719	109	124	37	140	—	180	47	82
1900	648	136	96	38	111	—	146	50	71
1901	642	210	96	39	103	—	104	20	70
1902	442	168	82	23	71	—	39	14	45
1903	387	125	55	25	87	—	44	15	36
1904	354	112	52	26	75	—	37	10	42
1905	358	106	67	29	70	—	31	11	44
1906	486	96	124	42	125	—	19	19	61
1907	601	112	153	64	134	—	22	29	87
1908	399	145	69	32	62	—	19	21	51
1909	436	207	59	29	62	—	15	19	48
1910	531	224	90	40	97	—	17	19	44
1911	903	179	133	46	255	—	27	99	164
1912	857	155	136	68	234	—	58	73	135
1913	1497	192	243	75	392	—	198	123	273
1914	972	175	97	50	232	—	177	53	187
1915	672	85	67	40	189	—	63	75	153
1916	532	75	74	44	105	—	73	44	117
1917	730	148	70	55	225	—	51	32	149
1918	1165	173	75	67	420	—	107	48	275

Table B.1: (cont.)

1919	1352	250	65	77	335	—	134	113	378
1920	1607	250	126	68	340	—	268	150	405
1921	763	173	28	29	151	—	158	42	182
1922	576	169	21	23	115	—	77	56	115
1923	628	197	35	24	103	—	65	61	143
1924	710	204	50	31	136	—	66	81	142
1925	603	175	59	31	94	—	58	54	132
1926	323	69	33	12	62	—	43	42	61
1927	308	115	27	10	69	—	34	16	37
1928	302	100	33	9	51	—	38	16	55
1929	431	162	58	17	80	—	40	21	53
1930	422	158	44	21	70	—	47	22	60
1931	420	155	38	21	61	—	57	17	71
1932	389	115	105	24	46	—	29	25	45
1933	357	117	43	20	68	—	20	30	59
1934	471	150	57	25	81	—	44	31	83
1935	553	233	64	28	73	—	46	36	73
1936	818	290	79	27	148	—	77	66	131
1937	1129	470	84	33	220	—	98	50	174
1938	875	374	42	36	138	—	110	49	126
1939	940	417	73	25	181	—	122	34	88
1940	922	386	60	34	229	—	81	36	96
1941	1251	482	42	20	472	—	77	58	100
1942	1303	555	47	13	476	—	66	51	95
1943	1785	862	52	23	612	—	71	68	97
1944	2194	1275	48	30	610	—	48	82	101
1945	2293	1319	41	29	591	—	36	156	121
1946	2205	1339	36	37	449	—	77	105	161
1947	1721	1066	25	22	291	—	35	119	163
1948	1759	1125	40	26	266	—	36	111	155
1949	1426	878	48		257	46	54	85	104
1950	1339	861	27		227	53	71	68	85

Tex & Cloth

1951	1719	1067	25		318	67	95	91	123
1952	1714	1226	18		220	48	94	55	107
1953	1746	1313	28		205	53	80	74	83
1954	1989	1466	31		207	46	75	125	83
1955	2419	1784	25		302	77	96	118	96

Table B.1: (cont.)

	Total	M&Q	Tex & Cloth	ME&S	Veh.	Cons.	Tran.	Misc.
1956	2648	2078	34	256	52	114	102	68
1957	2859	2226	37	275	71	126	121	87
1958	2629	1964	29	302	84	178	83	67
1959	2093	1311	25	397	135	171	88	101
1960	2832	1669	41	553	174	215	179	180
1961	2686	1466	41	548	157	286	138	209
1962	2449	1207	46	588	166	316	134	174
1963	2086	993	46	568	173	168	133	161
1964	2524	1063	57	766	217	222	180	242
1965	2354	743	44	856	221	261	179	274
1966	1937	556	30	703	214	265	178	208
1967	2116	399	61	908	272	256	208	293
1968	2378	227	69	1103	318	276	342	387
1969	3116	193	96	1434	374	285	540	577
1970	3906	165	118	1921	451	337	584	782
1971	2228	138	97	1107	304	234	269	383
1972	2497	229	97	1250	288	244	237	449
1973	2873	305	123	1342	382	217	298	591
1974	2922	196	125	1326	280	203	305	774

*The industrial groups are Mining and Quarrying (M&Q), Textiles (Tex), Clothing (Cloth), Metals, Engineering and Shipbuilding (ME&S), Vehicle Production (Veh.), included throughout the period in ME&S, but also given separately since 1949, Construction (Cons.), Transport and Communication (Tran.), and Miscellaneous Industries (Misc.), including numerous small manufacturing industries, agriculture, finance, distribution, and public employment. Since 1949, separate figures are not given for Textiles and Clothing separately, so the two are combined (Tex & Cloth).

Table B.2: Annual Number of Strikers by Industrial Group (000s)

	Total	M&Q	Tex	Cloth	ME&S	Veh.	Cons.	Tran.	Misc.
1888	119	59	33	4	19	n.a.	1	2	3
1889	337	38	50	19	60	—	6	144	19
1890	393	140	42	29	82	—	12	72	15
1891	267	51	45	41	61	—	25	33	12
1892	357	119	102	36	40	—	18	13	28
1893	599	476	43	102	29	—	19	15	7
1894	257	176	27	4	20	—	13	12	6
1895	207	54	57	49	32	—	8	2	5
1896	148	48	23	3	33	—	30	3	7
1897	167	38	25	6	67	—	13	12	8
1898	201	147	12	3	15	—	14	3	6
1899	138	27	52	1	14	—	27	12	5
1900	135	45	16	2	10	—	16	20	25
1901	111	62	12	4	14	—	9	3	9
1902	117	86	8	2	10	—	5	1	5
1903	94	50	5	2	28	—	3	2	3
1904	56	26	9	1	9	—	6	2	3
1905	68	34	10	3	7	—	6	2	5
1906	158	64	57	7	23	—	1	2	3
1907	101	36	28	10	12	—	1	8	6
1908	224	60	120	3	29	—	3	4	5
1909	170	150	5	2	7	—	1	4	2
1910	385	205	123	3	31	—	1	19	4
1911	831	68	198	10	74	—	2	439	41
1912	1233	922	48	29	66	—	5	143	19
1913	516	159	55	13	102	—	34	77	61
1914	326	199	16	5	37	—	28	9	31
1915	401	267	30	5	41	—	14	22	21
1916	235	54	52	14	64	—	5	24	22
1917	575	185	43	8	283	—	5	17	34
1918	923	317	222	21	200	—	30	49	85
1919	2401	857	452	26	373	—	20	529	143
1920	1779	1299	74	31	169	—	45	64	97
1921	1770	1234	373	5	62	—	29	27	40
1922	512	115	5	3	342	—	9	9	29

Table B.2: (cont.)

	Total	M&Q	Tex	Cloth	ME&S	Veh.	Cons.	Tran.	Misc.
1923	343	160	31	3	52	n.a.	18	49	30
1924	558	125	10	5	65	—	105	223	26
1925	401	124	156	5	22	—	5	26	63
1926	2724	1087	17	1	14	—	3	20	8
1927	90	58	3	9	9	—	7	2	1
1928	80	46	21	1	5	—	3	2	3
1929	493	66	390	1	23	—	3	7	3
1930	286	139	122	1	6	—	4	5	10
1931	424	239	146	1	9	—	11	5	14
1932	337	143	271	2	3	—	3	12	3
1933	114	59	5	2	13	—	1	26	8
1934	109	61	10	2	13	—	1	10	6
1935	230	168	8	2	13	—	3	23	12
1936	241	143	8	12	26	—	7	24	22
1937	388	250	15	6	69	—	5	33	8
1938	211	134	6	5	34	—	11	11	11
1939	246	151	6	4	48	—	26	9	9
1940	225	143	7	7	30	—	20	4	14
1941	297	128	6	5	127	—	9	13	11
1942	349	196	7	4	108	—	10	12	11
1943	454	200	5	3	139	—	11	43	13
1944	716	495	6	2	171	—	4	28	96
1945	447	205	3	8	104	—	3	107	17
1946	405	166	5	12	124	—	5	46	47
1947	489	242	3	3	87	—	4	110	39
1948	324	145	11	5	82	—	6	56	38
1949	313	179	7		38	8	7	68	15
1950	269	126	2		54	22	12	41	33
			Tex & Cloth						
1951	336	120	5		89	47	17	84	19
1952	303	199	2		62	28	17	8	15
1953	1329	163	13		1075	316	18	36	25
1954	402	184	4		66	2	33	101	16
1955	599	321	3		99	9	12	140	34
1956	464	221	6		175	80	12	19	32

Table B.2: (cont.)

1957	1275	249	9	824	158	15	157	21
1958	456	216	6	107	63	23	87	17
1959	522	179	4	138	76	20	29	151
1960	702	224	8	266	141	22	141	41
1961	673	233	9	252	106	46	52	81
1962	4297	135	12	3676	831	54	299	123
1963	455	129	8	181	80	70	38	31
1964	701	121	11	246	79	25	251	48
1965	673	76	9	344	160	28	131	86
1966	415	45	3	195	75	35	104	34
1967	552	33	9	306	118	36	104	63
1968	2074	21	14	1773	468	46	124	97
1969	1427	140	27	565	230	43	374	278
1970	1460	117	46	546	206	49	325	377
1971	864	18	14	397	208	37	289	110
1972	1450	339	21	454	140	195	215	227
1973	1103	44	26	467	232	24	139	404
1974	1161	286	29	389	118	21	130	307

Table B.3: The Reasons Given for Striking (Number of Strikes)

	WI	WD	OW	HRS	EPC	WC	TU	Sy&Mi	Total*
1893	258	161	56	10	92	122	73	10	782
1894	291	262	11	23	158	219	74	23	1061
1895	267	167	19	12	122	204	76	9	876
1896	325	106	139	26	53	164	103	105	1021
1897	329	72	131	20	121	119	49	23	864
1898	278	88	83	19	87	94	51	11	711
1899	321	48	91	17	102	69	46	26	719
1900	268	46	170	6	93	57	45	9	648
1901	166	101	135	29	84	79	38	10	642
1902	105	74	88	20	58	64	29	4	442
1903	92	59	81	17	54	56	25	3	387
1904	66	83	83	13	46	47	15	1	354
1905	84	69	82	14	47	37	21	4	358
1906	150	54	128	13	53	52	32	4	486
1907	190	46	148	16	88	57	50	6	601
1908	76	77	96	14	54	43	29	10	399
1909	105	44	107	27	63	44	31	15	436
1910	103	37	162	22	80	75	41	11	531
1911	374	41	161	31	140	66	79	11	903
1912	321	49	169	27	149	50	70	22	857
1913	776	36	170	49	236	73	133	24	1497
1914	425	47	131	28	180	56	82	23	972
1915	398	28	63	17	82	18	55	11	672
1916	332	18	48	16	70	22	17	9	532
1917	426	21	74	4	116	42	35	12	730
1918	659	26	85	25	200	73	78	19	1165
1919	679	63	115	137	196	82	51	29	1352
1920	888	51	140	41	259	93	89	46	1607
1921	72	393	95	31	91	40	24	17	763
1922	29	255	101	18	77	52	31	13	576
1923	76	148	129	16	87	52	91	29	628
1924	214	78	144	13	121	58	57	25	710
1925	116	83	106	15	141	54	72	16	603
1926**	54	33	61	16	80	29	28	36	323
1927	35	71	59	22	68	22	26	5	308
1928	26	63	80	15	69	29	13	7	302

Table B.3: (cont.)

1929	42	82	100	12	107	40	40	8	431
1930	38	91	120	19	79	45	28	2	422
1931	32	114	86	33	84	52	18	1	420
1932	21	131	78	10	89	43	14	3	389
1933	36	60	92	4	90	44	24	7	357
1934	79	49	100	18	121	62	37	5	471
1935	85	42	128	11	148	84	36	19	553
1936	162	34	173	23	221	99	84	22	818
1937	323	19	246	43	265	100	110	23	1129
1938	139	34	166	41	257	130	92	16	875
1939	226	51	205	25	217	124	74	18	940
1940	218	33	233	27	196	164	35	16	922
1941	332	55	362	55	188	212	33	14	1251
1942	394	55	363	47	166	234	18	26	1303
1943	381	94	501	52	214	439	31	73	1785
1944	339	78	733	57	229	674	40	44	2194
1945	291	—	699	89	291	782	76	65	2293
1946	254	—	707	63	287	778	81	35	2205
1947	182	—	625	89	230	527	30	38	1721
1948	167	—	563	65	249	647	48	20	1759
1949	83	—	528	54	229	457	46	29	1426
1950	78	—	509	37	202	436	35	42	1339
1951	190	—	643	37	257	535	28	29	1719
1952	115	—	611	58	260	618	32	20	1714
1953	97	—	694	45	227	640	30	13	1746
1954	116	—	811	47	242	735	30	8	1989
1955	196	—	1035	45	253	833	33	24	2419
1956	286	—	922	74	229	1078	35	24	2648
1957	327	—	952	117	271	1106	63	23	2859
1958	224	—	984	68	340	936	58	19	2629
1959	238	—	730	34	332	689	42	28	2093
1960	471	—	915	70	362	906	63	45	2832
1961	458	—	848	58	410	806	69	37	2686
1962	380	—	745	8	472	708	100	36	2449
1963	383	—	573	18	336	664	74	20	2068
1964	540	—	668	23	404	765	98	26	2524
1965	648	—	532	44	420	626	69	15	2354
1966	431	—	452	26	397	556	59	16	1937
1967	638	—	348	37	428	562	80	23	2116

Table B.3: (cont.)

	WI	WD	OW	HRS	EPC	WC	TU	Sy&Mi	Total*
1968	925	—	305	29	479	500	109	31	2378
1969	1543	—	240	32	486	569	179	67	3116
1970	2162	—	303	27	546	609	180	77	3906
1971	890	—	265	23	568	362	83	37	2228
1972	1216	—	261	42	461	398	83	36	2497

	***Wage	Ben.	Hrs.	Redund.	TU	WC	Man.	Dism.	Misc.	Sym.	Total
1973	1369	93	71	87	235	237	386	384	11	39	2873
1974	1797	125	53	85	184	156	263	259	—	23	2922

Notes

*WI refers to wage increases; WD to wage decreases; OW to other wage questions; HRS to demands concerning the length of the working day or week; EPC to the employment of particular persons or particular classes of persons; WC to working arrangements, conditions, discipline, etc.: TU to trade union status; SY&Mi to sympathy or miscellaneous causes.

**Figures for 1926 exclude the General Strike.

***In 1973 the Department of Employment's classificatory scheme was altered. The new categories were: wage rates and earnings level, extra wage and fringe benefits; duration and pattern of hours worked; redundancy questions; trade union matters; working conditions and supervision; manning and work allocation; dismissal and other disciplinary measures; miscellaneous; and stoppages involving sympathetic action included previously.

Table B.4: The Reasons given for Striking (Number of Strikers)*

	WI	WD	OW	HRS	EPC	WC	TU	Sy&Mi	Total
1893	188578	368326	10556	1191	18688	25667	19298	3588	634386
1894	117028	109302	8573	6105	25275	37763	15519	4680	324245
1895	94761	47038	1399	2858	17512	84393	6614	9183	263758
1896	69433	20714	25670	3658	7478	33121	13021	26582	198678
1897	69968	13419	22906	52769	19529	38311	8018	1347	230267
1898	15:747	10654	13991	777	9203	11742	2215	440	200769
1899	73700	6800	14100	3900	8200	17900	5100	8300	138100
1900	57269	7385	18259	718	10427	18956	19573	2568	135145
1901	19886	14852	24127	4198	10524	23185	11531	3134	111437
1902	15208	26053	15472	3044	11436	19849	25489	273	116824
1903	14412	12019	23126	4108	7822	13609	17602	817	93515
1904	4960	13323	14180	1970	6081	7601	7925	20	56060
1905	13735	11422	13580	3145	6408	5546	9377	4440	57653
1906	58942	5399	23532	7086	4734	6536	50750	833	157872
1907	25193	3849	27016	2080	13699	11802	16439	650	100728
1908	16261	141646	17982	8377	11078	12467	12218	3940	223969
1909	13803	9755	18470	87367	13492	8892	12935	5544	170258
1910	20748	7154	48572	91927	114793	62207	32777	6907	385085
1911	333647	16280	33288	13161	32639	68009	327588	6492	831104

Table B.4: (cont.)

	WI	WD	OW	HRS	EPC	WC	TU	Sy&Mi	Total
1912	114606	7967	897847	8961	34985	42068	120924	5658	1233016
1913	239874	16356	26916	13688	53714	20159	120470	24860	516037
1914	61000	106000	34000	11000	31000	14000	50000	19000	326000
1915	314000	6000	18000	2000	13000	9000	32000	7000	401000
1916	135000	4000	12000	15000	39000	14000	5000	11000	235000
1917	223000	26000	33000	3000	192000	21000	69000	8000	575000
1918	380000	32000	40000	162000	154000	29000	108000	18000	923000
1919	1051000	543000	90000	461000	129000	61000	25000	41000	2401000
1920	1353000	44000	53000	13000	176000	45000	27000	68000	1779000
1921	8000	1680000	17000	10000	23000	14000	7000	11000	1770000
1922	5000	169000	32000	6000	23000	263000	10000	4000	512000
1923	11000	94000	42000	6000	24000	43000	105000	18000	343000
1924	305000	79000	38000	2000	35000	26000	18000	55000	558000
1925	39000	217000	19000	9000	57000	22000	31000	7000	401000
1926**	9300	1057000	2100	1100	15900	8100	12900	18700	1444400
1927	5000	18000	8000	13000	29000	5000	6000	6000	90000
1928	6000	15000	17000	1000	13000	7000	1000	20000	80000
1929	4000	411000	25000	4000	25000	7000	15000	2000	493000
1930	11000	126000	19000	96500	17000	11000	5000	500	286000
1931	2000	218000	19000	24000	16000	140000	5000	***	424000
1932	2200	279000	10600	4700	15900	16900	5700	2200	337200

Table B.4: (cont.)

Year									
1933	4200	21800	19800	200	34000	25700	5400	2800	113900
1934	19300	5600	20700	2300	32100	15300	8500	4500	108300
1935	15300	8000	33300	4500	39800	34500	20100	74400	229900
1936	40600	3100	33600	7100	53300	34500	20200	48900	241300
1937	129700	2600	47900	40300	54100	23300	21800	68500	388200
1938	25500	4300	36300	6900	59800	34400	34500	9300	211000
1939	41000	7600	49200	8600	66000	25600	31300	16700	246000
1940	38300	5500	56100	7500	36800	28800	10000	42100	225100
1941	65100	10100	81400	13100	58300	37400	16200	14900	296500
1942	102300	17500	108300	13200	57300	33600	5200	12100	349500
1943	124400	21700	97500	10800	65000	49300	11900	73000	453600
1944	78000	9000	414000	11000	61000	104000	10000	29000	716000
1945	101000	—	118000	34000	50000	108000	17000	19000	447000
1946	82000	—	88000	15000	74000	78000	47000	21000	405000
1947	75400	—	83900	90300	55600	77000	4200	102300	488700
1948	55100	—	87000	18700	44600	73800	12200	32600	324000
1949	57400	—	102100	8800	53100	38100	12600	41000	313000
1950	79700	—	52400	4100	42300	51500	9500	29400	268900
1951	68300	—	89300	5000	69500	68800	11000	24000	335900

Table B.4: (cont.)

	WI	WD	OW	HRS	EPC	WC	TU	Sy&Mi	Total
1952	87500	—	79800	10100	57800	50900	6200	10900	303200
1953	1116900	—	83300	8800	47500	53300	11100	8200	1329100
1954	50200	—	105200	31200	65500	113400	13500	22500	401500
1955	118900	—	168200	7600	109700	96900	7900	89400	598600
1956	125700	—	114400	11800	64300	116800	4700	26500	464200
1957	926000	—	122800	13700	57400	122800	17300	15200	1275200
1958	88600	—	123800	13100	91700	115500	15100	8300	456100
1959	181200	—	107100	10400	94000	82700	11300	34900	521600
1960	225400	—	174800	24800	95900	134200	16200	30100	701500
1961	207100	—	122200	12800	145600	131400	40900	13000	672900
1962	3609700	—	84700	1000	446100	92900	49700	12600	4296600
1963	161900	—	85800	6000	71900	96500	27300	5600	455200
1964	293400	—	111300	12500	99200	145300	18500	21300	701500
1965	272500	—	104900	66100	100000	112600	14800	2600	673500
1966	122100	—	75700	6400	97800	82900	24000	6500	415400
1967	195600	—	66400	6200	110800	125100	27300	20300	551800
1968	1745600	—	63300	5500	131400	96700	20900	10700	2074000
1969	737100	—	72900	7600	133500	258300	75900	141400	1426600
1970	948000	—	84700	3400	200600	155500	47500	20500	1460100
1971	489000	—	104800	4000	140800	17800	27900	29500	863800
1972	854100	—	156700	8200	271300	99600	32400	28100	1450000

Table B.4: (cont.)

	Wage	Ben.	Hrs.	Redund.	TU	WC	Man.	Dism.	Misc.	Sym.	Total
1973	714000	35100	12500	40600	72900	51500	92800	80300	3500	9900	1103200
1974	877900	79700	14300	13300	41400	27000	55700	51500	–	5300	1160800

Notes: All abbreviations bear the same meaning as in the previous table.

* The figures in this table and in Table B.6 for the years up to and including 1897 refer to the number of workers involved both directly and indirectly in strikes, not simply strikers.

** The figures for 1926 include the national coal stoppage, but exclude the General Strike. An estimated 1,580,000 workers joined with the miners in the General Strike in May 1926, which would bring the total number of strikers for the year to 2,724,000.

*** Less than 500

Table B.5: Results of Strikes

Number of Strikes, the results of which were:

	Workers' Victories	Compromises	Employers' Victories	Unknown
1888	249	94	124	50
1889	502	404	209	96
1890	386	232	340	92
1891	372	182	272	80
1892	287	119	229	65
1893	304	165	271	42
1894	372	244	389	56
1895	303	206	343	24
1896	418	250	348	5
1897	202	215	307	11
1898	238	243	227	3
1899	230	236	245	8
1900	202	221	211	14
1901	163	192	280	7
1902	107	123	202	10
1903	88	110	179	10
1904	62	112	179	1
1905	70	118	166	4
1906	153	150	179	4
1907	193	161	246	1
1908	79	144	171	5
1909	79	153	199	5
1910	135	196	194	6
1911	227	387	287	2
1912	235	361	258	3
1913	428	687	382	—
1914	240	407	325	—
1915	157	267	248	—
1916	122	270	140	—
1917	229	340	161	—
1918	348	547	270	—
1919	345	701	306	—
1920	390	710	507	—

Table B.5: (cont.)

1921	152	296	315	–
1922	111	243	222	–
1923	187	258	183	–
1924	163	312	235	–
1925	154	260	189	–
1926	67	129	126	–
1927	61	129	118	–
1928	42	116	144	–
1929	89	178	164	–
1930	71	196	155	–
1931	108	146	166	–
1932	88	133	168	–
1933	75	134	148	–
1934	136	149	186	–
1935	149	191	213	–
1936	217	252	349	–
1937	252	331	546	–
1938	203	237	435	–
1939	245	245	450	–

Table B.6: Results of Strikes

Number of Strikers involved in Strikes, the results of which were:

	Workers' Victories	Compromises	Employers' Victories	Unknown
1888	65,598	17,602	30,585	5,488
1889	98,330	187,531	40,490	10,706
1890	213,926	66,079	102,057	11,183
1891	68,351	98,227	93,144	7,748
1892	98,205	183,414	71,026	4,154
1893	400,171	157,979	77,427	1,709
1894	71,661	111,078	136,373	5,133
1895	63,544	124,137	73,748	2,329
1896	78,486	53,598	78,486	283
1897	49,788	75,265	102,482	2,732
1898	45,490	34,501	120,667	111
1899	36,808	40,237	60,275	738
1900	40,612	56,390	33,516	4,627
1901	30,591	40,955	37,675	2,216
1902	36,917	41,645	35,515	2,747
1903	28,908	19,310	44,276	1,021
1904	15,413	17,441	23,180	26
1905	16,702	27,464	22,943	544
1906	67,159	51,618	38,547	548
1907	32,883	40,632	27,233	250
1908	19,185	146,850	56,437	1,497
1909	19,123	112,307	37,846	982
1910	63,000	267,000	52,000	2,000
1911	55,000	699,000	77,000	*
1912	918,000	136,000	177,000	2,000
1913	162,000	245,000	109,000	—
1914	64,000	213,000	49,000	—
1915	78,000	266,000	57,000	—
1916	53,000	112,000	70,000	—
1917	103,000	395,000	77,000	—
1918	204,000	503,000	216,000	—
1919	337,000	1,489,000	575,000	—
1920	189,000	1,401,000	189,000	—

Table B.6: (cont.)

1921	26,000	1,644,000	100,000	—
1922	23,000	425,000	64,000	—
1923	85,000	179,000	79,000	—
1924	54,000	404,000	100,000	—
1925	64,000	124,000	213,000	—
1926**	21,000	40,000	1,083,000	—
1927	25,000	37,000	28,000	—
1928	4,000	44,000	32,000	—
1929	23,000	436,000	34,000	—
1930	18,000	46,000	222,000	—
1931	154,000	204,000	66,000	—
1932	23,200	154,400	161,600	—
1933	14,200	51,800	47,900	—
1934	32,800	39,500	35,400	—
1935	113,300	54,100	62,500	—
1936	55,200	66,500	119,600	—
1937	42,700	98,600	246,900	—
1938	44,700	53,100	113,200	—
1939	66,000	54,000	126,000	—

* = less than 500 strikers.
** = excluding General Strike.

Table B.7: Wage, Price, and Real Wage Indices, 1851-1974

	Money Wages (Jan. 1956 = 100)	Retail Prices (Jan. 1956 = 100)	Real Wages (Jan. 1956 = 100)	Wholesale Prices (1952 = 100)	London Food (1900 = 100)
1851				23	
1852				24	
1853				29	
1854				31	
1855				31	
1856				31	
1857				32	
1858				27	
1859				29	
1860				30	
1861				30	
1862				31	
1863				31	
1864				32	
1865				31	
1866				31	
1867				30	
1868				30	
1869				30	
1870				29	
1871				29	
1872				31	
1873				32	
1874	17.5			31	
1875	17.3			30	
1876	17.1			29	
1877	16.9			30	151
1878	16.3			28	141
1879	15.9			26	135
1880	15.9	33.3	47.7	27	142
1881	16.2	32.6	49.7	27	140
1882	16.4	32.3	50.8	27	140
1883	16.4	32.3	50.8	27	140

Table B.7: (cont.)

1884	16.3	30.7	53.1	24	128
1885	16.0	28.8	55.6	23	116
1886	15.9	28.2	56.4	22	110
1887	15.9	27.9	57.0	21	105
1888	16.3	27.9	58.4	22	105
1889	16.7	28.2	59.2	22	108
1890	17.3	28.2	61.3	22	106
1891	17.5	28.2	62.1	23	109
1892	17.3	28.5	60.7	22	109
1893	17.3	27.9	62.0	21	103
1894	17.2	27.0	63.7	20	100
1895	17.1	26.7	64.0	19	95
1896	17.3	26.3	65.8	19	91
1897	17.4	27.3	63.7	19	98
1898	17.9	27.9	64.2	20	104
1899	18.3	27.6	66.3	20	97
1900	19.2	28.9	66.4	21	100
1901	19.0	28.6	66.4	21	—
1902	18.8	28.6	65.7	21	
1903	18.7	28.9	64.7	21	
1904	18.6	28.9	64.4	21	
1905	18.6	28.9	64.4	21	
1906	18.9	28.9	65.4	22	
1907	19.6	29.9	68.6	23	
1908	19.5	30.5	63.9	22	
1909	19.2	30.5	53.0	22	
1910	19.3	30.8	62.7	23	
1911	19.4	31.1	62.4	23	
1912	19.9	32.4	61.4	25	
1913	20.5	32.4	63.3	25	
1914	20.7	33.4	62.0	25	
1915	22.1	39.5	55.9	31	
1916	24.3	46.9	51.8	40	
1917	28.9	56.5	51.2	51	
1918	36.7	65.2	56.3	57	

Table B.7: (cont.)

	Money Wages	Retail Prices	Real Wages	Wholesale Prices	London Food
1919	42.8	69.0	62.0	63	
1920	53.6	80.0	67.0	78	
1921	53.0	72.6	73.0	50	
1922	38.8	58.8	66.0	40	
1923	35.9	55.9	64.2	40	
1924	37.0	56.2	65.8	42	
1925	37.3	56.5	66.0	41	
1926	37.1	55.2	67.2	37	
1927	36.8	53.9	68.3	36	
1928	36.3	53.3	68.1	36	
1929	36.2	52.7	68.7	35	
1930	36.0	50.7	71.0	31	
1931	35.5	47.5	74.7	27	
1932	34.8	46.2	75.3	26	
1933	34.4	45.0	76.4	26	
1934	34.5	45.3	76.2	27	
1935	34.9	45.9	76.0	27	
1936	35.7	47.2	75.6	29	
1937	37.0	49.5	74.7	33	
1938	38.1	50.1	76.0	31	
1939	38.2	50.7	75.3	31	
1940	43.0	59.1	72.8	42	
1941	46.6	63.9	72.9	47	
1942	50.6	64.2	78.8	49	
1943	52.7	63.9	82.5	50	
1944	55.0	64.5	85.3	51	
1945	57.3	65.2	87.9	52	
1946	61.9	65.5	94.5	53	
1947	64.1	65.8	97.4	59	
1948	67.6	70.2	96.3	67	
1949	69.6	72.1	96.5	70	
1950	70.5	74.4	94.8	80	
1951	76.2	81.2	93.8	97	

Table B.7: (cont.)

1952	82.8	88.6	93.5	100
1953	86.7	91.3	95.0	100
1954	91.2	93.0	98.1	101
1955	97.6	97.2	100.4	104
1956	105.4	102.0	103.3	108
1957	110.7	105.8	104.6	110
1958	113.4	109.0	104.0	107
1959	116.8	109.6	106.6	107
1960	119.9	110.7	108.3	108
1961	125.0	114.5	109.2	110
1962	129.3	119.4	108.3	111
1963	134.1	121.7	110.2	112
1964	140.7	125.7	111.9	116
1965	146.3	131.7	111.1	119
1966	153.7	136.9	112.3	123
1967	157.6	140.3	112.3	123
1968	168.8	146.9	114.9	130
1969	177.6	154.9	114.7	135
1970	195.0	164.7	118.4	143
1971	221.0	180.2	122.6	153
1972	248.2	193.1	128.5	161
1973	287.5	210.8	136.4	192
1974	344.3	244.6	140.8	263

Table B.8: Unemployment Rates, 1867-1974

	Trade Union Returns		Official Returns	Estimated 'Official' Rates
	Method A	Method B		
1867	7.4			9.1
1868	7.9			9.7
1869	6.7			8.2
1870	3.9			4.8
1871	1.6			2.0
1872	.9			1.1
1873	1.2			1.5
1874	1.7			2.1
1875	2.4			3.0
1876	3.7			4.6
1877	4.7			5.8
1878	6.8			8.4
1879	11.4			14.0
1880	5.5			6.8
1881	3.5			4.3
1882	2.3			2.8
1883	2.6			3.2
1884	8.1			10.0
1885	9.3			11.4
1886	10.2			12.5
1887	7.6			9.4
1888	4.6	4.9		5.7
1889	2.1	2.1		2.4
1890	2.1	2.1		2.4
1891	3.2	3.5		4.1
1892	5.8	6.3		7.3
1893		7.5		8.7
1894		6.9		8.0
1895		5.8		6.7
1896		3.3		3.8
1897		3.3		3.8
1898		2.8		3.3
1899		2.0		2.3
1900		2.5		2.9

Table B.8: (cont.)

1901	3.3		3.8
1902	4.0		4.7
1903	4.7		5.5
1904	6.0		7.0
1905	5.0		5.8
1906	3.6		4.2
1907	3.7		4.3
1908	7.8		9.1
1909	7.7		9.0
1910	4.7		5.5
1911	3.0		3.5
1912	3.2		3.7
1913	2.1	3.6	
1914	3.3	4.2	
1915	1.1	1.2	
1916	.4	.6	
1917	.7	.7	
1918	.8	.8	
1919	2.4	—	2.8
1920	2.4	3.9	
1921	14.8	16.9	
1922	15.2	14.3	
1923	11.3	11.7	
1924	8.1	10.3	
1925	10.5	11.3	
1926	12.2	12.5	
1927		9.7	
1928		10.8	
1929		10.4	
1930		16.1	
1931		21.3	
1932		22.1	
1933		19.9	
1934		16.7	
1935		15.5	
1936		13.1	
1937		10.8	

Table B.8:(cont.)

	Trade Union Returns		Official Returns	Estimated 'Official' Rates
	Method A	Method B		
1938			12.9	
1939			10.5	
1940			6.0	
1941			2.2	
1942			.8	
1943			.6	
1944			.5	
1945			1.3	
1946			2.5	
1947			3.1	
1948			1.9	
1949			1.6	
1950			1.6	
1951			1.2	
1952			2.2	
1953			1.8	
1954			1.5	
1955			1.2	
1956			1.3	
1957			1.6	
1958			2.2	
1959			2.3	
1960			1.7	
1961			1.6	
1962			2.1	
1963			2.6	
1964			1.7	
1965			1.5	
1966			1.6	
1967			2.5	
1968			2.5	
1969			2.5	
1970			2.6	
1971			3.4	

Table B.8: (cont.)

1972	3.8
1973	2.6
1974	2.6

Notes: Method A is the rate of trade union membership unemployed estimated from expenditure on unemployment benefit. Method B is the rate estimated by the number of actual unemployed at the end of each month. The official returns refer to the percentage of insured workers unemployed. The 'estimated official rate' was obtained by adjusting the trade union rates, based on the ratio of these to the official rate between 1913 and 1926.

Table B.9: Indices of Output, Employment and Productivity, 1855-1974

	Gross Domestic Product (1913=100)	Employ- ment (1913=100)	Total Productivity (1913=100)	Industrial Production (1913=100)	Industrial Productivity
1855	32.7	59.1	55.3	26.3	
1856	34.0	59.9	56.8	28.1	
1857	34.6	59.8	57.9	29.1	
1858	34.7	58.4	59.4	28.5	
1859	35.6	61.8	57.6	30.0	
1860	36.4	62.8	58.0	31.7	
1861	37.4	62.1	60.2	31.7	
1862	37.7	61.1	61.7	32.4	
1863	38.0	62.4	60.9	32.5	
1864	39.0	64.6	60.4	35.0	
1865	40.2	65.1	61.8	37.3	
1866	40.8	65.0	62.8	38.7	
1867	40.4	63.1	64.0	36.4	
1868	41.7	63.3	65.9	36.4	
1869	42.0	64.3	65.3	35.8	(1890-99
1870	44.6	66.2	67.4	40.2	=100)
1871	47.0	68.1	69.0	43.5	65
1872	47.1	69.0	68.3	44.8	70
1873	48.2	69.4	69.5	45.3	79
1874	49.0	69.5	70.5	46.4	75
1875	50.2	69.6	72.1	46.7	74
1876	50.7	69.2	73.3	47.5	71
1877	51.2	69.0	74.2	47.4	72
1878	51.4	68.2	75.4	47.3	66
1879	51.6	65.4	78.9	45.6	67
1880	53.1	69.9	76.0	50.3	69
1881	55.5	71.6	77.5	53.5	77
1882	57.1	73.2	78.0	55.7	77
1883	57.5	73.8	77.9	56.5	76
1884	57.6	70.3	81.9	54.4	76
1885	57.3	70.2	81.6	52.1	75
1886	58.2	70.2	82.9	51.0	79
1887	60.5	72.9	83.0	55.1	83
1888	63.2	75.7	83.5	58.3	90

Table B.9: (cont.)

1889	66.6	78.7	84.6	62.4	96
1890	66.9	79.5	84.2	63.3	93
1891	66.9	79.2	84.5	64.1	91
1892	65.3	77.8	83.9	61.0	89
1893	65.3	77.7	84.0	60.0	91
1894	69.7	79.1	88.1	63.5	103
1895	71.9	81.0	88.8	66.5	105
1896	74.9	84.0	89.2	71.4	102
1897	75.9	85.0	89.3	73.4	105
1898	79.6	86.4	92.1	77.0	110
1899	82.9	88.1	94.1	80.1	111
1900	82.3	88.7	92.8	80.1	104
1901	82.3	89.0	92.5	80.3	104
1902	84.4	89.2	94.6	81.7	108
1903	83.5	89.3	93.5	80.0	105
1904	84.0	88.9	94.5	81.0	103
1905	86.5	90.6	95.5	85.7	106
1906	89.4	92.7	96.4	89.3	108
1907	91.1	93.5	97.4	91.0	109
1908	87.4	90.3	96.8	83.7	103
1909	89.4	91.2	98.0	84.3	106
1910	92.2	94.9	97.2	85.5	106
1911	94.9	97.4	97.4	91.5	105
1912	96.3	97.9	98.4	93.9	109
1913	100.0	100.0	100.0	100.0	106
1914	101.0	99.7	101.3	93.7	
1915	109.1	102.9	106.0	95.5	
1916	111.5	104.4	106.8	90.4	
1917	112.5	105.1	107.0	84.4	
1918	113.2	105.8	107.0	81.5	
1919	100.9	104.2	96.8	89.8	
1920	91.3	99.9	91.4	97.9	
1921	83.9	88.2	95.1	79.7	

Table B.9: (cont.)

	Gross Domestic Product	Employment	Total Productivity	Industrial Production	Industrial Productivity
1922	88.2	88.0	100.2	92.2	(1925-29 =100)
1923	91.0	89.1	102.1	97.6	
1924	94.8	90.5	104.8	108.4	96
1925	99.4	91.5	108.6	112.7	98
1926	95.7	91.5	104.6	106.6	98
1927	103.4	94.2	109.8	122.8	101
1928	104.7	94.6	110.7	119.5	100
1929	107.8	95.9	112.4	125.5	103
1930	107.0	94.1	113.7	120.1	106
1931	101.5	91.9	110.4	112.3	106
1932	102.3	92.3	110.8	111.9	105
1933	105.3	94.2	111.8	119.3	107
1934	112.2	96.9	115.8	131.2	113
1935	116.5	98.7	118.0	141.2	120
1936	121.8	101.8	119.6	153.9	124
1937	126.1	105.2	119.9	163.1	125
1938	127.6	105.5	120.9	158.7	123
1939	128.9	109.8	117.4		
1940	141.8	113.7	124.7		
1941	154.7	118.2	130.9		
1942	158.5	122.1	129.8		
1943	162.0	123.1	131.6		
1944	155.6	121.6	128.0		(1952-9 =100)
1945	148.8	119.2	124.8		
1946	142.3	113.2	125.7	162.6	82
1947	140.2	113.7	123.3	171.3	80
1948	144.7	113.5	127.5	186.0	84
1949	150.0	113.6	132.0	196.8	88
1950	154.9	114.7	135.0	208.0	91
1951	159.5	116.1	137.4	214.8	92
1952	159.2	116.0	137.2	210.0	91
1953	165.5	116.7	141.8	222.0	95
1954	172.2	118.5	145.3	235.6	99
1955	178.7	119.9	148.9	247.6	101

Table B.9: (cont.)

1956	180.7	120.7	149.7	248.6	101
1957	183.6	120.5	152.4	253.1	102
1958	183.2	119.9	153.6	250.3	103
1959	190.6	120.1	158.7	263.1	108
1960	201.6	122.2	165.0	281.6	113
1961	207.0	123.8	167.6	285.1	113
1962	209.3	123.9	168.9	288.1	114
1963	217.6	124.1	175.3	297.9	120
1964	230.7	125.7	183.5	320.9	128
1965	237.8	126.9	187.4	330.2	130
1966	241.5	127.3	190.2	335.8	133
1967	245.8	125.5	196.4	339.8	138
1968	256.4	125.0	205.6	359.8	148
1969	261.2	125.0	209.5	369.5	152
1970	265.7	124.4	214.2	370.6	155
1971	269.9	122.3	221.5	372.1	161
1972	277.7	123.3	225.7	379.5	168
1973	293.6	125.8	234.1	407.3	178
1974	291.2	126.5	321.3	394.3	173

Note: The figures on Industrial Productivity for 1924-38 actually refer simply to productivity in manufacturing industry only.

Table B.10: Trade Union Membership, 1870-1974 (in Thousands)

	Membership of TUC-Affiliated Unions	Trade Union Membership
1870	250*	—
1871	289	
1872	256	
1873	750	
1874	1192	
1875	818/540**	
1876	558	
1877	691	
1878	624	
1879	542	
1880	494	
1881	464	
1882	509	
1883	520	
1884	598	
1885	581	
1886	636	
1887	674	
1888	817	
1889	885	
1890	1470	
1891	1303	
1892	1220	1576
1893	900	1559
1894	1100	1530
1895	1000	1504
1896	1076	1608
1897	1093	1731
1898	1184	1752
1899	1200	1911
1900	1250	2022
1901	—	2025
1902		2013
1903		1994
1904		1967
1905		1997

Table B.10: (cont.)

1906	2210
1907	2513
1908	2485
1909	2477
1910	2565
1911	3134
1912	3416
1913	4135
1914	4145
1915	4354
1916	4644
1917	5494
1918	6533
1919	7926
1920	8348
1921	6633
1922	5626
1923	5429
1924	5544
1925	5506
1926	5219
1927	4919
1928	4806
1929	4858
1930	4824
1931	4624
1932	4444
1933	4392
1934	4590
1935	4867
1936	5295
1937	5842
1938	6053
1939	6298
1940	6613
1941	7165
1942	7867

Table B.10: (cont.)

	Membership of TUC-Affiliated Unions	Trade Union Membership
1943		8174
1944		8087
1945		7875
1946		8803
1947		9145
1948		9362
1949		9318
1950		9289
1951		9535
1952		9588
1953		9527
1954		9566
1955		9741
1956		9778
1957		9829
1958		9639
1959		9623
1960		9835
1961		9897
1962		9887
1963		10067
1964		10216
1965		10323
1966		10260
1967		10188
1968		10189
1969		10468
1970		11174
1971		11120
1972		11349
1973		11444
1974		11755

* Actually 1869.
** Two Congresses held this year.

INDEX

'abnormal places' 176
'Affluent Worker' studies 27-8, 62;
  see also Goldthorpe, Lockwood
age structure: of dockers 182-3; of
  textiles workers 185
Allen, V.L. 8, 65-6
Ashenfelter, O. 29
Ashton, T.S. 180
Askwith, G.R. 100
Association of Scientific, Technical,
  and Managerial Staff (ASTMS)
  167-8; *see also* white-collar
  workers

Baldwin, S. 53
Barnes, G. 111
Bean, R. 76-8
Benbow, W. 46
Bevin, E. 129, 182
Blackburn, riot in 1878 46
'blackcoated worker' *see* white-collar
  workers
Black Friday 129
Boilermakers' union 94
boot and shoe makers 170; union of
  94
brick, glass, cement and pottery
  workers 168-8, 170, 172, 174-5,
  178
Briggs motors 140
British motors 62
builders *see* construction

'ca-canny' 97
casualism among dockers 181-2
Citrine, W. 128
City of London 131
Clack, G. 140
class consciousness, problems with
  concept of 67; *see also* workers'
  attitudes and expectations
Clegg, H.A. 24, 56, 127
clothing 54-5, 159, 166-70, 175, 178
coalmining 26, 48, 53, 56, 127, 140;
  see also mining and quarrying
Cole, G.D.H. 132, 139, 180
Cole, M.I. 129-30, 132, 139
collective action, pre-industrial 45-7,
  68n3; *see also* food riots

Commission of Enquiry into
  Industrial Unrest, 1917 110-11
Communist Party of Great Britain
  60, 132
community structure 26-7, 34, 112,
  158, 179-84
construction 45-55, 99, 157-9,
  166-9, 172, 174, 178
Cotton Factory Times 131
cotton workers *see* textiles
'Coupon Election' of 1918 60
Crowley, D.W. 98

Dagenham 143-4
Dangerfield, G. 99-100
demands of strikes 50-2, 54-5
determinants of strikes *see* multivariate analysis
Devlin Committee 180; *see also*
  dockers
dockers 10, 26, 28, 49-53, 98-9, 157,
  166-8, 174-7, 179-83, 187
Dunlop, J.T. 45, 56-7, 64

economic fluctuations 12-13, 23,
  170-4; *see also* long waves
economic theories of strikes 28-31
Economist, The 113
eight-hour day 50, 95-6
Ellesmere Port 144
engineering 49-54, 63, 95, 157,
  166-70, 172, 174, 176; lockout of
  1897-8 48, 59, 98; lockout of
  1922 127
Engineering Employers' Federation
  53, 58, 127, 140
expectations function 29; *see also*
  workers' attitudes and expectations

family structure among textile
  workers 184-5
Federation of British Industries 140
Financial Times 144
Fischer, D.H. 40
Flanders, A. 24
food, drink, and tobacco 166-8, 174,
  179
food riots 11-12, 45-6; *see also*